WOMEN UNDER COMMUNISM
Family in Russia & China

Women Under Communism

Family in Russia and China

by

PAUL CHAO
Ph.D.(N.Y.U.), M.Litt.(Cantab.)

GENERAL HALL, INC.
Publishers
23–45 Corporal Kennedy Street
Bayside, New York 11360

WOMEN UNDER COMMUNISM: Family in Russia & China

ISBN: 0-930390-00-8 (paper)
       0-930390-01-6 (cloth)

Library of Congress Catalog Card Number: 77—89932
Manufactured in the United States of America

To
My Mother

TABLE OF CONTENTS

PREFACE

This book explores the relationship between one influential system of ideas, socialism, and a major social institution, the family, as it has emerged in the Soviet Union and the Chinese mainland. Since both socialist societies have patterned their family system on the basis of Marxist doctrine, they provide an excellent laboratory for our enquiry. On account of serious deficiencies in the theory itself and certain outstanding features of the concrete historical events, very little of orthodox Marxism has survived intact in the family system in either of these socialist societies.

Embarking on this study, I surely had to review and analyze Marxist writings on the family, to place them in the main tradition of evolutionary theory, and with the aid of existing documentary sources, to demonstrate those characteristics of Soviet and Chinese social structure, function and values, that impose limits on the translation of doctrine into action, of vision into reality. Most of my sources especially press material, were written in Chinese and English, and cover the period from 1949 to 1977.

I was interested in this field of research because of its relevance to the actual political situation. In the course of the work I came to realize more and more clearly the significance of the material gathered from an extensive reading of Marxist works on the nature of the family. Newspaper accounts were also illuminating. Nowadays because political circumstances have permitted access, however limited, to Soviet Russia and People's Republic of China, personal reports and experiences have added much to this research. Moreover, the Communist authorities have no qualms about distributing their literature far and wide and beyond the seas. Thus we have relatively easy access to recent and relevant material and are able to keep abreast of changes in the family system both of Soviet Russia and People's Republic of China.

William Paterson College   PAUL CHAO
New Jersey, May 1977

ACKNOWLEDGEMENTS

In collecting the material for this work and in tackling the problems it raised I have been accorded lavish help from other scholars. I should like to express my gratitude to Dr. Marvin Bressler, my professor at New York University for devoting his valuable time and energy to guiding and supervising this research, and Dr. E.O. Smigel for his assistance in obtaining essential data. I have also to thank Dr. Robert Bierstedt and Dr. J. Bram for their advice and guidance. I wish to thank the scholars of Cambridge University, who have given me the benefit of their criticism and suggestions: for the fourth chapter, which treats the development of the Soviet family and woman's status, I particularly and gratefully acknowledge the help and advice of Professor and historian Edward H. Carr, Fellow of Trinity College and Mr. J.C. Hall, Fellow of St. John's College. I am also grateful to Dr. Reo F. Fortune, the anthropologist for reading and criticizing the manuscript. I am indebted to Professor Meyer Fortes, anthropologist and Fellow of King's College and Dr. Edmund R. Leach, Provost of King's College who encouraged me in this work. Dr. D. Lockwood, sociologist and Fellow of St. John's College and Dr. E.G. Pulleyblank sinologist and fellow of Downing College read the manuscript and offered me valuable criticism on many points. I convey my profuse thanks to Dr. John L. Thomas, S.J. research professor at Georgetown University, Washington D.C. for his advice and his kindness in helping me in the research. My thanks are also due to Mr. Charles Sweeting who helped me in proof-reading. If there are errors in this book, I alone am answerable for them.

May 1977   P. C.

INTRODUCTION

This study of socialist family doctrine particularly as it is presently understood and applied in the Soviet Union and the Peoples' Republic of China, will be widely welcomed both for its timeliness and scholarly analysis. Perspective China-watchers have frequently reminded us during the past two decades that there is a good deal of information available on China but the problem is to interpret it. I feel that few contemporary social scientists are as well prepared through family background, personal experience and scientific training as my former student and long-standing friend Professor Chao, to undertake this difficult task in regard to information relating to the contemporary Chinese family. Given the cultural differences and ideologically colored character of much of the data involved, his unique qualifications of lived experience and mature scholarship must be regarded as absolute prerequisites for balanced interpretation.

Although the present work discusses the development of socialist family programs in Soviet Russia as well as China, for reasons that I hope will become evident, my brief introductory remarks here will be concerned primarily with changes in the Chinese family. The typical Western conception of the Chinese family system is compounded of fictions as well as facts, of stereotypes derived from accounts of the limited "gentry" class. It seems obvious that to identify current ideologically induced changes in Chinese family patterns requires, at a minimum, a sensitive informed awareness of the actual form and functioning of the Chinese family system before these assumed changes occurred.

But there is an additional reason for special concern with the Chinese family and consequently, for welcoming the publication of Professor Chao's scholarly work at this time. The recent cautious decision of Chinese Communist leaders to initiate the gradual re-entry of that most populous of nations into more direct albeit limited communications with the outside world has quite understandably aroused serious scientific interest as well as widespread popular curiosity regarding the extent to which the structures of Chinese social institutions have changed under the Communist regime. More than 1,000 Americans have visited China since the former President Nixon's much publicized "journey for peace" to Peking in February 1972. Judging from the accounts that have already appeared, the motive and message of these reports will bear careful scrutiny. In making these needed evaluations, the balanced perspective and informed judgment provided by the present study will prove invaluable.

Although everything that has been happening in and to China under the Communist regime has become an object of considerable popular interest, there are a number of reasons why changes affecting family patterns will continue to enjoy priority of concern among social scientists. Up to the fall of the Ch'ing Dynasty in 1911 until the Communist takeover in the late forties, the entire Chinese social system was based on or profoundly influenced by the family. Essentially organized along patrilineal, patrilocal and patriarchal structural lines and grounded on the quasi-religious father-son relationship sanctioned by Confucian piety, this Chinese version of the "trustee-type" family was well designed to assure, among other things, sufficient male offspring for ancestor worship and a form of family solidarity based on descent from a same parent. The locus of family power was in the elders of the patrilineally extended kin group, that is, in the oldest ascendant generation; and inasmuch as this power was embodied in and operated through an intricate web of property and cultic relations, it was impervious to direct challenge and could continue to function more or less effectively as long as these relations remained substantially unchanged.

This traditional Chinese family system provided great social security, but the overemphasis on male prerogatives, the subordination of women, the limitation of freedom of marital choice and divorce, and the comprehensive power vested in parents and kin elders inherent in its structure was bound to bring it under increasing criticism and attack once alien Western views of marriage and freedom gained wider acceptance particularly among intellectuals and upper-class youth. Hence as Professor Chao reminds us, the traditional Chinese family system had become the target of reform long before the Communist takeover. As a matter of fact, new laws and written codes relating to the family appeared shortly after 1911, while the Republican Civil Code of 1931 contained most of the relevant provisions of the Communist Marriage Law of 1950, which is now substantially in force. Yet it must also be noted that owing to the illiteracy of the masses, the pervasive force of custom, and the failure to change the intricate web of institutionalized relationships supporting the traditional system, these earlier attempts to induce family change remained largely ineffective.

In light of these considerations, the question regarding the extent to which the Chinese Communist government has succeeded in altering the nation's traditional family patterns assumes central importance. The Communist regime has had over two decades to implement its 1950 Marriage Law, and this period in the life of a family endured for centuries is far too brief to reveal which officially induced changes will actually persist. The best response we can hope for under these circumstances is a kind of progress report that will bring us up-to-date regarding what has been happening on the family front since the Communist takeover in the late forties. The present study is well designed to serve this purpose since its author has made judicious use of all reliable information currently available to document the regime's experience in this regard up to the present.

Owing to their doctrinal presuppositions, of course, Chinese Communist leaders were fully committed to family reform. Marxist literature on the family, following the position developed by Engels in his work on the family and the origins of private property, uniformly contends that since the regnant bourgeois family is a social institution designed to perpetuate the power of the ruling classes as well as the subjugation and sexual exploitation of women, it must be changed or destroyed. But as orthodox Marxists, Chinese Communist leaders were also committed to approach the problem of family reform in the context of a theory of social change. When it soon became evident, however, that the Chinese family system, at least, did not automatically respond to the changes they had effected in the core structures of society, Chinese Communist leaders did not hesitate to introduce elaborate programs of family education and coercion, contending in typical Marxist fashion that such programs would be necessary only during the current transitional period.

Although we still have very little empirical information relating to the family values, attitudes, feelings, interpersonal relationships, and parenting practices of the great mass of the Chinese people, it appears that the nuclear unit of the family system persists and continues to fulfill its essential functions as the basic cell of society. What have come under increasing pressure and attack, however, are the social structures traditionally embodying the extensions of this nuclear unit through clearly defined patrilineal kinship lines and clan relationships. Considered either from the viewpoint of Chinese Communist leaders or in terms of the traditional Chinese family system, these changes must be regarded as both crucial and strategic. In his famous essay of 1927, Mao Tze-Tung had noted that man in China was routinely subjected to the domination of three systems of authority: political, clan, and theocratic. It now appears under the Communist regime that only the political remains fully operative.

The present study fully documents the gradual emergence of these

xi

structural changes in the Chinese family system, and given the current lack of reliable information on the subject, this undoubtedly constitutes one of its major contributions. But considered in its entirety and in a broader frame of reference, Professor Chao's research also provides ample material for mature reflection on how and to what extent family theory is related to practical programs of action in those concrete historical situations where socialist ideology is accepted as normative. The brief suggestive remarks that follow are offered in the hope that they may serve as relevant starting points for further reflection along these lines.

In the first place, it would be misleading to assume that Chinese Communist leaders proceeded to reform the family on the basis of some well-defined conception of what the family ideally should be. Like socialist theorists everywhere, their positive statements regarding the family are essentially negative in the sense that they are aimed at objectionable aspects of the traditional family system. Indeed, considering the nebulous quality of socialist thinking relative to what the family would or should be in the socialist society — even the prophet, Engels, remained silent on this point — we must conclude either that socialist theorists seriously underestimate the personal and social significance of the family or that they are presently unable to formulate a positive conception of the family consonant with the other components of a social system postulated in their ideology.

Second, it would be analytically naive to attribute exclusive causality in effecting structural changes in a family system directly to the distinctive family ideology (assumed to be) cherished by political leaders in a socialist society. We can use the example of Chinese Communist leaders to illustrate this point. Of necessity, their immediate major concern, reflected both in Mao's misconceived Great Leap Forward was to maximize production and assure China's economic independence. To achieve these goals they were well aware that they had to expand the Chinese economic system through extensive industrialization. But once economic development got under way, most of the family changes noted above became in some measure inevitable.

This assertion in no way implies that there is a simple correlation between stages of economic development and particular forms of family system. It is reasonable to conclude that China's traditional trustee-type form of family organization, at least, would undergo marked structural changes once it was exposed to the full impact of industrializaton and its accompanying urbanization. As in all similarly modernizing societies, one could safely predict, in particular, that extended kinship ties would become weaker, lineage patterns would gradually dissolve, and the nuclear family would begin to emerge as a more independent kinship unit. Although ideologies may play significant causal roles in effecting social change, it is extremely difficult to identify primary causal relations in a society characterized by extensive industrialization as well as highly centralized doctrinaire manipulation.

Thirdly, the above remarks regarding the pressing need to expand the economic system through industrialization does not signify that modern socialist regimes can affect a family system only by serving to facilitate or hasten its transition from an extended to a conjugal form. The peculiarly Chinese, or better, Maoist interpretation of Marxist socialism includes a set of social objectives whose concrete realization would require the complete subordination of conjugal, parental, and familial affections and concerns to the needs of the group or community as these needs are variously defined by those currently in control of the Party.

Essentialy Chinese Communist leaders are attempting to establish a society in which complete control over both the formation of policy and administrative structures is highly centralized, inasmuch as it is vested in top Party leaders whose power extends to every level of the entire system. To assure that the impact of this power on the individual remains proximate, every individual, in conformity with the Party's *mass line* method of organization, is integrated into various groups designed to channel this centralized power down through every sector of society and to provide for the implementation of its directives at all appropriate levels.

According to Maoist thinking, moreover, the individual's acceptance of this total, pervasive inclusion in organizations is to be motivated by unquestioning faith in the system rather than fear of coercion, by a sense of primary loyalty to the party rather than to family or friends, and by an ideal of comradeship. Since this typically Utopian conception of human nature and society relegates the family to a wholly secondary position in the social system and also in the lives of people, its effective implementation would require a complete restructuring of familial roles and functions, together with a radical reorientation of the emotions and affections traditionally associated with their fulfillment. This appears to be a big order, indeed, even though Chinese Communist leaders have available for reeducating recalcitrants the numerous labor camps, euphemistically called *May 7th Schools,* created during the Great Cultural Revolution.

Finally, if one may judge from the family experience of socialist societies in Europe, one may safely predict not only that the Chinese family system will evolve into some form of conjugal type organization but also that like families in other socialist societies it will maintain most of the family values, attitudes, and practices characteristic of the so-called bourgeois family of modern capitalist societies. In the practical order this means that like the family in other socialist societies it will remain unintegrated in the total system and consequently will constitute a perennial source of alienation. This follows logically from the fact that if the goals of the family as an institution differ markedly from the goals of society, the family finds it difficult to fulfill its function of socializing the children; that is, it is unable to mold the child into the type of person who will accept the values of the socialist system as self-evident and who will learn to pattern his behavior in conformity with the expectations that such a system has of the individual in his various roles.

In concluding statement to his work, Professor Chao reminds us that there is need for continuing study of future family development in Soviet Russia and China. Since reliable information regarding many aspects of these massive experiments in engineering social change is still limited, we are grateful to him for making the results of his own persistent research available to us at this time.

Georgetown University
Washington, D.C., 1977

JOHN L. THOMAS, S.J.
RESEARCH PROFESSOR

CHAPTER 1

Woman, Family and Philosophy

*The principle which regulates the existing
social relations between the two sexes - the
legal subordination of one sex to the other
- is wrong in itself, and now one of the
chief hindrances to human improvement;
and it ought to be replaced by a principle
of perfect equality, admitting no power or
privilege on the one side, nor disability on
the other.*

JOHN STUART MILL

This book aims to examine the stages of family development which,
directly or indirectly, bear on the Marxist doctrine of the family. Our
interest focuses particularly on the analysis of various concepts of the
family which are relevant to its emergence and evolution. Further, the
theories of social evolutionists and anthropologists which contribute to
understanding these concepts will be presented.

MATRIARCHATE

J.J. Bachofen in *Das Mutterrecht* formulated the theory of the matriarchate. His argument was that mankind had, at one time, lived in a state
of unregulated promiscuity, and that the difficulty of establishing paternity led to the reckoning of descent through the mother. As a result, the
mother-child bond was the only certain relationship. Although the social
system of matriarchy seems to be a cultural oddity, Bachofen contended
that it existed widely among primitive peoples. African cases of feminine
pre-eminence (Balunda, for example) and inheritance by a sister's son
among American Indians are illustrations of it.[1] The Lycians had a matriarchal social system; children were named after the mother and women
ruled both the household and the state. This reflects the existence of
gynaecocracy. In Bachofen's opinion, gynaecocracy was not the original,
primitive system, but a later development, superseding the earlier state
of promiscuity

What is the principle underlying the precedence of maternity over
paternity? Bachofen postulated that polyandry was the determinant factor. Poverty led to female infanticide, which in turn brought about a

shortage of adult women, and the final result was sexual promiscuity, followed by a mother-centered family life. The Polynesian Marquesans of the Eastern Pacific,[2] Tibetans and Todas of India are commonly known to be polyandrists. Tibetan and Eskimo polyandry has been attributed to female infanticide.

Further evidence about matriarchy was presented by ethnologists who reported mother-dominated families and societies among primitive hunting peoples. These discoveries, in conjunction with the frequent occurrence of the matriarchal family among pastoral peoples in early civilizations, lend support to the hypothesis that the earliest type of family life was mother-centered.[3]

Influenced by Bachofen's *Das Mutterrecht,* J.F. McLennan also claimed that maternal descent usually preceded paternal descent, citing the Iroquois as an example. However, McLennan was not wholly explicit; in adopting Bachofen's statement 'kinship was anciently traced through women only', he contended that descent and inheritance were traced exclusively through the female line.[4] Bachofen's hypothesis is also associated with Darwin's and Spencer's evolutionary theories. Spencer's principles of biological evolution assume a series of stages through which one form of life passes to another; the same principle can be applied equally to cultural evolution, particularly to that of the family institution. Similarly E.B. Tylor, J. Frazer and more recently, E.S. Hartland support the theory of the maternal precedence. L.H. Morgan contributed to the evolutionary theory of the matriarchate in his work *Ancient Society;* the gens of American Indians[5] were originally organized according to mother-right, out of which, later, there evolved the gens organized according to father-right. Among the Iroquois and Pueblo Indians, women were authorized to nominate a candidate for a vacancy on the council of chiefs and reserved the right to impeach an undesirable chief-elect. Further, as A.L. Kroeber notes, it is because of women's ownership of the house that there existed the so-called matriarchate among Zunis.

Adopting the evolutionary theory of the matriarchate, Marx and Engels seek to explain the supremacy of women in the houshold.[6] They maintain that exclusive recognition of the female parent, owing to the impossibility of identifying the male parent, must mean that the mother ruled the house.[7] In the communistic household, which they envisage, most, or all, of the women belong to one and the same gens, while the men come from various gentes - a situation which would favour female dominance.

PROMISCUITY

Social evolutionists contend that the family developed from a state of primitive communism to a higher, or monogamous, form. Sir John Lubbock held, with Bachofen, Morgan, A.W. Howitt and Spencer that prior to marriage there existed an original state of sexual promiscuity which he called 'communal marriage'. Communal marriage arose through the capture of women from other groups, and with marriage by capture, wives became private property.[8] The social phenomenon of 'marriage by capture', Marx inferred, meant that in the patriarchal family system the arrangement of a marriage was not the affair of the two partners, but of their mother. However, Bachofen, as we have seen, was the first to reveal some previously unknown primitive state of sexual promiscuity, and claimed that there was evidence in old classical literature of a marital form prior to monogamy among Greeks and Asiatics, when not only did a man have sexual relations with several women, but a woman associated with several men without offending against morality.[9] He contended that hetaerism, or tribal communal marriage, was the original form of sexual relations.[10]

It is hetaerism which led in time to maternal descent and maternal rule. The natural jealousy of the male - and observation of the monogamous habits of the anthropoid apes - led Darwin to doubt that promiscuity was universal.[11] McLennan maintained that the original sexual relationship was a promiscuous one, polyandry being the first general modification of promiscuity.[12] Promiscuity was modified when a small number of men attached themselves to a particular woman. Since the male partners of a woman bore no necessary relationship to one another under the polyandrous system, it is reasonable to conclude that under primeval conditions kinship could be reckoned only through the mother because paternity was uncertain.

R. Briffault proposed an evolutionary scheme of the development of the family; he employed the evidence of survival, arguing that such institution as the sororate, the levirate, sex hospitality[13] and the exchange of wives pointed to early stages of group marriage and that with the exigencies of property rights, patriarchal institutions followed.

In an attempt to draw together the many lines of progress, Morgan claimed that human mating was, in the beginning, promiscuous, and regarded as evidence of the survival of group marital arrangements among certain Australian tribes. He wrote in *Ancient Society*:

' . . . The consanguine family and the Malayan system of consanguinity presupposed antecedent promiscuity . . . The consanguine family is stamped with the marks of this supposed antecedent state. It is recognized promiscuity within defined limits . . . Promiscuity may be

deduced theoretically as a necessary condition antecedent to the consanguine family, but it lies concealed in the misty antiquity of mankind
beyond the reach of positive knowledge.'[14]

Influenced by the evolutionary theory of promiscuity, socialists believe
that the family developed out of sexual promiscuity and economic communism. The family, in fact, is the last stronghold of the pre-capitalistic,
self-sufficient patriarchal household. It offers a model to communism and
in the same way it is the pattern on which such forms of common life as
ecclesiastical monasticism and brotherhood of sects were moulded.[15]
Engels, moreover, asserted that the traces Bachofen found in historical
and religious survivals do not refer to a promiscuous stage of sexual
relations, but to a much later form, that is, group marriage.[16] Group
marriage, namely the form in which a whole group of men and women
possess one another, leaves little, if any, room for jealousy. Similarly
August Bebel (1840–1913) pointed out that the family began with a
primitive promiscuity; and a kind of improved and dignified promiscuity
has evolved in the socialist state.

E.A. Westermarck is opposed to the evolutionary theory of promiscuity. He argued that man was originally monogamous and adduced as
evidence selected examples of monogamy among the anthropoids and
hunting and food-gathering peoples.[17] Engels, however, inferred that
when Westermarck applied the term 'marriage' to every relationship of
the two sexes until the birth of the offspring, this sort of marriage reflected promiscuous intercourse. Furthermore, it is Westermarck's view
that promiscuity 'involves a suppression of individual inclinations' and
'the most genuine form of it is prostitution.'[18] In his indictment of capitalism, Marx contended that the promiscuity of hataerism in the past had
become, in our time, disguised prostitution, degrading the status of
woman.

VARIOUS FORMS OF THE FAMILY

Regarding various forms of marriage, Morgan undoubtedly exerted a
significant influence upon Marxist doctrine. Let us now look at this assumption. In his book *Ancient Society,* Morgan postulated that the family
has developed from a stage of primitive communism to a higher, i.e.,
monogamous, form. The first stage is the 'consanguine' family in which
there exists intermarriage of brothers and sisters or of cousins, in a
group. Then follows the 'punaluan' family, in which groups of brothers
share their wives and groups of sisters share their husbands.[19] This stage
serves to avoid the intermarriage of brothers and sisters, and abolishes
incestuous mating.

The third stage is the 'pairing' family, in which marriage takes place between single pairs without exclusive cohabitation. This is followed by the 'patriarchal' family, founded on the marriage of one man with several wives, over whom the head of the family has complete control.

The final form of marriage is monogamy, involving exclusive cohabitation of single pairs. Morgan assumed that consanguine, punaluan, and monogamous forms of family were all important. The various forms of family are not separated from one another by clearly defined lines, but have sprung successively from one another and thus represent collectively the growth of the family idea.[20]

Morgan's typology of the family institution evoked Marx's admiration. On the basis of Marx's notes on Morgan's *Ancient Society*, Engels wrote *The Origin of the Family, Private Property and the State* in 1884. He inserts 'the rule of men over female slaves and polygamy' between the pairing family and monogamy. The monogamous family is essentially an outgrowth of private property, he continues, and the existence of private property is no longer significant as it yields to collective and state ownership of the means of production. We will analyze this aspect of Marxist doctrine fully later on.

THE INFLUENCE OF THE EVOLUTIONARY THEORY ON THE MARXIST DOCTRINE OF THE FAMILY

There has been some evidence that the Marxist theory of the family is markedly influenced by social evolutionists. Lubbock, who held with McLennan, Bachofen, Morgan and many others that the first stage of marriage was communal, wrote:

"Bachofen, McLennan and Morgan, the most recent authors who have studied this subject, all agree that the primitive condition of man, socially, was one of pure hetaerism, when marriage did not exist, or, as we may perhaps for convenience call it, of "communal" marriage, where all the men and women in a small community were regarded as equally married to one another.'[21]

Under the influence of McLennan's theory, Lubbock ascribed exogamy to marriage by capture, which alone could explain the origin of individual marriage by giving a man the right to monopolize a woman. This led to the establishment of the Marxist doctrine in relation to the supremacy of man over woman. Bachofen and Morgan are held to represent the theory of ancient matrilineality. Among the scholars who admitted this theory as a keynote to the Greek and Roman gentes, the most conspicuous was the English anthropologist R. Briffault. In 1927 he published *The Mothers,* a three-volume synthesis of mythology that sought to establish the economic evolution of marriage.

Morgan's *Ancient Society* was of the greatest interest to Marx, and came to be viewed as a Socialist classic. On Marx's instructions, Engels attempted to acquaint European socialists with Morgan's discoveries. Engels said:

'No less a man than Karl Marx had made it one of his future tasks to present the results of Morgan's researches in the light of the conclusions of his own, within certain limits, and thus to make clear their full significance. For Morgan in his own way has discovered afresh in America the materialistic conception of history discovered by Marx forty years ago, and in his comparison of barbarism and civilization it had led him, in the main points, to the same conclusions as Marx.'[22]

In 1844 Engels wrote *The Origin of the Family, Private Property, and the State,* subtitled *In the Light of the Research of Lewis Henry Morgan.* Engels outlined its contents and enriched them with new materials on early German and Celtic tribes. Engels wrote in 1891:

'The fourteen years which have elapsed since the publication of his (Morgan's) chief work have greatly enriched the material available for the study of the history of primitive human societies. The anthropologists, travelers and primitive historians . . . contributed either new material or new points of view. As a result, some of Morgan's minor hypotheses have been shaken or even disapproved. But not one of the great leading ideas of his work has been ousted by this new material.[23]

In proving that private property and the state were related in history, Morgan had demonstrated that both were only passing phases in the evolution of human society. Herein lies the agreement between Morgan and Marx; and thus the implications for socialists were obvious. It is their belief that the society which organizes production anew on the basis of free and equal association of the producers will put the whole state machinery where it will then belong into the museum of antiquities.

In declaring *Ancient Society* a model of materialist history, Engels was, to a certain extent, justified; today Socialists follow Engels in his estimation of *Ancient Society.* In 1891, for example, Kautsky translated it into German; Bebel applied Morgan's theory of the matrilineal gens[24] to predict the equality of women under socialism; Daniel de Leon frequently cited Morgan's writings and claimed him as a Socialist prophet. In 1918. the centenary of Morgan's birth, the *Weekly People,* the organ of the Socialists Labour Party, published a special issue to commemorate his work.[25]

Marx and Engels adopted Morgan's notions and evolutionary theories in treating the origin of bourgeois sex life and family morals together with the emergence of private property. Morgan's influence in this sphere was considerable, but he was unpopular with bourgeois scientists because of his reflections upon the moral foundations of their society.[26] Soviet anthropologists' belief in the communistic nature of primitive society is further reinforced by N.Y. Marr, the virtual director of Soviet linguistics until 1950.[27] Marr is convinced that there will be in the future a re-emergence of an archaic socialist society, namely a classless society.

This brief review should demonstrate sufficiently the relationship of evolutionary theories and Marxist doctrine on the family. They are but two aspects of the same socio-cultural reality and change in two historically different periods and in divergent interests.

In the first part of my investigation, an attempt will be made to analyze in greater detail the Marxist doctrine on the family, which includes the main theories of the family. Our interest will be focused on the analysis of various Marxist ideas of the family and woman's status, including also those of Engels, Bebel, Lenin, Stalin and Mao Tze-tung.

NOTES

[1] Robert H.Lowie, *The History of Ethnological Theory*, New York: Rinehart and Company, Inc., 1937, p. 42.
[2] E.S. Craihill Handy, *The Native Culture of the Marquesas*, Bernice P. Bishop Museum Bulletin 9, Honolulu, 1923, p. 101.
[3] Joseph K. Folsom, *The Family*. New York: John Wiley and Sons, Inc., 1934, p. 114
[4] J. F. McLennan, *Studies in Ancient History*. London: Macmillan and Co., 1886, p. 323.
[5] From the time of Morgan until the present most American anthropologists have used the term 'clan' to designate a matrilineal sib in contradistinction to a patrilineal sib for which the term 'gens' has been used. George P. Murdock, *Social Structure*. New York: The Macmillan Company, 1949, p. 145.
[6] 'The Woman Question' *Selections from the Writings of K. Marx, F. Engels, V.I. Lenin and J. Stalin* (New York: International Publishers, 1951.), p. 12.
[7] *Ibid.* p. 12.
[8] J. Lubbock, *Origin of Civilization* (London, 1870), pp.66-84.
[9] F. Engels, *The Origin of the Family, Private Property and the State* (New York: International Publishers, 1942), p. 10.
[10] Johann J. Bachofen, *Das Mutterrecht*, (Basel, 1897), pp. xviii xix, xx, 10.
[11] Charles Darwin, *The Descent of Man* (New York: D. Appleton and Co., 1872), pp. 600-605.
[12] John F. McLennan, *Studies in Ancient History* (London, 1896), pp.50-55.
[13] Sex hospitality is not equivalent to promiscuity. The passing union with a guest is permitted solely on condition that it in no way infringes the law of exogamy. Maxim Kovalevsky, *Tableau des origines et de l'évolution de la famille et de la propriété*, (Stockholm Samson and Wallin, 1890.) p. 14.
[14] Lewis H. Morgan, *Ancient Society* (New York: Holt, 1907), p.67.
[15] Carl Brinkman, 'Family', *The Encyclopedia of the Social Sciences*, Vols. V-VI, p.67, 1931.
[16] Engels, *Op. cit.*, p.28.
[17] Carl Brinkman, 'Family', *Op. cit.*, p.65.
[18] Engels, *Op. cit.*, p.32.
[19] *Ibid.*, pp.394-95.
[20] John Lubbock, *The Origin of Civilization and the Primitive Condition of Man* (London, 1870, 2nd edition), p.77.
[21] John Lubbock, *Op. cit.*, p.77.

[22] F. Engels, *Op. cit.*, p.5 - Preface to the First edition.

[23] *Ibid.*, p.17.

[24] Morgan's discovery of the true nature of the 'gens' and its relation to the 'tribe' laid bare the inner organization of the primitive communistic society. Along with the dissolution of the primitive communities, society begins to be differentiated into separate, unequal and finally antagonistic classes.

[25] *Daily People*, September 6, 1905; *Weekly People*, November 23, 1918 and November 22, 1919.

[26] Engels, *Op. cit.*, pp.64,67.

[27] N.Y. Marr advanced a scheme of linguistic evolution in which the 'plural' preceded the 'singular' and thought it was collective awareness of collective production with collective tools.

P. Tolstoy, 'Morgan and Soviet Anthropological Thought', *American Anthropologist*, 54(1954), p.10.

CHAPTER II

Engels' and Bebel's Ideas on the Family

Anyone who knows anything of history knows that great social changes are impossible without the feminine ferment. Social progress can be measured exactly by the social position of the fair sex.
MARX, *Letter*, 1869.

Discussion of Engels' *The Origin of the Family, Private Property and the State* has criticized his use of Morgan's data on family evolution. Engels supported Morgan's thesis, however, and maintained that, though some of Morgan's hypothesis have been found untenable in the light of present research techniques, this should not vitiate his reputation as the positive value of his contribution has been influential. Morgan's greatest contributions were his findings afterwards interpreted and used by Engels himself in support of his views on the emancipation of women. Engels' original assumption was that group marriage evolving to monogamy served as an approach to the study of the subjugation of women in modern capitalist society.

Morgan's *Ancient Society* was used as a rationale for a stern indictment of male superiority and dominance over women. The inequality between the sexes is bitterly attacked. On the basis of his extensive knowledge in many fields, Engels condemned the capitalistic conventions which have abased women. In so doing, he argued that the capitalist family system is inherently founded upon private property, the supremacy of men, and the indissolubility of the marriage pact. Once private property has been abolished, the remaining two will be deprived of their vital support and will inevitably dissolve. Engels' analysis is rich in insight and establishes many important and fundamental principles of sociological analysis.

1. ENGELS' GENERAL IDEAS

The general propositions in Engels' work are impressive. Although not explicitly formulated, they lay the foundation of his approach to the study of the family, and organize his method of analysis. As a useful index one may summarize the main points of his *The Origin of the Family Private*

9

Property, and the State. It should be noted, however, that although the central interest of this study lies in exploring the general propositions with regard to the family, the interconnection of property ownership and the family must be taken into consideration.

(1) The first form of the family was based, not on natural, but on economic conditions - on the victory of private property over primitive - natural communal property.[1]

(2) Changes in methods of production result in changes in the relations of production and thus they modify the totality of social relations within the family. To procure the necessities of life had always been the business of the man; the taming of the animals and the subsequent care of them were the man's work.[2]

(3) The division of labor between the two sexes is determined by few other causes than by the position of woman in society, which is to say that the division of labour is characteristic of all societies.[3]

(4) Authority and property relationships between the sexes in the family are determined by the role which men and women play in the productive process. As it was man's part to obtain food and the instruments of labour necessary for the purpose, he was the owner of instruments of labour.[4] In proportion as wealth increased, the man's position in the family became more important than the woman's.[5]

(5) The establishment of the exclusive supremacy of the man had its effects first in the patriarchal family, which was an outgrowth of the domestication of animals and the breeding and care of flocks and herds.[6] This economic innovation developed into a hitherto unsuspected source of wealth and created entirely new social relations.[7] According to the social custom of the time, i.e., the division of labour, the man was the owner of the new source of subsistence, the cattle, and later of the new instruments of labour, the slaves.[8]

(6) Individual sexual love, in the modern sense of the term, itself plays a small part in the rise of monogamy (patriarchal),[9] the aim of which is, on the basis of economic conditions, to make man supreme in the family, and to propagate as the future heirs to his wealth, children indisputably his own.[10]

(7) Both polygamy and polyandry are simply exceptional 'historical luxury products.'[11]

(8) With the patriarchal family, and still more with the single monogamous family, household management lost its public character. The wife, the head-servant, excluded from all participation in social production.[12]

This resulted in her economic disadvantage as well as in social and sexual discrimination.

(9) Co-existent with the rise of monogamous marriage, there emerged 'hetaerism', i.e., sexual intercourse between men and unmarried women outside marriage, which develops more and more into open prostitution.[13] As a consequence of 'hetaerism' there developed the pattern of neglected wife, wife's attendant lover, and cuckolded husband.[14]

(10) Sexual love in the relationship with a woman becomes the real rule among the proletariat, i.e., romantic love between mates is a modern concept depending for its realization upon the degree of equality of rights of the sexes. Such love can only develop when as a result of the abolition of property, marriage is no longer marriage of convenience for the preservation and inheritance of property.[15]

(11) In Protestant society, the son of the bourgeois family is theoretically free to choose a wife on the basis of mutual love. But this is an instance of bourgeois hypocrisy, since, in view of property relations, parents still preserve the power to choose mates for their children from their own class.[16]

(12) The lady of civilization, surrounded by false homage and insulated from all real work, has an infinitely lower social position than the hard-working woman of barbarism.[17]

(13) The emancipation of women is possible only when women can take part in production outside the home on a large, communal scale, and domestic work no longer claims anything but an insignificant amount of time. Now that large-scale industry has taken the wife out of the home into the labour market and into the factory, no basis for male supremacy is left in the proletarian household.[18]

(14) Under capitalism, when the wife remains excluded from public production and unable to earn, if she wants to take part in public production and earns independently, she cannot carry out family duties. Thus the modern individual family is founded on the open or concealed domestic slavery of the wife, and modern society is a mass composed of these individual families as its molecules.[19]

(15) With the transfer of the means of production into common ownership, the single family ceases to be the economic unit of society. The care and education of the children becomes a public affair whether they are legitimate or not; this relieves the wife, now socially employed, of oppressive home burdens.[20]

(16) The transformation of permanent heritable wealth-the means of production-into social or common property will reduce to a mimimum all anxiety about bequeathing and inheritance.[21] Full freedom of marriage

can only be established in the absence of all the economic considerations which exert a powerful influence on the choice of a marriage partner. Then there is no other motive (money, for example) left except mutual inclination or love.[22]

(17) As sexual love is by its nature exclusive, marriage based on sexual love is by its nature individual; hence if the economic considerations that now force women to submit to the habitual infidelity of men, disappear, women will be placed on an equal footing with men. This equality thus achieved will tend more effectively to make men monogamous than to make women polyandrous.[23]

The preceding excerpts and generalizations are impressive and demonstrate a wealth of ideas. Most of them foreshadowed the formulation of policy aimed at modifying the family institution after the Bolshevik Revolution. Despite the manifest weakness of Engels' work in the selection of data on primitive societies, it provides numerous valuable suggestions from which later researchers on the subject of the family might profit considerably.

2. THE MARXIST DOCTRINE ON HISTORICAL DEVELOPMENT

Engels, under the influence of the evolutionists, such as McLennan, Lubbock, Briffault, Bachofen, and Morgan, undertook an investigation of the historical development of the family. His interest focused on the monogamous form in the capitalistic social structure where the female sex is allegedly oppressed.

1. The first is the "un-family" stage in which sexual relations were absolutely unregulated, and any permanent relationship between husband and wife and parent and child was unknown. Out of this condition arose a form of the family known as "consanguine". To quote Engels' statements on the consanguine family:

> Here the marriage groups are separated according to generations; all the grandfathers and grandmothers within the limits of the family are all husbands and wives of one another; so are also their children; the fathers and mothers; the latter's children will form a third circle of common husbands and wives; and their children, the great-grandchildren of the first group, will form a fourth. . . . At this stage the relationship of brother and sister also includes as a matter of course the practice of sexual intercourse with one another.[24]
> There is a lack of historical evidence for the existence of this form of

family, even among the most primitive peoples. However, Engels assumed that this form reflects the previous unorganized stage of promiscuity which foreshadowed the subsequent development of the family.

2. The second is the "punaluan" family,[25] which excludes brothers and sisters from marriage, and later the brothers' and sisters' children and grandchildren. As a result of these prohibitions, this group developed into a gens, that is, a firm circle of blood relations in the female line, between whom marriage was prohibited.

There is a clear indication that Engels was influenced by Morgan in proposing this form of family. Morgan described the punaluan family in *Ancient Society* as follows:

. . . Founded upon the intermarriage of several sisters, own and collateral, with each others' husbands in a group; the joint husbands not being necessarily kinsmen of each other. Also, on the intermarriage of several brothers, own and collateral, with each others' wives, in a group; these wives not being necessarily of kin of each other, although often the case in both instances. In each case the group of men were conjointly married to the group of women.[26]

In support of the existence of the punaluan family advanced by Morgan, Engels held that this form was symbolic of the American system. He disagreed with Spanish missionaries who viewed this family system with horror. In defending the position of Engels, however, Marx asserted that if Bachofen considered these punaluan marriages "lawless", a man of that period would consider most present marriages between near and remote cousins on the father's or mother's side to be incestuous marriages contracted between blood brothers and sisters.[27] Caesar's report of the Britons, who were in the middle stage of barbarism, is best explained as group marriage, since every ten or twelve men had wives in common, especially brothers with sisters and parents with children.[28] The group marriage, as it prevailed in ancient times, is a primitive form, while the punaluan family is considered a higher stage of development. The former also appears to represent the social level of vagrant, savages, whereas the latter presupposes relatively stable settlements of "communistic" communities and suggests a higher phase of development.

3. The third stage is the "pairing" family, in which one man lived with one woman in a temporary unit, although polygamy and infidelity remained the right of man. However, an extremely strict fidelity was imposed on the woman as long as she lived with the man, and any adultery on her part was cruelly punished. The pairing family[29] was to grow more stable and widely accepted as the "gens"[30] developed. Among the Iroquois, for example, at the lower stage of barbarism, we find that marriage

was prohibited among all relatives, including several hundred degrees of kinship.

The pairing marriage was dissoluble at the desire of either partner, but among many tribes, such as the Iroquois, public opinion was against separation. In this respect, after the first decade of the Russian Revolution the legal position of marriage reflected what Engels had called the "pairing" marriage. The only difference was that the Communist Party, now in power, maintained its rights to aver, by propaganda and internal discipline, automatic divorce among citizens.[31]

The pairing family was unable to abolish the "communist" household inherited from ancient times, where the supremacy of women was strong. Engels believed that the key factor which caused the deposition of women from the superior status was a change in the economic system. The production of wealth, which exerted an irresistible impact on pairing marriage brought it about. Since it was the man's role to obtain food and instruments of labour, he was the owner of the new sources of subsistence (the cattle), and later of the new instruments of labour (the slaves). Proportionately as his wealth increased, the man's position in the family became more important than the woman's, and the traditional order of inheritance was overthrown in favour of his children. As a result, mother-right was disrupted.[32]

The overthrow of mother-right represented the historical defeat of the female sex. Man became the master in the home and woman was relegated to servitude. She became the slave of his lust and a mere instrument for reproduction. This change was especially conspicuous among the Greeks.

4. The fourth stage is the patriarchal family; the establishment of the supremacy of the male. Engels quoted Morgan's description of the essential features of this form of family as follows:

. . . The organization of a number of persons, bound and free, into a family, under paternal power, for the purpose of holding lands, and for the care of flocks and herds. . . . The chiefs, at least, lived in polygamy. . . . Those held to slavery and those employed as servants, lived in the marriage relation.[33]

Marx added:

The modern family contains in germ not only slavery (servitus), but also serfdom, since from the beginning it is related to agricultural services. It contains in miniature all the contradictions which later extend throughout society and its state.[34]

The patriarchal family emerged as an intermediate form between the pairing family and monogamy,[35] and formed the transitional stage between the matriarchal unit, evolving from group marriage, and the single family of today. In the German family system the economic unit was composed of several single families. The Roman family typically illustrated this type; the father exercised absolute power and other membes had no rights. The Semitic family was patriarchal; the patriarch himself lived in polygyny, while other members lived in monogamy. The Chinese society, as Mao Tze-tung points out, was characterized by small-scale production based on individual labour, dominated by the patriarch.[36] In this family system all the members of the family subordinate themselves absolutely to patriarchal rule.

The patriarchal family system has been bitterly attacked in Communist societies, because under this system woman has been excluded from social production, i.e., from employment outside the home. As an illustration, in Chinese society one of three qualifications in the selection of a mate is the wife's ability to endure household drudgery. Under the Communist regime in China, the new Marriage Law has emancipated young people, but especially women, from the traditional family bondage. For example, in mass meetings and public trials, the maltreatment of wives and daughters-in-law is severly condemned.

5. The final stage is the monogamous family which developed from the loose pairing family and the patriarchal family household.[37] As indicated before, Engels believed that monogamy, the first form of the family, was based not on natural, but on economic conditions, that is, on the victory of private property over primitive, natural communal property or collectivism.[38] Consequently, the supremacy of man in the family, and the inheritance of his property by children, were inevitable. Monogamous marriage was not historically a reconciliation of man and woman; on the contrary, it came as the subjugation of one sex by another. This antagonism between the sexes was unknown in all previous history. To quote Engels:

> In an old unpublished manuscript, written by Marx and myself in 1846,[39] I find the words "the first division of labour is that between man and woman for the propagation of children". And today I can add: "The first class opposition that appears in history coincides with the development of the antagonism between man and woman in monogamous marriage, and the first class oppression coincides with that of the female sex by the male".[40]

Monogamy represented great historical progress in relation to the previous forms of marriage. The Communists contend, however, that with the institution of private property which gave man economic power, monogamy became adulterated. Man enslaved woman, but remained polygamous, while woman was prevented from being polyandrous. Engels quoted Morgan's statement on this subject:

The old conjugal system, now reduced to narrower limits by the gradual disappearance of the punaluan group, still environed the advancing family, which it was to follow to the verge of civilization. . . . It finally disappeared in the new form of 'hetaerism', which still follows mankind in civilization as a dark shadow upon the family.[41]

Engels claimed that since monogamy arose as a consequence of the concentration of wealth in the hands of man, it would eventually disappear with the transfer of private property to collective ownership. The triumph of the proletariat revolution would destroy the economic foundations of the so-called monogamy of the bourgeois as well as the legal form of family and marriage relations, riddled as it is with hypocrisy, which is recognized by capitalist states. Under Socialism men would be compelled to be true monogamists because women would not tolerate unfaithfulness. This reflects Bachofen's dictum that monogamy was brought about through the desire of women to Morgan's statement that the family must advance as society advances, and change as society changes, as it had done in the past.[42] Also the transformation of private property into collective property,[43] will mark the end of wage-labour, and the spectacle of women surrendered for money.

In addition, through the disappearance of male supremacy, which originated from property relations, the indissolubility of marriage will be abolished. Engels' rationale was that marriage based entirely on love is the only relationship that is moral. In other words, the marriage in which love alone survives has meaning and value; but, owing to the variable of individual sexual love, expecially in men, separation will be beneficial for both partners if their affection terminates. It will be seen that Engels' ideas were considerably altered in the Soviet Union in the law of September 28, 1935 with reference to divorce. A divorce case must now be recorded in the passport and birth certificates of those involved. This obviously discourages the filing of a petition for divorce.

3. THE ENSLAVEMENT OF WOMEN

Marx asserted that 'men make their own history', but do so 'under circumstances directly given and transmitted from the past'. In line with Marxian ideas, Stalin interpreted the enslavement of woman as man-made history. History teaches that the social group which takes the principal part and performs the main functions in social production must inevitably control the means of production. Under the matriarchate, women controlled agricultural production, while men roamed the forests for food. Eventually, with the advent of stock-breeding and the invention of the spear and the bow and arrow, the principal role passed to men.

With the increase of means of production and thus of wealth, the great social division of labour for the first time engendered the cleavage of society in two classes: masters and slaves, exploiters and exploited.[44]

A. The Division of Labour and the Status of Women

Throughout Engels' *The Origin of the Family, Private Property and the State*[45] the term 'the mode of production' provides a framework for analysis. His contention was that the development of modes of production proceeded through a regular series: primitive communism, slavery, feudalism, capitalism, and communism, the last belonging to an indeterminate future. In a society which was called 'asiatic'' and "gentile" by Marx and Engels respectively, classes did not exist. They appeared to be the products of division of labour,[46] which was identified, in the *German Ideology* with the institution of private property.

In *the Origin of the Family* a distinction is made between three great social divisions of labour, of which the first two occurred in the "barbaric" stage. In the beginning, as a consequence of domesticating animals, men were able to produce more than was necessary for immediate subsistence. Engels thought that herds were originally possessed by the community, but they drifted, for unknown reasons, into the hands of private individuals. This led to the division of society into masters and slaves and, accordingly, destroyed the equality which existed previously between the sexes. Men owned the herds, while women were now confined to the tasks of the household. The division of labour within the family gave rise to the division of property between the sexes. The domestic work of the woman became insignificant in comparison with the acquisition of the necessities of life by the man; thus the woman became subordinate to the man. To emancipate woman and make her the equal of man is impossible if she is restricted to private domestic labour. To quote Engels: "In the family the husband is the bourgeois and the wife represents the proletariat".[47]

B. Private Property and the Enslavement of Woman

A no less interesting analysis in the light of the Marxist doctrine of the family is made by August Bebel.

In presenting the Marxian doctrine of the family, Bebel, like most other evolutionary theorists, contended that the present human family began with the "horde". As in the cattle herd, human sexual impulses were gratified according to opportunity. Bebel was convinced that among primitive peoples men and women were equal in bodily strength; nevertheless primitive women were subordinate to men because of their weakness during the periods of pregnancy, birth, and lactation.[48] By exploiting women's natural weakness, men enslaved them; thus woman was a slave before slavery existed.

Before the time of enduring union between pairs, women were regarded as private property or slaves of tribes, and used for communal purposes. In this stage, promiscuity was limited to the group which possessed property in common. One man employed one or more women as his own slave or property, and later provided them with the status of wife; it was out of the improvement in the condition of woman that marriage emerged. This social situation also contributed to the foundation of private property, of the family, tribe and state.[49]

Since monogamy would emerge as a result of the concentration of considerable wealth in the hands of individuals with subsequent inheritance, the shift from private property to common or socialist ownership would eliminate the need for both monogamy and prostitution. Bebel's logic is that monogamy among women and polygamy among men result from the economic condition in capitalist societies.

C. Participation in Social Production and the Emancipation of Woman

As industries developed and bourgeois society grew, women gradually tended to gain their individuality. The next step would be directed towards the emancipation of women when a different form of family was evolved to suit the industrial way of making a living. It is explicitly recognized by the Marxists that the general independence of women can be attained only in a free and equal society. In other words, the great achievement will rest with the productive forces.[50] Moreover, when private property is liquidated in a socialist society, class struggle will lose its validity and, accordingly, the problem of women's emancipation will be solved; this is the true meaning of Marxism.[51] However, in Bebel's view there is grave doubt that a complete solution to sexual equality could be anticipated merely by the solution of the labour problem in a capitalist economic system. Bebel proposed an organized effort for the attainment of political and legal rights for women and argued that not until the overthrow of the capitalist system and the establishment of a socialist society could the full emancipation of woman be attained. Furthemore, Bebel suggested that the attraction of women to industry should be encouraged as a step towards their freedom. This is intended to counteract the isolation and the backwardness of women under the pre-capitalist patriarchal family.[52] In like manner, Engels claimed that the required condition for the liberation of the wife is to bring the entire female sex into public industry. This would abolish the economic dependence of woman upon man for the necessities of life.[53]

Bebel and Engels exerted a profound influence on Lenin in formulating the programme and policy for women's emancipation in Russia after the Bolshevik Revolution. Again, Lenin and the international communists saw the struggle for woman's rights as an aspect of the class struggle and maintained that complete emancipation of the sex was dependent upon the abolition of class exploitation.[54]

4. THE MARXIST IMAGE OF THE BOURGEOIS FAMILY

The Capitalist Institution and the Bourgeois Family

The discussion of the family institution in the *Communist Manifesto* is not extensive; nevertheless, the idea of the family has been developed in the *Selected Works* of Marx and Engels.

Marx indicated that the contemporary bourgeois family which implies the economic dependence of women of the upper classes and the prostitution of women[55] of the lower classes reflects the property relationships of a class-laden society. The basic logic rests on the fact that the social sub-system, that is, to say, the economic institution, evolves in a lineal direction, and that the family, a dependent variable in causal-functional relationship, is merely adapted to and affected by changing economic conditions. In view of the impossibility of existence for the bourgeoisie without a constatnt renewal of the means of production, Marx declared that the bourgeoisie stripped the sentimental veil from the family and reduced it to a mere mercenary contract.[56] Marxists hold that the culture of any society is based on the means of production. Because the proletarian is propertyless, his relationship to his wife and children no longer has anything in common with bourgeois family relations.[57] Marx wrote in the *Communist Manifesto*:

> On what foundation is the present family, the bourgeois family, based? On capital, on private gain. In its completely developed form this family exists only among the bourgeoisie. But this state of things finds its complement in the practical absence of the family among the proletarians, and in public prostitution.[58]

Clearly related to the above Marxist doctrine, the *Communist Manifesto* rejects the contention of its adversaries that communists attempt to eliminate the family institution. They concede, however, that they seek to end a form of family founded on a mercenary basis, but they strive instead to abolish the unjustifiable exploitation of children by their parents. They advocate the transfer of the responsibility for education from the home to society. It is stated in the *Communist Manifesto*:

> Do you charge us with wanting to stop the exploitation of children by their parents?. To this crime we plead guilty. But, you will say, we destroy the most hallowed of relations, when we replace home educa-

tion by social. . . . The Communists have not invented the intervention of society in education; they do but seek to alter the character of
that intervention, and to rescue education from the influence of the
ruling class.[59]

Moreover, in answer to the charge that Communists intend to make
women common property they retort:

The bourgeois sees in his wife a mere instrument of production. He
hears that the instruments of production are to be exploited in common, and, naturally, can come to no other conclusion than that the lot
of being common to all will likewise fall to the women. He has not even
a suspicion that the real point aimed at is to do away with the status
of women as mere instruments of production.[60]

Again, Marx and Engels repudiated the accusation that Communists introduced a community of women. They wrote:

For the rest, nothing is more ridiculous than the virtuous indignation
of our bourgeois at the community of women. . . . The Communists
have not need to introduce community of women; it has existed almost
from time immemorial . . . Our bourgeois, not content with having
the wives and daughters of their proletarians at their disposal. . . .
take the greatest pleasure in seducing each other's wives.[61]

Is it not also all very well to stigmatize Marxists as seducers?

Bourgeois Marriage

Marx and Engels remarked that bourgeois marriage degenerates into
a commercial transaction and thus has lost all characteristics of tender-
ness and sincerity. The bourgeois dismisses the sanctity of marriage and
becomes a concealed adulterer, just as the merchant ignores the sanctity
of property as he deprives others of their property by speculation and
deception. It is stated in the *Communist Manifesto*:

Bourgeois marriage is in reality a system of wives in common and thus,
at the most, what the Communists might possibly be reproached with
is that they desire to introduce, in substitution for a hypocritically
concealed, an openly legalized community of women.[62]

Engels ascertained that it is an error to speak of "the" family without
qualification. Historically, in the family as conceived by the bourgeoisie,
the only ties are those of boredom and money.[63] The character of this
kind of family is reflected by its officially sacred status and in everyday
hypocritical phraseology. In fact, it seems that the concept of the family
wanes, though genuine family feelings based on concrete conditions can
still be found. In the eighteenth century, the concept of the family was
greatly modified. The individual roles within it, such as obedience, affection, and conjugal fidelity were vanishing. However, the essential compo-

nents of the family, such as property relations and life in common, the conditions that were necessary because of the existence of children, the structure of modern towns, and the development of capital, persisted.[64] As an illustration for a short period, during the French Revolution the family was virtually abolished.[65] In the nineteenth century, the family continued to exist even though its dissolution was becoming apparent owing to the expanding and accelerating development of industry and competition.[66]

Bourgeois marriage has been also discussed by Marx and Engels in the *Holy Family*.[67] They wrote:

Adultery, seduction is an honour to the seducer and is looked upon as quite the thing. . . . But the poor girl! Infanticide that is a terrible crime! If she clings to her honour, she must destroy the evidence of dishonour; but when she sacrifices her child to the prejudices of the world she is regarded as even more blameworthy, and is herself in a vicious circle in which all the mechanism of civilization moves. . . .

The debasement of the female sex is an essential character-trait of civilization, no less than of barbarism, with the difference, that under civilization all the vices which barbarism practises in a simple and straight forward way, are now preserved in complicated, ambiguous, and hypocritical semblance. . . . [68]

According to Marx and Engels, during the nineteenth century, prostitution and trafficking in human flesh became a noticeable branch of commercial enterprise. All these phenomena resulted from the institution of the bourgeois family and marriage.

The Exploitation of Women

The effects on the family when a change occurs in the means of production can be illustrated by the case of the shift from locally self-sufficient agricultural economy, such as domestic handicraft production, to large-scale factory production under commercial and industrial capitalism.[69] Under such conditions the home was separated from the place of work, and joint domestic labour by family members gave way to the sale of individual labour to employers who owned the means of production and utilized them for profit. Men and women, husbands and wives, were frequently compelled to compete for the same jobs in the labour market.

Engels deprecated the laxity of girls' morality in factories, and, according to the factories Enquiry Commission, he cited the statement of a witness from Leicester that he would rather see his daughter beg than go into the factories, which were complete hell holes.[70] Elsewhere, Engels quoted a statement by a Manchester witness that three-quarters of the girls aged between 14 to 20 who worked in factories were unchaste;[71] and he asserted that manufacturers had immoral relations with their female employees.[72] It was his belief that the employment of women ultimately would dissolve the family. When the wife spends twelve or thirteen hours everyday in the mill, he stated, and the husband works the same length of time there, the children are inevitably deprived of proper care.[73]

The Impact of Capitalism on Family Stability

In *The Condition of the Working-Class in England in 1844* Engels described the condition of the proletarian family. He indicated that drunkenness and debauchery were conspicuous vices among the workers who had not yet become class-conscious, and who submissively accepted the bourgeois social order. Elsewhere, with respect to the deplorable status of women in bourgeois society, Engels asserted:

If people are relegated to the position of animals, they are left with the alternatives of revolting or sinking into bestiality. Moreover the middle classes[74] are themselves in no small degree responsible for the extent to which prostitution exists-how many of the 40,000 prostitutes who fill the streets of London every evening are dependent for their livelihood on the virtuous bourgeois? How many of them were first seduced by a member of the middle classes, so that they now have to sell their persons to passers-by in order to live?[75]

Marx and Engels assumed that forcing women and children to work in factories undermined the family relationship and completely transformed the relationship between parents and children and between man and wife. For example, as a result of the employment of women in the factory, children were left unattended and grew wild like weeds by the wayside. Engels wrote:

The employment of the wife dissolves the family utterly and of necessity, and the dissolution . . . brings the most demoralizing consequences for parents as well as children. A married woman cannot really be regarded as a mother if she is unable to spare the time to look after her child, if she hardly sees the infant at all, and if she cannot satisfy her baby's elementary need for loving care . . . Children who grow up under such conditions have no idea of what a proper family life should be. . . . When they grow up and have children of their own they feel out of place because their own early experience has been that of a lonely life . . . In brief, the children become emancipated and regard their parents' house merely as lodging, and quite often if they feel like it, they leave home and take lodging elsewhere.[76]

There was another unfortunate aspect of the industrial situation. As the operation of spinning and weaving machinery required little muscular strength, capitalist employer tended to engage women and children for this work, to the exclusion of able-bodied male workers, whose earnings were thereby reduced. Engels stated:

> In spinning mills women and girls alone work the trottle spindles. . . . The piecers are nearly always women and children, but occasionally one finds young men aged between 18 and 20 and even an older spinner who would otherwise be unemployed. . . . [77] Power looms are generally worked by young women aged between 15 and 20 or a little more.[78]

According to Engels, if the wife provided the greatest part, or even the whole of the common possession, the form of ownership was abnormal; she would become arrogant about contributing the greatest share of livelihood. In this case, the binding tie of the family would not be affection, but private interest lurking under the cloak of a pretended community of possessions.[79] On the other hand, compulsory work would replace play for the children who would provide free labour at home. This mode of production, while augmenting the materials of life, at the same time increased the degree of exploitation. As the capitalist mode of production eliminated the economic basis of parental authority, it is clear that all traditional family ties would be broken. Marx asserted:

> It was not, however, the misuse of parental authority that created the capitalist exploitation, whether direct or indirect, of children's labor; but on the contrary, it was the capitalist mode of exploitation which, by sweeping away the economic basis of parental authority, made its exercise degenerate into a mischievous misuse of power.[80]

Furthermore, Engels maintained that as a consequence of continuous employment of children and unmarried women, female workers became unsuitable as future housewives. It seemed to Engels that a girl who worked in a mill from her ninth year would be unfit for domestic work. Employment outside the home prevented unmarried women from learning knitting, sewing, cooking and washing, which were the most ordinary duties of housewives.[81] It did not seem to Engels that the disintegration of the feudal family would lead to a higher form of family organization.

The Exploitation of Children

A further factor contributing to family instability was the employment of children. This resulted in factory legislation which began to interfere in and regulate "home-labour". This was viewed as a direct attack on parental authority, and the inevitable result was that children were exploited. It must be acknowledged that the modern industrial and factory system, in destroying the economic foundation on which the traditional family was based, also loosened all traditional family ties. In *Capital,* Marx described the ways in which children reacted against parental control. He wrote:

The system of unlimited exploitation of children's labour in general, and the so-called home-labor in particular is maintained only because the parents are able, without check or control to exercise this arbitrary and mischievous power over their young and tender offspring. . . . The children and young persons, therefore, in all such cases may justifiably claim from the legislature, as a natural right, that an exemption should be secured to them from what destroys prematurely their physical strength and lowers them in the scale of intellectual and moral beings.[82]

Further, Marx held that following the dissolution of the feudal family system, modern industry necessarily creates a new economic foundation for a higher form of family and new relations between the sexes. In other words, on the strength of the collective working group composed of individuals of both sexes and all ages, modern industry is capable of making social progress. However, from the point of view that the labourer works in the interest of the process of production rather than in his own, it is a breeding-ground for corruption and slavery.[83]

It should be noted that Engels' views have been fundamentally revised and amended by Marx in his *Capital*. Marx did not, however, modify his indictment of capitalism for its introduction of new technology. The core of Marx's thesis is that, while he and Engels keenly desired to see the capitalist system abolished, they did not condemn it, nor could they do so without vitiating and destroying their own case.[84] Indeed, they paid tribute to it, and in doing so they turned sharply on such writers as Proudhon and Sismondi, whose opposition of the capitalistic system led them to advocate a return to a more primitive economic system.[85] By contrast, Marx stated in his letter to P.V. Annenkov, December 1846, that when new productive forces were achieved, men would change their method of production and subsequently their economic relations.[86] The handmill, for example, was a characteristic of feudal society, while the steam-mill society appeared with the industrial capitalist. It follows that when men change their mode of production-their way of securing their livelihood-they change all their social relations within the family.[87]

5. WOMEN AND SOCIALISM

Marxist doctrine on the family seeks to indicate that the emancipation of mankind, particularly the realization of the ideas of women's liberation, could not be achieved unless capitalism was overcome, and a socialist society established. The Bolshevists have attempted to achieve this, and the Marxist doctrine on the family is well suited to the task of undertaking a consistent anti-feudal revolution with all its socialist implication. The same Marxist doctrine has been fully developed by a number of socialists and analyzed in the Constitution of socialist society. Lenin said:

> There is not a trace in our Soviet Russia of inequality between woman and man. The worst, the most disgraceful and hypocritical discrepancy in the marriage and family law, the inequality with regard to children, has been completely abolished by the Soviet government. This is only the first step to the liberation of woman.[88]

According to S. Wolffson, the legal and political equality of women does not mean complete equality in the family. There are a number of impediments which prevent its realization. A considerable majority of women are not equally engaged in communal production; female labour is less productive than male labour; Lenin quoting Marx, said that in the early stages of the Communist society the distribution of goods would be according to the amount of work performed by the individual. This would necessarily constitute inequalities, as no two human individuals perform the same amount of work.[89]

In view of the importance of the equality of women, a special provision was introduced into the new Constitution of the U.S.S.R. on the initiative of Stalin. Article 122 of the draft Constitution says:

> Woman in the U.S.S.R. has equal rights with man in all branches of economic, cultural, social, and political life. The implementation of these rights of women is assured by granting women the same rights as men to work, to pay, to holidays, to social insurance and education, by government protection of mothers and children, by allowing women holidays with pay during pregnancy, by a wide network of maternity homes, children's crèches and kindergartens.[90]

Woman's Struggle for Freedom

With regard to the family, the Soviet attitude has been influenced by two elements: (1) conditions in Russia under the Tsars, and (2) the Marxist doctrine which inspired Bolshevists in reforming these conditions. On the assumption of political power by the Bolshevists, the first task was the introduction of modern legislation.[91] One of the basic tenets of the Soviet Republic was to abolish all restrictions on the rights of women and to bring about complete equality between the sexes. To achieve this, a programme for the transference of the economic and educational functions from the household to society was enacted. For women this meant freedom from household drudgery and independence from men. Lenin condemned the aspect of household slavery, emphasizing that "no real emancipation was possible while women were oppressed by the pettiest, dirtiest, heaviest, and dullest toil, that of the kitchen and of the individual family household in general".[92]

As a result, feelings and thoughts were revolutionized in the relation between men and women, particularly in the sphere of sexual relationship and of marriage and the family. The decay and corruption of bourgeois marriage, with its difficult divorce, its freedom for men and enslavement for women, elicited this attack by Lenin:

> The Soviet government has completely abolished the source of bourgeois filth, repression and humiliation-divorce proceedings. For nearly a year now our completely free divorce laws have been in force. We issued a decree abolishing the difference in the status of children born in wedlock and those born out of wedlock, and also the various political disabilities.[93]

In defending freedom of divorce, Engels did not approve of the idea of frivolous sex relations, nor of quick, casual and unstable marriage. He insisted that under socialism marriage must not be transitory and short-lived. Marx and Engels did, however, state that in exceptional cases where, for various reasons, cohabitation became unbearable, the freedom of divorce might be sought, but this is not the same freedom as that of bourgeois legislation. In this light the Soviet Constitution is written:

> During the lifetime of both parties to a marriage the marriage may be dissolved either by the mutual consent of both parties to it or upon the "ex parte" application of either of them.[94]

Elsewhere, on the abrogation of church marriage, Lenin asserted:

> In our cities and factory settlements the law (abolishing the inferiority of women) on the complete freedom of marriage is taking root, but in the countryside it very frequently exists only on paper . . . There, church marriage still predominates. This is due to the influence of the priests, and it is more difficult to fight this evil than the old laws.[95] His main theme is that the bourgeois family grants all privileges and all rights to the man at the woman's expense. Apart from this, church marriage occupies a definite and important position in all bourgeois countries, even those where church is separated from state, as for example, in France. This inequality of sexes is not to be tolerated in a socialist society. In fact, the Family Code of 1918, which deprived church marriage of any significance and validity, granted civil recognition only to the civil Soviet marriage. This was regarded as a fundamental revolution in Russia. It is interesting to note that the new Code, which replaces the clergy's parish registers in recording births, deaths and marriages, is firmly established in the life of the people.

With regard to the important role of women in a socialist society, Lenin added:

It has been observed in the experience of all liberation movements that

the success of a revolution depends on the extent to which women take part in it. The Soviet government is doing everything to enable women to carry on their proletarian socialist activity independently.[96]
In this connection Stalin added:
Not a single great movement of the oppressed in the history of mankind has been able to do without the participation of working woman . . . It is not surprising that millions of working women have been drawn in beneath the banners of the revolutionary movement of the working class, the most powerful of all liberation movement of the oppressed masses.[97]

The Way to the Emancipation of Women

1. In accordance with the fundamental ideas of Bolshevism and of the Russian Revolution, the first step is to involve women, who were oppressed under capitalism, in political and social activities. They were exploited and oppressed by the capitalists in both monarchic and democratic bourgeois societies. What underlies this oppression and exploitation is the existence of private property. This deplorable situation was described by Lenin as follows:
And it is impossible to draw the masses into politics without also drawing in the women; for under capitalism, the female half of the human race suffers under a double yoke. The working women and peasant women are oppressed by capital; but in addition to that, even in the most democratic of bourgeois republics, they are, firstly, in an inferior position because the law denies them equality with men, and secondly, they are "in domestic slavery", they are "domestic slaves. . . .[98]
This statement might be interpreted to show that women now enjoy complete equality of rights with men in Soviet society. The law of June 27, 1936, which was drafted on the basis of Marxist doctrine, abolished the subordination of wife to the husband. Soviet legislation provided freedom of divorce, equated *de facto* marriage with registered marriage and removed the stigma from "illegitimate" children.

2. The second step is the abolition of private ownership of land, factories, and so on. This is the only road open to the complete and real emancipation of women from domestic slavery-the conversion of the small, individual economy into a large, communal one.[99] In his *Women and Society* Lenin emphasized this principle, and asserted:
The aim of the Soviet government was to create the conditions in which the toilers could built their own lives without the private ownership of the land, without the private ownership which everywhere . . . even in the most democratic republics, has actually placed the

toilers in conditions of poverty and wage slavery, and women in a position of double slavery.[100]

It should be noted that the complete abolition of *de facto* inequality between women and men cannot be reached until the fundamental political and economic problems of the proletarian dictatorship have been solved. But drawing women into politics and socialist communal production is one of the chief means of effecting their real, complete liberation. This attempt can make them equal with men and at the same time relieve them of the burdens and drudgery of the small household by establishing communal mess halls, laundries, children's crèches, and kindergartens.

A further implication of the emancipation of women is their participation in the collective-farm system of socialism. This aims at the eventual liquidation of *de facto* inequality between men and women on the land. Stalin remarked:

> As for the women collective farmers themselves, they must remember the force and importance of the collective farm for women; they must remember that they have a chance of an equal footing with men in the collective farms alone. Without the collective farms, inequality; with the collective farms, equality of rights![101]

Moreover, under the conditions of socialist ownership and production, marriage ceases to be an economic contract, and becomes a bond of personal affection and disinterested love. According to Engels:

> A generation of men who never in their lives have known what it is to buy a woman's surrender with money or any other social instrument of power; a generation of women who have never known any occasion for giving themselves to a man from any other considerations than real love, or for refusing to give themselves to their lover from fear of the economic consequences.[102]

Lenin held the view that the transition from a bourgeois to a socialist society is complicated, for it must modify the most deep-rooted bourgeois habits. Nevertheless, the transition has been attempted. It is quite clear that the emancipation of women is moving irresistibly forward and will be achieved eventually throughout the entire world.

Socialism and the Emancipation of Women

Engles said that woman's exclusion from social production has not only been her economic disadvantage but has also involved social and sexual discrimination. Emancipation is possible only when women take part in production outside the home in large-scale industry.[103] The Constitution of the U.S.S.R. is patterned after Engels' proposition.

Real Equality

1. The Marxist doctrine states that capitalism cannot establish real

equality, equality before the law, equality between the well-fed and the hungry. One of its manifestations is the inferior position of women. In the tradition of Marx and Engles, Lenin declared in 1919:

Not a single bourgeois state, not even the most progressive, republican democratic state, has brought about complete equality of rights. But the Soviet Republic of Russia promptly wiped out, without any exception, every trace of inequality in the legal status of women, and secured her complete equality in its laws.[104]

Elsewhere he wrote:

Notwithstanding all the liberating laws that have been passed, woman continues to be a domestic slave, because petty housework crushes, strangles, stultifies and degrades her, chains her to the kitchen and to the nursery, and wastes her labour in barbarously unproductive, petty, nerve-racking, stultifying and crushing drudgery. Public dining rooms, crèches, kindergarten. . . . which can in fact emancipate women, which can in fact lessen and abolish their inferiority to men in regard to their role in social production and in social life.[105]

Lenin's main contention is that the conditions of real freedom for marriage partners would be established when private property and the property relations which have accompanied economic considerations in choice of a marriage partner were removed. Accordingly, houselold duties would not preoccupy the worker's wife. Under such circumstances it is probably that the majority of women would remain in social production even after marriage. Such a state of affairs would be an adequate basis for equality of access to the majority of better-paid professions and equality of income for men and women doing similar work. In the U.S.S.R. much work has been devoted to alleviating the economic and domestic drudgery that prevents the housewife from engaging in social production. Lenin repeated the same idea in his famous article "The Great Beginning".[106]

Influenced by Engels' theory[107] A. Kollontai presented a similar point of view with regard to the ways in which true equality may be attained. The reduction of woman's fruitless labor in the household is one of the means of her emancipation. Care of babies, economic protection of children, and proper establishment of social education were undertaken by the Soviet government through the Sub-department of Safeguarding Motherhood and Babyhood, headed by Comrade V.P. Beledeva, and through the Narkompross(People's Commissariat for Education) Department for Social Education.

2. The concept of "equality" particularly in regard to payment, has been interpreted variously in our time in the Soviet Union. Strict equality of wages was introduced in the early days of the Revolution, when high

officials received no more salary than bench workmen. This policy had to
be discarded later in order to influence greater production, because it
proved an inadequate incentive to the workmen. Sharply differentiated
wages were introduced in the early 1930's. The *Soviet Encyclopedia* states:
"Socialism and egalitarianism have nothing in common". In like manner,
Lenin stated that, without a material stake for all personnel in the results
of their work, the country's productive capacity could not be raised and
a socialist economy could not be built. Socialism means "to each according to his work." (See the Soviet Constitution). Khrushchev also disa-
grees with egalitarian distribution. According to him socialist distribution
must be based on the principle of equal pay for equal work. This means
that the same legal yardstick is applied to different people, and because
socialism excludes class inequality there remains only the inequality of
wages received by individuals. Inasmuch as different people have different skills, talents, and working ability, it is natural that with equal work
for equal pay there would be in fact unequal incomes. The bourgeois law
recognizes individual, private ownership of means of production, while
socialism converts them into public property. Under socialism all people
stand on equal footing with the means of production and are paid in
accordance with their work. The rule is: "If a man does not work, neither
shall he eat". In a capitalist society, however, according to Khrushchev,
distribution is in reality based not on work, but primarily on capital. Thus,
greater income is received not by those who work more, but by those who
have capital.[108]

Socialism and the Abolition of Prostitution
In arguing that socialism alone creates all necessary conditions for real
monogamy, Engels wrote:
> As the means of production becomes communal ownership, hired
> labour, the proletariat, will also disappear and consequently the neces-
> sity for a certain number of women to surrender themselves for money.
> Prostitution disappears; monogamy, instead of collapsing, at last
> becomes a reality also for men.[109]

Engels' theory is that there is no real monogamy under capitalism, even
though the bourgeois hypocritically acclaim the sanctity of marriage.
Polygamy and men's sexual relations with many women flourish under
capitalism. Under socialism, however, where marriage is concluded on
the basis not of material possession, but of love, woman ceases to sell
herself into marriage or into prostitution. In Engels' opinion, man must
be a true monogamist in a socialist society because polygamy may lead
the free woman to break up the marriage. In the *Communist Manifesto*,
Marx and Engels pointed out that communal possession of women, in
fact, exists under capitalism, taking the form of official and unofficial

prostitution, but that it will never exist in a communist society. According to Lenin, prostitution is one of the evils of a bourgeois society, and it is to be ascribed equally to the evil property system and the moral hypocrisy. Lenin stated:

> . . . One can judge what disgusting bourgeois hypocrisy reigns at these aristocratic, bourgeois congresses. The mountebanks of charity and the police protection of mockery at want and misery go together to fight against prostitution, which is maintained precisely by the aristocrats and the bourgeois.[110]

The October Revolution had a marked effect on prostitution, but did not put an immediate end to it. With the victory of socialism the economic foundations of prostitution were almost completely eliminated. The reduction of unemployment, the progress of women's economic independence, the collectivization of the village, the large-scale participation of women in industrial production, the equal pay for men and women, have all served to the same end. However, in spite of this, Lenin recognized that the problem remained in some degree even under socialism. He declared:

> Besides, the question of prostitutes will give rise to many serious problems here. Take them back to productive work, bring them into social economy. That is what we must do . . . It will give us a great deal of work here in Soviet Russia. The Party must not in any circumstances calmly stand by and watch such mischievous conduct on the part of its members.[111]

There can be no question that prostitution has diminished in Soviet urban areas, but there is serious doubt whether it has been ended, or whether its decrease resulted entirely from the abolition of private property. Payment for prostitution need not be made only in money; it may take the form of privileges, power, food, and clothing.[112] These exchangeable commodities exist in any complex society. This subject will be discussed in detail later.

The Relation of the Sexes

Engels maintained that because sexual love is by its nature exclusive, marriage based on love is inherently individual marriage. This clearly reflects Bachofen's conviction that the transformation from group marriage to individual marriage depends on the status of the women. If economic considerations, which make women tolerate the habitual infidelity of their husbands, vanish, the equality of women will be more likely to make men monogamous, rather than women polyandrous. Engels' conception of the love between men and women under socialism is essentially different from ordinary sexual attraction.[113] Where love in marriage under capitalism, as Engels put it, either was not in existence or was not

mutual, and a woman's affections are not taken into account, under socialism love is mutual.[114] Engels' ideas have been adopted in socialist
society and applied in the formulation of family policy.

Free Love

The two letters[115] written by Lenin to Iness Armand are valuable
documents representing the Communist attitude to two important issues,
that of the life and morals of the workers and that of family and marriage.
Lenin demands a Marxist approach to these problems, and castigates a
frivolous attitude to them. He issues a warning against any active interest
in various fashionable ideas which seem revolutionary but are in reality
bourgeois. For example, he cites certain demands for "free love". According to Koltsov's report, a young mother registering her new-born
baby was ignorant not only of the surname of his father but even of his
forename.[116] In Pilnyak's *Mahogany,* a woman who expects a child by an
unknown father, says:

> In the centre of my attention was neither love nor my partner, but I
> myself and my emotions. . . . I did not want to become pregnant; sex
> is joy; I did not think of the child. But I will manage it, and the State
> will help me. As to morals, I don't know what it means. I have been
> taught to forget it. . . . [117]

Such a frivolous attitude towards marriage, on the part of people who
enter upon it with insufficient knowledge of each other, should not be
tolerated in the Soviet State.

In analyzing such situations, Lenin claims that "bourgeois marriage"
understands "free love" to be "freedom from seriousness in love", and
"childbirth" to be "freedom of adultery". Thus he condemns "Free love"
as a bourgeois attitude of exploitation or oppression in the matter of sex
relations. Further, Lenin contrasts "base and vile marriage without love",
not with "freedom of love" or with "short-lived passion and liaison", but
with "Proletarian Civil Marriage with Love". He attacks the "free love"
attitude and regards it as being representative of the decay of bourgeois
society. This attitude has become the official interpretation of the problem of sex in a socialist society. When the essay on "free love" or "sex
morality" written by A. Kollontai from the viewpoint of radical feminism
was seen to express the social and moral disintegration under the New
Economic Policy, it was rejected as a deviation from the Party's point of
view. This lurid interpretation of sex relations is discussed in the current
literature of that period. P. Romanov wrote:

> We have no lover, we have only sex relations. And those who seek in
> love something more than physiology are looked upon with contempt,
> as though they were mentally deficient and ill.[118]

There is no need to conceal the fact that young people have evidently absorbed many bourgeois attitudes towards sex. These obsolescent vestiges, these remnants of capitalism must be completely eliminated from one's character and one's life.[119] In place of free love the Russian government attempted to substitute the so-called Stalinist Virtue. Stalinist Virtue is portrayed as a brave attempt to regiment individuals through regulation of sexual impulses. A Soviet journal *Novyi Mir* reveals the meaning of Stalinist Virtue as follows:

> A Soviet person cannot "simply" love someone without criticism, without political and moral watchfulness. . `. . Our Soviet citizen can no longer love only because of a natural drive. He wants his beloved to be worthy of his feeling, to possess the best Soviet qualities.[120]

This is to say that political watchfulness cannot be related even in the most intimate moments between lovers, and that doctrinal orthodoxy must play a formative role in the love relationship.

Thus, the Stalinist Virtue which was instituted in order to replace original Communist free love, indicates, first, the deterioration of love, and second, the subordination of the sexual impulses to the political and economic exigencies of the Soviet State.[121]

Sex and Bourgeois Morality

Lenin clearly believes that many problems related to sex and marriage arise in a bourgeois society based on private property. The war and its consequences created conflicts and suffering for woman in sexual matters. The old world of feeling had begun to shake. There is some indication of a reaction against falseness and hypocrisy.[122] Marx believes that the forms of marriage and family, which depend upon the economic structure of bourgeois society and form an integral part of it tend to collapse.[123]

The constraint of bourgeois marriage and the family laws based on the power of sacred property produces conflict and evil. Lenin said in his conversation with Klara Zetkin:

> Sex and marriage forms, in their bourgeois sense, are unsatisfactory. A revolution in sex and marriage is approaching, corresponding to the proletarian revolution. It is easily comprehensible that the very involved complex of problems brought into existence should occupy the mind of youth, as well as women . . . They are rebelling with all the impetuosity of their years. . . . It is particularly serious if sex becomes the main mental concern during those years when it is physically most obvious.[124]

Thus the decadence and corruption of bourgeois enslavement, with its freedom for the men and its shackles for the women, and the distastefully hypocritical nature of sexual morality fill all thinking people with abhorrence.

There is some indication that a large part of Soviet youth showed a tendency toward the bourgeois conception of sexual life. They labelled their attitudes as "revolutionary" and "Communistic". In the view of Lenin, this "new sexual life" of the young or the "glass of water" theory, simply seems another aspect of bourgeois prostitution. "This cannot be identified with freedom of love as we communist propose it", Lenin comments. Young people are mistaken if they believe that, in communist society, the satisfaction of sexual desires will be as simple as drinking a glass of water. Its adherents maintain that it is Marxist. But Marxism attributed all these phenomena in the ideological superstructure of society to its economic basis. In this connection, Lenin wrote:

> I think this glass of water theory is completely un-Marxist, and more-over, anti-social. In sexual life there is not only simple nature to be considered, but also cultural characteristics, whether they are of a high or low order. In his *The Origin of the Family* Engels showed how signifi-cant is the development and refinement of the general sex urge into individual sex love. . . . Drinking water is of course an individual affair. But in love two lives are concerned, and a third, a new life, arises. It is that which gives it its social interest, which gives rise to a duty towards the community. [125]

A large part of unstable sex morality is noticeably found among the more adult sections of the population. This group, brought up in a bourgeois society, has not yet completely eliminated the old bourgeois attitude towards women, whom they regard as toys. According to the reports in Rabotnitsa, a certain Bagirov, in the village of Mikrakha (Daghestan) accepted *kalym* (payment of ransom for the bride): 9 puds of wheat, 2 puds of rice, and some money. In Uzbekistan, on one of the collective farms in the village of Beglyar in the Kagan region, Dzhura Tashev, son of Kulak and husband of the best shock-collective farmer, forbade his wife Khamra-oi-Nazarova to be present at the first Confer-ence of the Female Youth of Uzbekistan, and when she ignored his instructions, tried to kill her. [126] In six months of 1935 there were heard, in the court of the Kasum-Kent region (Daghestan), five charges of bigamy, ten charges of beating girls of the mountain tribes, four charges of having married off minors and four charges of accepting *kalym*. [127] Similarly, Chinese Communist literature points out that freedom of mar-riage and love is a weapon for releasing the people, especially women, from the sufferings caused by the feudalist marriage system. However, many citizens, especially the young, fail to understand correctly the prin-ciple of freedom of marriage and love. As a result, they have adopted an intolerably casual attitude towards marriage and divorce. [128] In an article entitled "treat marriage seriously," the *Peking People's Daily* tells us:

We have observed that young men and women have often treated love

lightly, considered money and position as its conditions, given no regard to political, ideological and labour achievements. We are deeply concerned that treating love as a trifle or play is an expression of the corrupt bourgeois thought.[129]
With respect to bourgeois morality, a comrade Wolffson[130] came to the conclusion that as far as family life is concerned, the overwhelming majority of the workers adopt a serious attitude to marriage. Those who prefer a frivolous, transient liaison to a stable union form a much smaller proportion.

Woman's Right to Divorce

One of the Marxist doctrines is that, with the disappearance of private property, the only motive for marriage would be individual sexual love. In the absence of such love, freedom of separation would be beneficial both to the partners and to society.[131] The dictatorship of the proletariat has abrogated the institution of compulsory monogamy for life and broken the rusty chains of the indissolubility of marriage. This can be achieved by freeing people from the unnecessary difficulties of divorce. In the U.S.S.R., for example, no one is authorized to force people who no longer love each other to continue living together. Lenin clearly stated:

> . . . This question of divorce is a striking illustration of the fact that one cannot be a democrat and a socialist without immediately demanding full freedom of divorce, for the absence of such freedom is an additional burden on the oppressed sex, woman, although it is not at all difficult to understand that the recognition of the right of women to leave their husbands is not an invitation to all wives to do so! . . . [132]

It is of course hardly necessary to mention that under capitalism divorce is difficult because the female is enslaved economically and because she remains fettered with the care of children, nursery, and kitchen. However, only those who are not familar with the Marxist doctrine would think that facile freedom of divorce is impossible. There can be no doubt that, in the view of the Marxists, democracy has not shattered class oppression, but made the class struggle more intense. The more clearly a woman sees freedom of divorce, the clearer will it appear that the source of her "slavery" is not lack of rights but capitalism. Thus both Marxism and Leninism have always been antagonistic to the principle of the indissolubility of marriage,[133] and have pleaded for the unconditional right to divorce. This is not aimed at destroying the family, but at providing the conditions necessary for its reconstruction on a new basis. Lenin wrote in 1914:

Reactionaries are against freedom of divorce: they clamour for its 'careful treatment' and cry out that it implies the 'disintegration of the family'. Democracy, on the other hand, regards these reactionaries as hypocrites who in fact uphold . . . the privileges of the one sex and further oppression of woman; it holds that in reality freedom of divorce means, not the "disintegration" of family links, but on the contrary their strengthening on the only stable and democratic bases tolerable in civilized society.[134]

Elsewhere, Lenin argued that the right to divorce is difficult to exercise under capitalism. Yet, respectable social democracy is but the exercising of rights.[135] Unless these rights are fully exercised, socialism would be impossible. Hence in response to the Marxist doctrine, the Soviet government passed the law of divorce on December 19, 1917. According to Document 2,[136] a marriage shall be annulled when either one or both parties appeal for its termination. Document 3 reads: "Marriage may be dissolved by divorce so long as both parties are living."[137] The same document reads: "The mutual consent of husband and wife, as well as the desire of one of them to obtain a divorce, may be considered as a ground for divorce."[138]

The Marxist theory of freedom of divorce has been similarly adopted and developed by the Communist Party in China. Article 6 of their *Common Programme* says:

> The People's Republic of China abolishes the feudal system which holds woman in bondage. Women shall enjoy equal rights with men in political, economic, cultural, educational, and social life. Freedom of marriage for men and women shall be enforced.[139]

Likewise, according to the Marriage Law, divorce should be granted when husband and wife both desire it.[140]

On the subject of the present state of the family in Soviet Russia, it should be pointed out that young people see a wife as something on a par with a kitchen stove or an article of personal comfort, and a husband as a money producer, a pay envelope.[141] This attitude will be discussed later in detail.

Woman's Role in Socialist Construction

It is the Marxist doctrine that not until the road is open for woman's participation in large-scale social production will her emancipation be possible.[142] Modern large-scale industry not only permits the extensive employment of woman's labour, but demands it in order to develop service industries.[143] In the early years after the October Revolution, Lenin pointed out that woman's real emancipation would be brought about by engaging her in the social production of the country. He declared:

> This is the main task to bring women into socially productive work, to

get them away from 'domestic bondage', to liberate them from the deadening and humiliating subordination to the eternal and exclusive background of kitchen and children.[144]

This doctrine and policy were confirmed. In 1931, the general labour force was composed of 305, 161 persons of whom 61,140, or 20 per cent, were women. In 1935 there were 377,191 workers and clerks, of whom 96,345 or 25.7 per cent were women.[145] Later, in his speech at the First All-Union Congress of Shock Workers from collective farms in 1933, Stalin emphasized both the importance of woman's participation in the collective farms and the role played by the kolkhoz system in achieving full equality for the woman peasant. This has been verified by statistical evidence. About 6,000 women collective-farmers are chairmen of their farms. More than 60,000 are members of management boards of collective farms; 28,000 are group leaders, 100,000 are branch organizers, 9,000 are managers of collective farm dairies and 7,000 are tractor drivers.[146]

In November 1935, at a reception given to women shock collective farmers on the sugar-beet fields, Stalin repeatedly stressed the importance of the collective farms in attaining complete equality for women. He maintained that the female had been degraded to the lowest status of worker, either by her father before marriage or by her husband after marriage; and only the system of collective farming could possibly offer her freedom and release from the burdens of the primitive peasant small holding and the intolerable bondage of the household.[147]

As a socialist, Kollontai attempted to develop the Marxist doctrine on women's participation in social production. Expressing the view that, with the transfer of the means of production to communal ownership, the family would no longer be an economic unit in society. Instead, housekeeping would be transformed to a social, collective establishment, and the care and education of children would become a public concern.

Kollontai criticized the bourgeois feminist movement in the nineteenth century. Its chief objective was the achievement of woman's equal rights in all spheres of life within the confines of a bourgeois capitalist society. The adherents of the feminist movement, while attempting to imitate men in all possible ways, seemed determined to aggravate the sex-war. Furthermore, they failed to tackle in any constructive spirit the problem of reconciling and simplifying the dual responsibilities of women towards motherhood and the home on the one hand, and towards employment outside the home on the other. In a socialist society Kollontai believed that motherhood alone, i.e., woman's ability to bear children, is not in itself sufficient reason for placing her on an equal footing with men, who carry all the responsibility of production. Only when women share with the men in contributing to production, will their additional social responsibilities entitle them to special care and treatment.

There are two reasons why the Soviet government encourages women to join in social production —its keen interest in emancipating women from household drudgery, and its desire to develop the country's productive power. The first requirement is, therefore, to release as much manpower as possible from unproductive work, and utilize the full labour force; secondly, to secure the future supply of young workers, i.e., to protect the natural increase of population. In other words, the care of children is no longer a task limited to the family but rests on the community. [148]

It is clear that motherhood should be safeguarded, not only in the interest of women, but particularly to meet the difficulties of the national economy during its transformation to a socialist system. It is therefore necessary to prevent women's strength from being entirely expended on the family, and to utilize it more effectively for the benefit of the society. During the period 1930-31, there were increasing possibilities of employment for women. The State made systematic efforts to provide women in industry with every facility for gaining higher qualifications. In some important industries women responded enthusiastically to their increased opportunities, even surpassing their male fellow-workers. However, except in the textile and printing industries and some branches of teaching, it was difficult for women to compete with men.

In conclusion, the Workers' Republic aims at changing the social system with the object of giving women the opportunity to combine motherhood with the rearing of children for the Republic and to arrange the necessary maternal care and attention. In the *Communist China Digest*, the organ of Communist policy, it is noted that the large numbers of women directly participating in production outside the home mark a victory for the socialist system and the emancipation of women from patriarchal bondage. This implies that women have yet to participate in social manual labour en mass. [149]

The study so far has touched upon many of the ideas in the evolutionary and Marxist doctrines of the family which have interested social scientists. With a view to verifying the contribution to social science, a systematic formulation of all of the arguments will be attempted. Such an appraisal might be based on the method called the "logical problem of fit". The testing of hypothesis bears on the problem of fit. The fundamental hypothesis here is that, in the view of evolutionists, mother-right or matriarchate appeared before the father-right (McLennan, Bachofen, Morgan, and Lubbock). Monogamy developed from hetaerism or promiscuity owing to the development of economic conditions with a resultant undermining of the old or primitive communism; monogamy also developed with the overthrow of mother-right and resulted in polygamy for men. If, after an analysis of most societies, there appears to be no high correlation among the elements, the hypothesis is invalid.

NOTES

[1] F. Engels, *The Origin of the Family, Private property, and the State*, p. 57.

[2] *Ibid.*, p.147.

[3] *Ibid.*, p. 43.

[4] *Ibid.*, p. 48.

[5] *Ibid.*, p. 49.

[6] *Ibid.*, p. 50-51.

[7] *Ibid.*, p. 47.

[8] *Ibid.*, p. 49.

[9] *Ibid.*, p. 42.

[10] *Ibid.*, p. 57-58.

[11] *Ibid.*, p.54.

[12] *Ibid.*, p.65.

[13] *Ibid.*, p.59.

[14] *Ibid.*, pp.59-60.

[15] *Ibid.*, p.63.

[16] *Ibid.*, p.62.

[17] *Ibid.*, p.43.

[18] *Ibid.*, p.148.

[19] *Ibid.*, p.64.

[20] *Ibid.*, p.67.

[21] *Ibid.*, p.67.

[22] *Ibid.*, p.72.

[23] *Ibid.*, p.72-73.

[24] *Ibid.*, p. 32.

[25] The Maori word "puna" means a spring of water, but "punarua" means the practice of having two wives, generally sisters. The Maori word "punarua" is identical with the Hawaiian punalua (Rualue-two).

[26] Lewis H. Morgan, *Ancient Society*, pp. 383-84.

[27] F. Engels, *Op. cit.*, p. 35.

[28] Engels, *The Origin of the Family, Private Property, and the State*, New York International publishers, p.35. Some theorists call group marriage "sexual communism", but a close examination shows that in every known case there is a sharp definition of rights and responsibilities in relation to children. J. Lubbock, *The Origin of Civilization and the Primitive Condition of Man*, 5th ed. (New York, 1892), pp. 86-98; W.H.R., Rivers, *Social Organization* (New York, 1924), p. 80

[29] Engels distinguished between monogamy in the historical sense, in Morgan's sense of control of the wife by the husband, and in the etymological sense, indissolubility of the marriage being regarded as the criterion distinguishing monogamy from "pairing" marriage. F. Engels, *Op. cit.*, p. 55.

[30] Emile Burns, *Handbook of Marxism* (London: Victor Gollancz, 1935.)

[31] Rudolf Schlesinger, *Changing Attitudes in Soviet Russia-the Family* (London: Routledge and Kegan Paul, Ltd., 1949), p. 19.

[32] F. Engels, *Op. cit.*, pp. 48-49.

[33] Lewis H. Morgan, *Ancient Society*, p. 474.

[34] F. Engels, *Op. cit.*, pp. 51.

[35] According to Morgan and Engels the union of one man with one woman represents the "pairing" as well as the "monogamous" marriage.

[36] Fan Jo-yu, "Why We Have Abolished the Feudal Patriarchal Family System", *Peking Review*, Vol. III, No. 10 (March 8, 1960), p. 10.

[37] Carle C. Zimmerman, *Family and Civilization* (New York and London: Harper & Brothers, 1947), p. 26.

[38] F. Engels, *Op. cit.*, p. 57.

[39] This refers to the *Deutsche Ideologic* (German Ideology), written by Marx and Engels in Brussels in 1845 and first published in 1932 by the Marx-Engels-Lenin Institute in Moscow.

[40] Engels, *Op. cit.*, p. 58. According to Engels, division of labour and private property are identical expressions, for the division implies from the beginning the division of conditions of labour, of tools and materials and the splitting up of accumulated capital among different owners. *German Ideology*, p. 165.

[41] Morgan, *Ancient Society*, p. 511. Hetaerism co-existent with monogamous marriage is understood as the practice of sexual intercourse between men and unmarried women outside marriage. Engels interpreted Morgan's concept of hetaerism as a result of the emergence of the inequality of property.

[42] Morgan, *Op. cit.*, p. 499.

[43] Plato foreshadowed Engels' idea of the evil of property and wrote that property must go, for it embodied 'mine' and 'not mine' *The Republic*, Book V, p. 462.

[44] Engels, *Op. cit.*, p.147.

[45] Alexander Gray, *The Socialist Tradition* (New York: Longmans, Green and Co., 1946), p.306.

[46] T.B. Bottomore, "Some Reflections on the Sociology of Knowledge", *British Journal of Sociology*, 7(March 1956), p. 53.

[47] Engels, *Selected Works*, Vol. I, pp. 211-12, Moscow: Progress, 1970.

[48] Carle C. Zimmerman, and Merle E. Frampton, *Family and Society* (New York: D. Van Nostrand Company, Inc., 1935), p. 36.

[49] August Bebel, *Women in the Past, Present and Future*, trans. by H.B.A. Walther (London, 1902), 4th ed.

[50] Max Eastman, *Marxism, Is It Science?* (New York: W.E. Norton and Co., Inc., 1940), p. 99.

[51] Bourgeois marriage is a product of bourgeois property and will disappear with it.

[52] Bernhard J. Stern, *The Family, Past and Present* (New York: D. Appleton-Century Company, 1938), p. 185.

[53] Engels, *Op. cit.*, p. 30. In Engels' view the exclusion of women from better-paid jobs is the result of their inferior position in capitalist society.

[54] Bernhard J. Stern, *Op. cit.*, p. 185.

[55] Edward H. Carr, *Karl Marx-A Study in Fanaticism* (London:J.M. Dent and Sons, Ltd., 1934), p.76. Marx writes that marriage implies prostitution, just as private property implies pauperism.

[56] Karl Marx and F. Engels, *Selected Works*, 2 vols, Vol. I(London: Lawrence and Wishart, Ltd., 1943), p. 208.

[57] *Ibid.*, pp. 216-17.

[58] K. Marx and F. Engels, *Communist Manifesto* (Chicago: Charles H. Kerr & Co., 1947), p. 37.

[59] *Ibid.*, p. 34.

[60] K. Marx and F. Engels, *Communist Manifesto*, p. 35.

[61] *Ibid.*, p. 37.

[62] *Ibid.*, p. 39.

[63] *Communist Manifesto of Karl Marx and Frederick Engels with an Introduction and Explanation by D. Ryazanoff* (New York International Publishers, 1930), pp. 162-63.

[64] *Ibid.*

[65] In 1791 Title II, Article 7 was inserted in the French Constitution, which was opposed to the family. The Constitution defines marriage as only a civil contract. (253). The law of 1792 made divorce absolute, by mutual consent. (254), for incompatibility of temper, at the request of either spouse, and for seven other reasons. Ernest Glasson, *Le mariage civil et le divorce* (Paris: A Durant et Pedone-Lauriel, ed., 1880), pp.252-276.

[66]   Karl Marx on Stirner, *Dokumente des Sozialismus*, III, pp.126-127.

[67]   *The Holy Family*, i.e., *Die Heilige Familie* was written against the group of young hegelians, such as B. Bauer and D. Strauss. Marx attacked Bauer's idealistic philosophy, his negativism, his individualism and his aversion from action. T.B. Bottomore and M. Rubel, *Karl Marx-Selected Writings in Sociology and Social Philosophy* (London: Watts and Co., 1956), 58n. F. Gregoire, *Aux Sources de la Pensée de Marx-Hegel, Fauerback* (Louvain: De l'Institut Supérieur de Philosophie, 1947), p.13.

[68]   K. Marx and F. Engels, *Die Heilige Familie*, Ch. VIII, Sec.6, reprinted in Nachlass, II, pp.308-309.

[69]   Wilbert E. Moore, *Industrial Relations and the Social Order* (New York: The Macmillan Co., 1951), pp. 419-421.

[70]   *Factories Enquiry Commission*, First Report, 1833, C.2,p. 8, evidence taken by A. Power.

[71]   Engels, *The Condition of the Working-Class in England in 1844*, trans. and ed. by W.O. Henderson and W.H. Chaloner (Oxford:Basil Blackwell, 1958), p. 5.

[72]   Engels accused Edward Akroyd of Halifax of immorality with his female employees, but no evidence could be brought forward to substantiate the charge. J.F.C. Harrison, *Social Reform in Victorian Leeds. The Work of James Holl* (1820-Thoresby Society Monography, No. 3, 1954), p. 66.

[73]   Engels assumed that all social change resulting in industrial capitalism is a social evil. Engels' doctrine that the whole female sex should be back in public industry is not compatible with his notion that this would not adversely affect the family.

[74]   Engels always uses the work 'mittelklass' in the English sense of 'middle class' or 'middle classes' in the plural-the most common form. By the 'middle class' he means the class which owns property. The French word 'bourgeoisie' has the same meaning. Engels, *The Condition of the Working-Class in England in* 1844, p.5. According to Carr, 'class', in Marx, remains on the whole an objective conception to be established by economic analysis. In Lenin, the emphasis shifts from 'class' to 'party' which forms the vanguard of the class and infuses into it the necessary element of class-consciousness. E.H. Carr, *What is History?* A Pelican Book, 1961), pp.137-138.

[75]   Sir Archbald Alison, *The Principles of Population* (London: T. Cadell,1840), 2 vols. He said: 'When we reflect that thirty or forty thousand young women have embarked on a mode of life in London, which entails degradation in themselves and dissolute habits in others, and that in New South Wales there were, in 1833, 44,688 men and only 16,173 women, it is impossible not to wish for the despotic powers of an Eastern Monarchy who . . . would fill up the void of one hemisphere, and reform the character of so large a number in the other'. Vol. II, p.147.

[76]   *Ibid.*, pp.161-162.

[77]   Leonard Horner's report for the quarter ending September 30th, 1843 in Reports of the Inspectors of Factories. . . . for the half year ending 31st, December, 1843-1844, p. 4. In Lancashire there are hundreds of young men, between 20 and 30 years of age, in the full vigour of life, employed as piecers and otherwise, who are receiving not more than eight or nine shillings a week.

[78]   Engels, *The Condition of the Working-Class in England in 1844*, p. 158.

[79]   Engels, *Ibid.*, pp. 164-65.

[80]   Karl Marx, *Capital*, Vol. I.

[81]   Engels, *The Condition of the Working-Class in England in 1844*, p. 147.

[82]   Marx, *Capital*, Vol. I, Paul trans., p. 528.

[83]   *Ibid.*, p. 528.

[84]   Engels, "Review of Capital", (March 1868), *Selected Works*, I, p.425.

[85]   On Proudhon, Marx, "The Housing Question", *Selected Works*, I, 1968, p. 513, and on Sismondi, Marx, *The Poverty of Philosophy*, p. 73, and "Communist Manifesto' in *Selected Works*, I, p. 54. Marx spoke of English large-scale industry and did not intend to alter its methods, but only opposed their application to private undertakings. While Marx had in mind an organized factory system, Proudhon regarded land as the great natural economic basis of human existence. Pierre J. Proudhon, *Qu'est-ce que la propriété?*(Paris, 1840), p. 28.

[86]   *Correspondence*, p. 8, *Letter to P.V. Annenkov*, dated December 28 1846.

87 Marx, "Wage, Labour and Capital", *Selected Works,* I. p. 83.
88 Lenin, *Works,* Russian ed., Vol. XXVI, pp. 193-94.
89 Lenin, *The State and Revolution* (Moscow, 1935), p. 90.
90 *The Draft Constitution,* art. 122.
91 By the law on Obligatory civil registration of December 18, 1917, *Collection of Laws and Decrees of the Workers' and Peasants' Government,* 1917, No. 2, art. 160.
92 Lenin, *Programme and Statute of the Communist International,*XXVI, 193.
93 Lenin, *Women and Society* (New York: International Publishers, 1938), p. 11.
94 *Document 7,* 18. Mutual consent and irremediable breakdown as grounds have at last reached western countries.
95 Lenin, *Women and Society,* p. 11.
96 *Ibid.,* p. 12.
97 Joseph Stalin, *A Political Biography* (London: Hutchinson and Co., 1943).
98 Lenin, *International Woman's Day,* 1918.
99 Lenin, *Works,* Vol. XXVI, 1941, p. 194.
100 Lenin, *Women and Society,* p. 16.
101 Stalin, *Problems of Leninism,* 10th edition, p. 535.
102 Engels, *The Origin of the Family,Private Property and the State,* p. 73.
103 *Ibid.,* p. 65.
104 Leni, *Women and Society,* p. 26.
105 *Ibid.,* p. 14.
106 Lenin, *Programme and Statute of the Communist International,* XXIV.
107 Engels, *Op. cit.,* p. 46.
108 Nikita S. Khruschev, "The Future of Communist and World Society", reprinted from "New Stages in Communist Construction and Some Problems of Marxist-Leninist Theory", Part IV of Speech to the Extraordinary Twenty-First Congress of the Communist Party of the Soviet Union, *Pravda,* January 28, 1959, pp.2-10, trans. in *Current Digest of the Soviet Press,* Vol. II, No. 5, pp. 5-19.
109 Engels, *Op. cit.,* p. 67.
110 Lenin, *Women and Society,* p. 31.
111 Clara Zetkin, *Lenin on the Woman Question* (New York: International Publishers, 1934), p. 6.
112 Kingsley Davis, "The Sociology of Prostitution", *American Sociological Review,* 2 (October 1937), p. 752.
113 Engels, *Op. cit.,* p. 68.
114 This idea is still emphasized today in Russia. Permyak says that the closer we come to communism the purer will be the love between man and woman and the more lasting will be marriage, for it will be based only on mutual love. Yevegeni Permyak, "Long Engagement", *The Soviet Review,* Vol. 2, April 1962, p. 38.
115 The two letters were written by Lenin in January 1915.
116 *Pravda,* April 10, 1936. Cited by Schlesinger, *Op. cit.,* p. 342.
117 Vera Sandomirsky,"Sex in the Soviet Union", *The Russian Review,* 10(1951), pp. 199-209.
118 P. Romanov, "Without a Bird-cherry Tree", *Mydra,* Moscow, 1930, p. 8.
119 This is the statement of comrade S.V. Kosior delivered at the Tenth All Union Congress of the L.K.S.M.U.-Lenist Communist Union of the Youth Organization.(trans.).
120 Vera Sandomirsky, "Sex in the Soviet Union", *Op. cit.,* pp. 199-209.
121 *Ibid.*
122 Klara Zetkin, *Op. cit.,* p. 7.
123 Engels, *Op. cit.,* pp. 63-64. Now that large-scale industry has taken the wife out of the home into factory, no basis for male supremacy is left in the proletarian household.
124 Klara Zetkin, *Lenin on the Woman Question,* p. 10.
125 Klara Zetkin, *Op. cit.,* p. 11.
126 Rabotnitsa, Nos. 20-30, 1935. Cited by Schlesinger, *Changing Attitudes in Soviet Russia-the Family,* p. 344.
127 *Ibid.,* No. 21, 1925, pp. 4-5. Cited by Schlesinger, *Op. cit.,* p. 344.

[128] Wu Ch'eng-chen, "The Principles of 'Freedom of Marriage' Should not be Abused", Peking *Kuang-min Jih-pao*, February 27, 1957.

[129] Liu Tung-kao, "Treat Marriage Seriously", Peking *Jen-min Jih-pao*, May 29, 1959.

[130] S. Wolffson is a socialist. See Schlesinger, *Op. cit.*, pp.280ff.

[131] Engels, *Op. cit.*, p. 73.

[132] Lenin, *Collected Works* (London: Martin Lawrence; printed in United States of American, 1927).

[133] Engels holds that the indissolubility of marriage is an outgrowth of economic condition in which monogamy arose. Engels, *Op. cit.*, p. 73.

[134] Lenin, *Works*, Vol. XVII, p. 448.

[135] Engels, *Op. cit.*, p. 64. As a result of oblieration of private property, the wife has regained the right to dissolve the marriage. Today in the Soviet Union many women are absorbed in household matters. Taryana Vlasova's Report on 'Love and the Years', in M. Motzenck, "Youth Has Its Say on Love and Marriage"m in *The Soviet Review*, August 1962, p. 34.

[136] *Document 2*, paragraph 86. *Collection of Laws and Decrees of the Workers' and Peasants' Government*, 1918, Nos. 76-77, art. 818. These decrees include valid ecclesiastical and religious marriages contracted up to December 20, 1917

[137] *Document 3*, paragraph 87, *Ibid.*

[138] *Ibid.*

[139] *The Common Programme of the Chinese People's Political Consultative Conference* adopted by the first plenary session of the Chinese People's P.C.C. on September 29, 1949.

[140] *The Marriage Law of the People's Republic of China*, art. 17.

[141] M. Motzenck, "Youth Has Its Say on Love and Marriage", *Op. cit.*, p. 31.

[142] Engels, *Op. cit.*, p. 148.

[143] *Ibid.*, p. 64.

[144] Lenin, *Works*, Vol. XXV, pp. 63-64.

[145] *Revolutsia i Natsionalnosti*, 1936, No. 3, pp. 51ff. Cited by Schlesinger, *Op. cit.*, p.204.

[146] Stalin, *Selected Writings*.

[147] Stalin, *Problems of Leninism*, 1934, p. 534.

[148] Kollontai, *The Family and the Communist State*, 1920, pp. 15, 17. Engels, *Op. cit.*, p. 67. When the family ceases to be the economic unit of society, the care and education of children will become a social responsibility.

[149] 'Changes in the Family System will Benefit Productive Capacity' in *Communist China Digest*, November 11,1958 and August 29,1959, p.93.

CHAPTER III

Marxist Theories of Family Development

Women are not altogether in the wrong when they refuse the rules of life prescribed to the world, for only men established them and without their consent.
MONTAIGNE: *Essays* III,v.

1. EVOLUTIONARY THEORY OF THE FAMILY

Matriarchate refers to the socio-political pre-eminence of woman in the sense that women govern according to tribal customs, though the administrative authority rests in their brothers' hands. Matrilineal descent means of course descent reckoned through the mother-line. The evolutionary theory suffers from lack of historical evidence, and critics hold that its flaw, particularly in Bachofen and McLennan's outline, consists in their over-identifying matrilineal descent with the matriarchate. Modern anthropologists have unanimously disagreed with that identification or inference. Their premise is that one cannot safely infer matriarchate from matrilineal descent even though there is a tendency for matriarchate to correspond to mother-right.

Many scholars say that few, if any, groups use matriliny and completely exclude an individual from taking part in some aspects of the father's kin group. There seems to be some form of relationship and some kind of sentiment between children and their father's group. The Dobu father in Melanesia, for example, is described as being able to provide his son with a good line of yams despite the fact that the son's main status depends on the matrilineal principle.[1] There exist matrilineal communities in which women are found to exercise either dominant property rights or play an important role in social life. The best known illustrations are the Egyptians, the Iroquois, and Pueblo Indians. All landed property descended in the female line from mother to daughter. Ancestors were always traced farther back in the female than the male line, the father was only the holder of office, while the mother was the family link.[2] Among the Iroquois, women were entitled to arrange marriage and own property, houses as well as land. A.L. Kroeber noted that the women's ownership of the house constitutes the so-called matriarchate of the Zuni.[3] These illustrations, however, are not sufficient to warrant the evolutionary conclusion that the importance of women's position can only be interpreted by the female line of descent.[4] On the other hand, no social research has yet discovered a community in which women ruled alone. The female chief is either the sister or mother of the male chief of the whole tribe, and exercises her authority in his name and within a limited sphere.[5]

The preceding cases, however rare, are enough to prove that matriarchate in a strict sense is nowhere to be found, although in a few areas women have gained noticeable prerogatives. Still, the existence of such prerogatives in the case of matrilineal descent does not justify the inference that material descent constitutes the basic cause of privileges.

A close comparison of various cultures shows that women remain, in differing degrees, subordinate, even though they participate in more productive activities. South Africa and South America find women are in a markedly subordinate, if not humiliating, position. L.T. Hobhouse maintained that the patrilineal system prevails more significantly among pastoral than among agricultural savages. This would seem to argue against the priority of the matrilineal system. American anthropologists such as J.R. Swanton[6] and Kroeber[7] attacked the generalization that the matrilineal system preceded the patrilineal, and they supported the priority of the patrilineal.

Since the evolutionary theory of the matriarchate cannot be safely established, whatever the theory based on it is questionable. Here the Marxist doctrine that the overthrow of mother-right was the world's historical defeat of the female sex[8] lacks scientific foundation.

As regards promiscuity, the evolutionists' claim for its existence among primitive peoples seems illusory. The bias of our own deviant traditional sex mores has not only distorted the interpretation of sexual taboos but tempted some writers to impute to primitive peoples the sexual laxity, such as 'hetaerism', 'promiscuity' or 'sex communism'. Murdock's study reveals that evidence from the world-wide sample of 250 societies bears out the prevalence of a generalized taboo against all sex relations outside marriage. Only two societies, the Kaingang of Brazil and the Todas of southern India show a great freedom of sex and provide a justification for describing them as promiscuous.[9] However, in neither of them is there a complete lack of sexual regulation. R. Lowie indicated that while marriage among the Dieri is permanent, the actual state of concubinage is temporary. If we interpret this aright, the term 'sexual communism' is obviously misleading. And in matriarchate, promiscuity is stark pure fiction; it represents only an assumption of the evolutionary approach: before order, chaos; before regulation, no regulation.[10]

Darwin was critical of assumed promiscuity and contended that promiscuity among human beings was unlikely. This is supported by the evidence that anthropoid apes were not promiscuous and that aboriginal man probably lived in small communites with one wife, or, if he was powerful, with several, whom he jealously guarded against all other men.[11] E.A. Westermarck also argued that man was originally monogamous; his argument is based on selected examples of monogamy among the anthropoids and among hunting and food-gathering peoples, whom social evolutionists consider economically most primitive, and who were predominantly monogamous.[12] R. Briffault, in his book *The Mothers,* provided evidence of the killing, or threat of killing, of white travellers who refused an offer of 'hospitality prostitution'.[13] In the light of survivals, Briffault argued that such institutions as the sororate, the levirate, sex hospitality,[14] and wife swopping reflected the relic of group marriage upon which matriarchal institutions were superimposed. Lubbock suggested that primitive man did not live in a state of promiscuous intercourse, either from inclination or from a sense of duty. According to Starcke, this is also the essence of Lubbock's position.[15]

There is little doubt, as Lowie put forward, that promiscuity existed when primitive peoples had not yet developed a cultural norm used in judging sexual behaviour. This suggests that in the absence of such a norm, monogamy would also be regarded as promiscuous, that is, unbridled by any law. But we must bear in mind that the crucial issue is not whether at some remote period of history there was promiscuity, but whether evolutionary schemes are validly formulated.[16] In connection with evolutionary schemes, it could hardly be argued that monogamy is not the end-product of an evolutionary series arising from primitive promiscuity. The very primitive Andaman Islanders and the Semangs of the Malay forests were monogamous, but the Semangs married in serial monogamy.[17]

Morgan might argue that there was at one time an unorganized state in the relation between the sexes, upon which the actual marriage form was superimposed. In other words, the habit of promiscuous and licentious intercourse was once extremely common in all cultures, and the actual form of marriage would only be gradually developed.[18] Nonetheless, Morgan's argument is not convincing. Promiscuity in a strict sense could not be found anywhere.

Even Morgan himself admitted that as an inevitable condition before any form of marriage, promiscuity might only be inferred. But, he said that it lay concealed in the mists of antiquity, beyond the reach of positive knowledge.[19] Müller-Lyer wrote that whether prehistoric mankind had ever lived in promiscuity or whether it had separate families and separate marriages in primitive tribes remains speculative.[20]

There is, of course, some evidence that savages were extremely licentious and that communal marriages were popular. Nevertheless, there is also evidence that many tribes practised some form of marriage. Polygamy was almost universally accepted by the chiefs of every tribe. Hambly told that in Angola a headman of Ngalangi had eleven wives and eleven huts for them in his compound.[21] Moreover, there were some tribes, standing nearly at the bottom of the cultural scale, which were found to be strictly monogamous, like the Veddas of Ceylon. According to Lubbock, they married 'till death do husband and wife part'.[22]

Since primitive promiscuity cannot be adequately established, the opinion of some evolutionists that primitive tribes practised promiscuous relations or hetaerism appears arbitrary; and, similarly, the view that monogamy emerged primarily out of women's longing for the right of chastity would seem to be fallacious.

2. THE MARXIST FAMILY

It should be noted that it is absurd to criticize Marxist doctrine by comparing it with statements issued by Marx in his time. The Marxist doctrine would be irrelevant for our contemporary society if current research should show that not only a considerable number of his tenets, but also the method by which they were formulated, had been discarded. The criticism will be reasonable if the Marxist doctrine is defined in such a way as to be relevant *a priori* to the conditions of Western Europe in the nineteenth and early twentieth centuries. George Lichtheim defines capitalism as 'the economic system characteristic of bourgeois society, the latter being the fully developed form of Western civilization', and Marxism as being in opposition to that capitalism. In the second half of the twentieth century the major changes are taking place outside Western Europe.[23] Thus, by the above definition, Marxism is untenable.[24]

The Marxist Theory of Family History

Consanguinity means relatives by blood, as distinguished from affinity, or relatives by marriage; the consanguine form of family, if it ever existed, is at least not widely distributed. Failure to provide adequate evidence of the consanguine family in many cultures necessarily makes it unreliable. Incest taboos, on the other hand, are universally found among all people, the most primitive as well as the most civilized. The exceptions to this universal rule are few, or are not in any case applicable to the entire population of any society. The exceptions to the brother-sister taboo are the well-known cases of the royalty of Egypt, Hawaii, and Inca Peru;[25] Except in these cases the penalties for incest are severe.

Engels assumed that in group marriage, the punaluan form of family clan nomenclature and the customs of levirate and sororate[26] could be inferred by postulating the existence of an earlier form of group marriage; such inference is arbitrary. Discussing group marriage, Engels was rather ambiguous in the differentiation between the family itself and the clan; the term 'clan' is the official name and classification of kin groups, which functioned universally in the economic sphere and the kinship system.[27] After the clan has been formalized, the bilateral family relationship, though noticeably weakened, does not completely disappear. On the other hand, it is now discovered that monogamy exists among simple hunting and food-gathering societies, such as the Andamanese and the Fuegians.

The supremacy of men over women, which is presumably the consequence of capitalism, is the special target of Communist critics. According to Marxist doctrine, monogamy degrades women into intolerable slavery and a subordinate status. Marx and Engels extrapolated general principles and particular phenomena in the monogamous marriage. Two points should be taken into account concerning this issue.

(a) If monogamy is found to be obsolete in its social function, it is likely to be dismissed. On the other hand, if it is found to preserve and perpetuate socially prescribed values more efficiently than any other known form of marriage, it will probably be retained. This is not to deny, as in other areas of social and moral conduct, the existence of some deviators who act against the basic values of a society. Pointing to all possible defects of monogamy in capitalist society, Marxists attempt to use it as an ideological instrument to indict the capitalist social system and substitute the Communist state. In fact, investigations of Soviet matrimonial legislation adopted in 1929, such as *de facto* marriage and automatic divorce at the demand of either party leads one to conclude that there were noticeable deviations in Soviet monogamous marriage.[28]

(b) If the Marxist allegations that monogamy relegates women to slavery were true, if the mutual confidence and companionship of exclusive marriage were really yokes instead of free expression of personality, and if monogamy were such an institution as to introduce the supremacy of man and the oppression of woman, there would be no sense in monogamy at all. If most people believe that the general framework of the monogamous system is satisfactory, it seems that the best procedure would be, not to destroy this institution, but to change certain parts to increase the well-being and happiness of the members of the family.

In conclusion, if the family were subject to economic force, it would lose its *raison d'être*. For the family then is not 'natural', i.e., it is not a determinant and independent variable. If the end of higher capitalism is state capitalism, which has not need of the family institution, it is imperative for us to dismiss the family and develop a new social organization of an entirely different form.

Marxist Methodology in the Development of the Family

In Marx, history meant three things, which formed a coherent and rational whole: the motion of events according to objective, and primarily economic laws; the corresponding development of thought through a dialectical process; and corresponding action or execution, in the form of the class struggle,[29] which unites the theory and practice of revolution. What Marx offers is a synthesis of objective laws and of conscious action to carry them out in what are sometimes though misleadingly called determinism and voluntarism.

Now we come to account for the relationship of Marx's economic laws and the change in the family and the status of woman. The Marxist functional theory of the family, i.e., economic determinism, which brings about the change in the family system, may seem spurious. Marxists believe that economic conditions are an independent variable, while the family is a dependent variable. Similarly they maintain that man has an economic 'first cause'; this theory involves unidimensional limitations. Critics agree that although Marx is politically biased and functional, no serious historian can deny his great influence. This, however, does not warrant the acceptance of Marxist interpretation of change in the family. It is noted that a technico-economic development exerted a great influence on the most primitive form of social organization, which impels Marxists to frame their outlook in the most primitive form, hence their monist explanation. Similarly, Engels, in his study of ancient types of the family, introduced the idea that the forms of the family evolve in the fashion of the means of production. Thus since other dimensions also play a role in the changing family system, the derivation of historical materialism from the unique economic force as an independent variable is not justified in all its implications. Thus Engels' adherents attempt to 'supplement' the monism of socio-economic explanation by another equally potent factor, i.e., 'sex'.[30]

The second flaw of economic determinism lies in the fact that the co-existence of two phenomena is inadequate to prove a causal relation. The particular monogamous type, that is to say, the bourgeois family and the capitalist economic institution, may emerge simultaneously, influencing each other, but one does not inevitably cause the other. As a consequence, no primary and monistic approach can be legitimately construed. Granting the primacy of the economic institution on the ground that it provides the livelihood, it is the family that performs the biological or reproductive function.

The third shortcoming in the idea of economic determinism is that it is the only cause which has brought about the change in family relations. But in another way, the family is a result, a dependent variable in the economic-causal relational scheme. This reflects Morgan's assertion:

. . . . The question at once arises whether this (monogamous) form can be permanent in the future. The only answer that can be given is that it must advance as society advances, and change as society changes, even as it has done in the past.[31]

Being metaphysical in its essential elements, the concept of causal relation is improperly applied to many social phenomena which are not unilateral but mutually dependent. For this reason present-day natural sciences use the method of functional relations which supersedes that of one-sided and metaphysical determinism.[32] The scientific view is that associated phenomena are functionally related or are correlated in terms of the coefficient of a certain probability.[33]

The concept of functional relations enables one to treat any factor as a variable and to determine to what extent it is correlated with another factor. Also, it permits one to invert such an 'equation', i.e., taking 'economic' as a variable and attempting to find its functions, religious, political and so forth. For example, one may take an 'economic' factor as a variable and investigate to what degree is is correlated with religious phenomena(Marx). Similarly, one may take religious phenomena as a variable and endeavor to study their functions in connection with economic behaviour or phenomena(Weber).[34]

It is conceded that, as far as social and cultural change is concerned, a 'self-regulating' system of the family is to be excluded. The family does not change only 'within' itself without being influenced by other factors. The family system may play an important role in social organization but as alternatives, other social institutions, such as religion and politics may likewise operate in changing the family organization. Christianity effecting change in marriage, family and women's status has also spread into non-Christian cultures causing them to abandon their earlier polygamy. By a constant effort to reduce ploygamy, and in his preaching against the taking of too many wives, Mohammed contributed manifestly to strengthening the family among the Arabs.[35]

The extremely vital bio-social and cultural functions that the family performs explain its paramount role in influencing, not only its members, but also sociocultural processes. In Chinese society most institutions are patriarchal and paternalistic.[36] In this case the statement 'what the family is, so will society be' challenges Morgan's assertion: 'the family must advance as society advances'.[37] Again, after the Communists gained political power in the China mainland the Chinese traditional family system was drastically altered. However, it would be misleading to attribute this change to economic or industrial development; rather, it is the political institution that influences this system. It is altogether clear that encouraging children to denounce their parents in the interest of the state tends to disrupt the family as the last stronghold of solidarity and stability!

One would concede that the economic factor may be reconciled with functional interdependence, but neither Marx nor Engels recognized the impact of other social institutions, such as religious, political, and rules of taboo or mores, on the family. In fact, the Marxists contend that the economic factor shapes the institution of the family and stresses social class interest. However, even though the scheme of 'class-interest' is elaborated and counts for much in the outcome, this assumption is unconvincing, since, for one thing, the institution of the family has not changed quite as class interest would require.[38]

Today Marxists do admit that the economic factor is only one among many others;[39] this points to erroneous foundations in Marxist theory, and some of the evolutionary fallacies which result from such reasoning. In brief, the foregoing analysis reveals the flaw of simple correlation between economic development and the change of family system and woman's status. However, modern events lend support to the theory that wherever the economic system changes through industrialization, the family patterns alter accordingly. Extended kinship ties are set loose, old lineage organization is affected and some forms of the conjugal family come to the fore.

Woman's Social Production and her Emancipation

Marx and Engels raised these points on exploitation of women's labour:

(a) There is some tendency in Western societies to discourage women from being employed outside the home. In Fascist countries, such as Italy and Germany, the housewife's role in the home was recognized as a new social philosophy of woman's status. In reality, this programme was simply an intensification of the forces at work in other industrial capitalist countries. Given this trend it would be unlikely that capitalist countries were inclined to indulge in the exploitation of women.[40] Marx and Engels might argue that 'the first condition for the liberation of the wife is to bring the whole female sex back into public industry', and elsewhere Marx had declared (in a letter to Kugelmann in 1868) that 'social progress can be measured with precision by the social position of the female sex'.[41] This principle has determined the policy of the Soviet Union in regard to the employment of women. The State Planning Commission of the 2nd Five-Year Plan announced its intention of increasing the proportion of gainfully employed women to 33.9 per cent by 1937.[42] However, it should be kept in mind that the Marxist theory of 'the whole female sex is brought back into public industry' would seem applicable only to countries about to be highly industrialized. The point is that the conscious planning of the Soviet Union for the extension of women's employment in the total national economy is but an application of what occurred in industrialized capitalist countries during the period from 1880 to the first decade of the twentieth century.[43]

(b) Various protective legislations have been drawn up and enacted to eliminate inequalities and special hazards for women in industry.[44] In England legislation was proposed as an expression of the growing discontent against the overworking of women and young girls. Similarly, after World War I, the international Labour Organization at Geneva, established by the Treaty of Versailles as a part of the League of Nations, served the same purpose. In the United States the chief of Ordinance in 1917 issued orders to arsenal commanders and ordinance contractors that the standard of prevailing wages should not be lowered when women render equivalent services.

It may be concluded that the Marxist attack on capitalist society has undoubtedly arisen from a preoccupation with social class interests. Marx's analysis of the capitalist system in which the family plays a vital and fundamental part induced him to predict that, whereas the exploiting class would shrink, the exploited class would grow proportionately. It follows that the revolution in the family system would explode in the most advanced industrialized countries, and conditions fomenting a revolutionary movement would develop first there. Marxist predictions have not materialized. By the end of the nineteenth century there was increasing economic independence for women arising from the feminist movement and the demand for suffrage and emancipation in most countries. This promulgation of political rights and social legislation had rendered the Marxist indictment of exploitation of women unjustified. On the contrary, it is only in industrially backward countries, such as Russia and China among others, that the Marxian doctrine could have been applied.

It is of interest to notice that in his *Anti-dühring*, Engels offers a different explanation for the stages through which the division of labour has passed. The first is the separation of town and country and establishes a separation between agriculture and industry. The second is the origin of the family and refers to the higher stages of barbarism. Yet, in the *German Ideology* it is indicated that the division of labour materializes only when mental labour is divorced from physical labour.[45] Marx and Engels wrote:

. . . . The greatest division of the two mental and physical labours was the separation of town and country, which is stated to have begun with transition from barbarism into civilization, and indeed can scarcely have taken place in any intelligible sense at an earlier stage.[46] In this event, the first great division of labour which Engels refers to in the *Origin of the Family* would not seem to have been a valid division.

That the development of the productive forces engendered the exploitation of one class by another was the central issue in Engels' controversy with Dühring, who argued that political relationships caused class conflict and exploitation. Private property was not the actual result of productive force, but of altered conditions of production and exchange in the interest of increased production, i.e., as a result of economic causes.[47] Likewise the emancipation of women, which can only be achieved, in the Marxist doctrine, by their equal participation in social production, has not quite been evidenced in the Soviet Union; they, too, have the marriage-career syndrome. In the Soviet Union it is still premature to claim a reconciliation between the feminist demand for sex equality based on equal participation in social production and on motherhood, which is also an important social function. The fulfilment of motherhood should be remunerated not by the partner in the reproductive act but by the society in whose interest the function is performed. Schlesinger raised the question: is it true that once property inheritance and economic motives have ceased to play a decisive role in choosing a man, there is no other motive for marriage left except mutual inclination or love?[48] On the basis of Marxist doctrine, after the abolition of private property in the means of production, no immediate emergence of an egalitarian society would be possible.[49]

3. THE BOURGEOIS FAMILY

No one would deny that there were some pathological phenomena in the bourgeois marriage and family, such as commercial transactions, secret adultery, seduction, debasement of the female sex, and exploitation of women and children in production. These emerged in capitalist society with the advent of the industrial revolution. Employers using lower class children in England were fairly numerous during the seventeenth end eighteenth centuries. The cotton factories established in the countries of Lancashire and Yorkshire towards the close of the eighteenth century recruited workers largely from London pauper children. The atrocities inflicted upon these boys and girls and the overcrowded and unsanitary dormitories in the mills constitute one of the most sombre chapters in history, until the reforms of Lord Shaftesbury and others.

Marxist theory seems defective in assuming that social pathological phenomena seldom get remedied in time by adaptive changes and measures. The significance of adaptive change is derived from suggestions by Lowie of the importance of 'time'[50] and particularly from the sociological hypothesis of a 'strain towards consistency' and 'culture lag' between the constituent elements of a culture, advanced respectively by Sumner and Ogburn.[51] Historically, the social evils mentioned above were not left unnoticed forever. In 1794 public attention in England was called to the conditions of child labour in factories. In 1802 came the enactment of the first protective legislation with the passage of the Health and Morals Act, sponsored by Sir Rober Peel, to regulate the labour of children employed in cotton factories. This Act prohibited the binding out of children younger than nine years, restricted participation to twelve actual working hours a day and outlawed night work.[52]

In the United States various organizations were engaged in remedying the deplorable conditions of child labour. For example, the National Consumers' League, founded in 1899, was outstanding in its efforts in this field.[53] In 1904 the National Child Labour Committee was organized, and devoted itself to enlightening the public on certain deplorable conditions. It was also concerned with activating more and better laws which could be enforced. The American Federation of Labour participated in various attempts to enact Federal Child Labour Legislation.[54] Marxists were manifestly reluctant to admit that recent reforms in the two industrial countries had improved the lives of workers.

The Marxist doctrine reacted strongly to prostitution and adultery which it criticized as the results of monogamy and private economic production in capitalist societies. Engels said that "the more the hetaerism of the past is changed in our time by capitalist commodity production and brought about into conformity with it, the more . . . it is transformed into undisguised prostitution".[55]

It is conceded that prostitution is widespread in capitalist societies: one is led to believe that prostitution has ended in Soviet Russia. In her book *Red Virtue,*[56] Ella Winter has a chapter titled: Ending Prostitution. At its head there is a quotation from a Soviet physician: 'Soviet life does not permit prostitution', a dictum intended to illustrate one of virtues of the communist as against the capitalist system. There is little doubt that in Soviet Russia, especially in cities, prostitution diminishes in the early years after the Revolution. But there is grave doubt whether it has ended completely or whether the reduction has simply been a result of the abolition of private property.

It should be noticed that prostitution existed before the rise of capitalism. In the Soviet Union, the government has abolished social class,[57] but there still exists the incentive to trade sexual favours for non-sexual advantages. But prostitution is less prevalent because demand for it was reduced by the tendency towards greater freedom in sexual matters in the immediate post-Revolution years.

4. EQUAL STATUS OF MEN AND WOMEN AND THE CAPITALIST SOCIAL SYSTEM

The Marxists contended that under capitalism women carry the double responsibility of being workers and wives and that this problem can be solved only under socialism. The logic of this assumption is suspect. Under capitalism the role played by trade unions and modern political activity has made for more effective participation by women in economic as well as political affairs. Historically, the position of women in society and in the home has clearly shown the prevailing attitudes towards human rights. Even in recent instances of reaction against women, as in Germany, where there were organized efforts to confine them to childbearing and the household, women could not be completely degraded to their feudal status. On the contrary, despite its planned programme, the Nazi government was unable to remove women from industry.[58] American sociologists have deplored modern progressive trends in the family and predict that unless some unforeseen restoration occurs, the family system will continue headlong in its present decline. This view has been corroborated by the work of Lundberg and Farnham,[59] which glorifies medieval values. Recent developments in the United States have directed family trends away from those advocated by these writers and challenged Marxist doctrine on this issue. The manufacturing of new appliances has markedly assisted women's participation in industry, as was illustrated by the great rise in the employment of women during World War II. These developments have greatly affected the distribution of authority in the American family. They have increased women's demands for the attainment of equal rights in the sexual as well as the economic and intellectual sphere. To assist women who carry on the double task of domestic and outside work, husbands are expected to participate in many home duties. But, in spite of considerable progress, the participation of women in industry has not yet resulted in actual equality for them in the United States. Even in Soviet Russia, which was the first to adopt Marxist doctrine in terms of the emancipation of women, the absolute equality of men and women has not yet been achieved. A young Soviet army officer writes that in the highest level of family life, even under communism, there can never be complete equality between men and women.[60] In support for Marx-Leninism and the equality of men and women, a socialist writer, A.G. Kharchev maintains that Marxist doctrine has never claimed that equality means levelling of the sexes. However, since the doctrine fails to indicate to what extent there should be equality between the sexes, it lacks a sound argument to attack capitalist society in this respect.

Again, the Marxists demand economic emancipation of women which they regard as a prerequisite for the freedom of women in family relations. They maintain that the real problem of freedom and equality for both partners to contract, or to continue in, marriage would remain unsolved even if the abolition of the capitalist economic system, and of property relations created by it, removed all the accompanying economic considerations. It is Marxist belief that even after the nationalization of the means of production, no immediate realization of an egalitarian society and thus of equality of men and women would be possible.[61] The reasons for this are: first, women may be inclined from economic motives, to select a man with a high income and social prestige. Therefore, so long as a state, for example, the U.S.S.R. encourages economic inequality as an incentive for increasing production, there will be no inclination, for ideological reasons, to consider women's social status as completely independent of that of her husband. In brief, it is far from easy to achieve the complete equality of men and women.[62] Second, with respect to equality in sex relations, there are complicated problems of marriage and family life envisaged by Marx and Engels in a socialist society. It is, however, less the problem of 'sex emancipation' or 'free love' or 'glass of water' theory[63] than a question of whether monogamy is not a permanent institution[64] and should remain the standardized form of sexual relations. It is apparent that, apart from the subjective viewpoint,[65] Engels' s statement 'sexual love is by its nature exclusive' fails to answer the question of whether sexual love alone can guarantee the stability of marital unions when all economic considerations are discarded. It may be argued that sexual love is unlikely to provide a basis for an enduring marriage, since the life-span of that emotion varies from one individual to another.[66] Failure to achieve stability in marriage through sexual love alone would be correlated either with rigid social legislation, as in Soviet Russia, or by developing love for work or identifying love with duty and with friendship, as Kharchev maintains.[67] He said:

> It is hardly necessary to argue that a sense of duty should be fostered so that people should not regard the disappearance of passion as the end of love and should not rush headlong into search for a new passion.[68]

Evidently, the single-minded people who constitute revolutionary groups would find expression in revolutionary tasks as well as in their political work; and thus the happy and stable marriages of both Marx and Lenin might have resulted from their political ideology.[69] However, we should not identify the attitudes of communist leaders with those of the rank and file, or a pattern of behaviour calculated to further the revolutionary struggle with that which is likely to appear in a socialist society. There are some cases where ardent communists became so involved in their Party work as to sacrifice any stable personal relations; but an account of such cases, presented not as portraits of sacrifice in the interests of revolution, but as normal behaviour for a socialist society, seemed at all times abhorrent to the average Bolshevist mind.[70] In such cases one would be inclined to suspect the objectivity and authenticity of Karchev's report on the actual status of Soviet family.

5. WOMEN'S EMPLOYMENT AND THE DISRUPTION OF FAMILY RELATIONSHIPS

Marx's error rests in his insistence that capitalism is a universal law which could be used to interpret the origin of any social change. Vast change in family relations, such as female and child labour, with resulting male unemployment, could not occur unless the productive forces of a given system had reached the full extent of their development. Marx dated capitalism in the form of manufactures from the middle of the sixteenth century, and referred to it as a change in the status of the organization of labour only. Hence, what differentiated early capitalism from feudalism was a change in the status of the worker, i.e., in the relations of production. In other words, capitalism affected the relations of production even before it developed into productive forces.[71] Marx pointed out, in *Wage Labour and Capital,* that it is the technology of production, the productive forces that determines the relations of production just as it is the type of weapon used that determines the organization of an army.

According to Engels, large-scale industry dated from 1815, but it was not until 1830 that the productive forces of capitalism had developed to the point at which the proletariat first emerged as an element in the class struggle.[72] In other words, the productive forces had been fully developed before the capitalist system could properly be said to have existed at all. Our argument is that it is the productive forces, not necessarily capitalism that modified somewhat the traditional family system. There is no doubt, of course, that the modern capitalist system has exerted a noticeable impact on the family and later on the relations within it. Nevertheless, to say that only this system is accountable for the condition *sine qua non* of the modification of family relations, seems misleading. In the Soviet Union, though much less capitalized before World War II than some Western societies, the emancipation of women has been accomplished not so much owing to capitalism as to the state usurpation of

family functions. This does not deny the influence of industrial development for which women have been recruited and their participation in the
Five-Year Plan.

Although Marxists condemned capitalism for the evils visited upon the
family, they emphasized the advantageous consequences of industrialism
as an advance or earlier economics. They acknowledged the beneficial
effects of women's employment outside the home, of their emancipation
from household drudgery, and from depending on the earnings of their
husbands. Nevertheless, they declared that these advantages could not be
developed under capitalism without dealing with the dilemma of women's double responsibility as both the worker outside the home and the
wife in the home.[73] Their view condemns the capitalist system without
due regard to what it has contributed to human welfare. In such cases,
the Marxist impeachment of capitalist evils arose from class conflict and
is arbitrary.

It may be argued that the employment of married women would be
incompatible with their duties in looking after children. The argument
against the capitalist social system is based on idealizing a state-controlled family institution. However, it is an indeniable fact that nurseries,
which are increasingly used in Western societies, undoubtedly share the
duties of mothers in the home. Also it is likely that in the society of the
future, parents, especially the mother, will have shorter working hours
and more time to look after their children. Given everyone's modern
kitchen, with all kinds of labour-saving devices in many Western societies,
it seems probable that most women will remain in employment after
marriage. Dr. Klein, a social research worker of the London School of
Economics writes:

> It is not an urge for emancipation that causes more and more women
> to seek jobs. Rather, it is a result of smaller families, the general
> reduction in housework following the modernization of household
> techniques and a desire to improve the standard of living.[74]

Marxists contended that the rapid rate of the employment of women
had instigated the dissolution of family ties; it had, for instance, begun
the reversal of the role of the sexes.[75] Now, a careful investigation into
available evidence certainly suggests that detractors of the family system
overestimated the effects on family life of women's employment outside
the home. Engels' statement involves a contradiction. In one place he
argued that the first condition for the liberation of the wife was to bring
the whole female sex back into public industry.[76] He supported the idea
that women's employment could fulfil their personalities, give economic
satisfaction and psychological and legal equality with their husbands. In
another place, however, he deplored women's employment as a perver-
sion of nature.[77]

According to Engels, the natural consequence of the factory system was that the woman became the family bread-winner, and thus gained supremacy over her husband.[78] He wrote that 52 per cent of all factory workers were females, while 48 per cent were males,[79] a differential in the labour force that indicates a female encroachment upon male prerogatives and employment. As a result, women were likely to be employed because they would work for lower wages than men and be exploited.

Now it should be borne in mind that there was great distress and unemployment among men and women at the end of the eighteenth century. The labourer's wage was then below the level of family subsistence and even children had to work to supplement the father's inadequate income. In addition, as urbanization was accelerated along with the introduction of power-drive machinery due to the Industrial Revolution, more and more women flocked to the cities to sell their labour as factory workers.[80] The introduction of machines might be expected to lead, in the long run, to more jobs rather than unemployment. Engels, however, rejected this possibility. There are economists who believe that machinery inevitably depresses the wages of manual labour, but they admit that machinery has tremendously increased population, and afforded many other means of employment.[81]

To sum up, Marx had one theory of women and family life, how a woman should be emancipated and given more dignity and status, political equality, property rights, the right to pursue a career and a say in her children's education and upbringing, and completely equal rights before the law. But Marx did not foresee all the future shrewdly. His classical theories, also modified by Engels, have undergone profound revision even after the Socialist Revolution in the Soviet Union and China. Both these Communist societies have moved away from early libertarianism towards a strict regard for monogamous unions, safeguarded, however, by considerable emancipation of women and progress for advances into full citizenship. I am speaking as a scholar in Chinese who has researched these matters in China and in the West for three decades.

NOTES

[1] R.F. Fortune, *Sorcerers of Dobu*. London: George Routledge and Sons, Ltd., 1931, pp.18-20.
[2] W.M.F. Petrie, *Social Life in Ancient Egypt*, London, Constable and Co., Ltd., 1923, p. 119.
[3] A.L. Kroeber, *Zuni Kin and Clan*, Anthropological Papers of the American Museum of Natural History, Vol. 18, Part II, 1917.
[4] A. Giraud-Teuton, *Les origines du mariage et de la famille*, Genève et Paris, 1884, p. 215.
[5] S.N. Starke, *The Primitive Family in Its Origin and Development*, New York: D. Appleton and Company, 1889, p. 65.

[6] J.R. Swanton, "A Reconstruction of the Theory of Social Organization", in *Frank Boas' Anniversary Volume* (New York, 1906), pp. 166-178. Also his "The Social Organization of American Tribes", *American Anthropologist*, Vol. VII (1905), pp. 663-73.

[7] A. Kroeber, *Anthropology*. New York: Harcourt, Brace and Co., 1923, p. 331.

[8] Engels, *Op. cit.*, p. 50.

[9] George P. Murdock, *Social Structure* New York: The Macmillan Co., 1949, p. 264.

[10] A. Goldenweiser, *Anthropology-An Introduction to Primitive Culture* (New York: F.S. Grofts and Company, 1946), p. 516.

[11] Charles Darwin, *Descent of Man*. New York: D. Appleton and Co., 1872, p. 604.

[12] Margaret Mead, 'Family', *Encyclopedia of the Social Sciences*. New York: The Macmillan Co., 1931, Vols. 5-6, p. 65.

[13] R. Briffault, 'Group Marriage and Sexual Communism', in V.F. Calverton (ed.), *The Making of Man*. New York: The Modern Library, 1931, p. 223.

[14] M. Kovalevsky, *Tableau des origines et de l'évolution de la famille et de la propriété*. Stockholm: Samson and Wallin, 1890, p. 14.

[15] C.N. Starcke, *Op. cit.*, p. 172.

[16] Robert H. Lowie, *Social Organization*. New York: Rinehart and Co., Inc., 1949, p. 122.

[17] E. Adamson Heobel, *Man in the Primitive World*, New York: McGraw-Hill Company, Inc., 1958, p. 324.

[18] Morgan's theory relies on the classificatory system of kinship terminology as underlying widespread community of wives. A community of wives exists in some cases, but it should not necessarily be elaborated as supporting a primitive form. J. Layard, 'The Family and Kinship', in the *Institutions of Primitive Society*, Glencoe, Ill.: The Free Press, 1954, pp. 61.

[19] Morgan, *Ancient Society*, p. 502; A Kardiner and E. Preble, *They Studied Man*, New York, 1963, p. 90.

[20] F. Müller-Lyer, *The Family*, trans. by F.W.S. Brown, London, 1931.

[21] W.D. Humbly, 'Source Book for African Anthropology', *Field Museum of Natural History*, Anthropological Series, Vol. 26, Part II, 1937.

[22] John Lubbock, *Prehistorical Times*, 1869, p. 424.

[23] R. Schlesinger, 'Marxist Theory and the New Program of the Soviet Communist Party', *Science and Society*, Vol. XXVI, No.2, Spring, 1962.

[24] The definition of capitalism is given by G. Lichtheim, *Marxism: An Historical and Critical Study*. London, 1961, p. 165, n4.

[25] In these three societies marriage between brother and sister of royal lineage was mandatory. Its purpose was mystical and was intended to preserve supreme and divine royalty by prohibiting the marriage of royal members with mortals.

[26] The levirate is a cultural rule prescribing that a widow marry by preference the brother of her deceased husband. The sororate is a cultural rule instituting the marriage of a widower to the sister of his deceased wife. George P. Murdock, *Social Structure*, p. 29.

[27] Julian H. Steward, 'The Economic and Social Basis of Primitive Bands', in *Essays in Anthropology Presented to A.L. Kroeber*, University of California Press, pp. 331-347, 1936.

[28] R. Schlesinger, *Changing Attitudes in Soviet Russia—the Family in the U.S.S.R.; p.18.*

[29] 'The Proletariat', declared the *Communist Manifesto*, 'will use its political dominance to strip the bourgeoisie step by step of all capital, and concentrate all means of production in the hands of the state'.

[30] R. Schlesinger, *Marx, His Time and Ours*. London: Routledge and Kegan Paul, 1950, p.203

[31] Engels, *Op. cit.*, p.74.

[32] Kingsley Davis and W.E. Moore, 'Some Principles of Stratification', *American Sociological Review*, 10 (April 1945), p.244.

[33] A Cournot, *Essai sur les fondements de nos connaissances*. Paris, 1851; *Considérations sur la marche des idées* (Paris, 1872); *Traité de l'enchaînement des idées fondamentales dans les sciences et dans l'histoire* (Paris, 1908)

[34] Robert K. Merton, *Social Theory and Social Structure*. Glencoe, Illinois: The Free Press, 1957, p. 595.

[35] Koran, Sura IV on 'Women', New York: Everyman Library; Mansourx Fahmy, *La condi-*

tion de la femme dans la tradition et l'évolution de l'Islamisme. Paris, 1913, pp. 3-5; Robertson Smith, *Kinship and Marriage in Early Arabia.* London, 1903, pp. 121-22.

[36] C.L. Nieh, *China's Industrial Development: Its Problem and Prospects.* Shanghai: China Institute of Pacific Relations, 1933, p. 7.

[37] Engels, *Op. cit.,* p. 74.

[38] Thorstein Veblen, *The Place of Science in Modern Civilization.* New York, 1942, pp. 313-314.

[39] Marx, in his letter writings, and Engels discarded in practice their earlier claims and, in superseding 'the economic interpretation' recognized it as one among many others. 'Letter of 1894' *Der Sozialogische Akademiker.*

[40] Marx and Engels detested the capitalist social system and collected evidence to condemn it. If women were employed in factories, then they said that this practice would disrupt family bonds and utterly alter family life; if women remain at home, they denounced the capitalist system for preventing the emancipation of women.

[41] Bernhard J. Stern, *The Family, Past and Present,* New York: D. Appleton and Co., 1938, p.184. Bebel held that the encouragement of women to industry is a progressive step towards eliminating the backwardness of women under pre-capitalistic family.

[42] Mary van Kleek, 'Women in Industry', *Encyclopedia of the Social Sciences,* Vol.15, p.452. The proportion of women among the gainfully employed was 16.9 per cent in 1897 in Tsarist Russia, while in the Soviet Union it was 29.9 per cent in 1932.

[43] *Ibid.*

[44] Mary van Kleek, 'Women in Industry', *Op. cit.,* p.454.

[45] *Marx-Engels Gesamtausgabe,* abt. I, Band 5, p.21.

[46] *Ibid.,* p.39.

[47] Engels, *Anti-Dühring* (1877), p.146, 148.

[48] R. Schlesinger, *Op. cit.,* p.12.

[49] *Marx's Critique of the Gotha Programme,* English ed. (Marxist-Leninist Library).

[50] Robert H. Lowie, *Culture and Ethnology.* New York: Peter Smith, 1920, p.173

[51] W.G. Sumner, *Folkways.* Boston, 1906, pp.5-6; W.F. Ogburn, *Social Change.* New York: The Viking Press, 1952, pp.202-203.

[52] Raymond G. Fuller, "Child Labour", *Encyclopedia of the Social Sciences,* Vol. 2, p. 414.

[53] *Ibid.,* p. 418.

[54] *Ibid.*

[55] Engels, Op. cit., p. 66.

[56] Ella Winter, *Red Virtue*—Human Relationships in the New Russia. New York: Harcourt, Brace and Co., 1933. Chap. II.

[57] The Party forms one class and enjoys privileges. K. Davis, 'The Sociology of Prostitution', *Op. cit.,* p. 752.

[58] Alfred Meusel, 'National Socialism and the Family', *British Sociological Review,* 28 (1936), pp. 389-99.

[59] Ferdinand Lundberg and M.F. Farnham, *Modern Women: The Lost Sex,* New York, 1947, p.105.

[60] Bogdanovich is an officer of the Soviet army, aged 24, married; he is in the sixth year of marriage. This statement is found in M. Motzenok, 'Youth Has Its Say on Love and Marriage, *Op. cit.,* p.24.

[61] *Marx's Critique of the Gotha Programme,* English edition—Marxist-Leninist Library.

[62] That women are paid less than men for performing the same service should not be regarded as justifying a lower wage for women unless statistics show that the output is less when women are employed than when men are employed. M. van Kleek, 'Women In Industry', *Op. cit.,* p. 455.

[63] The emancipation of women accompanied by free-love vogue was condemned by Lenin as un-Marxist. Alexander Werth, 'Love Among the Russians', *New Statesman* 61, No. 1556, January 1961, p. 10.

[64] In Engels' view monogamy improves the personality of both partners as they complement each other.

[65] The subjective attitude of the Marxists is certainly relevant to a consideration of the question whether a libertine approach to the sex questions of a socialist society can be

sensibly inferred from its general outlook or is, from the point of view of Bolshevists, a relic of certain reactions to the conditions which predominate in a capitalist society.

[66] As a counter-measure to 'free sex love', the restoration or cult of the family was proclaimed in 1936 and 1944. A Werth, 'Love Among the Russians', *Op. cit.*, p.10.

[67] A.G. Kharchev, 'The Soviet Family', *The Soviet Review*, May 1961, p.10.

[68] *Ibid.*, p.11.

[69] Schlesinger, *Op. cit.*, p.15.

[70] *Ibid.*

[71] Gideon Sjoberg, 'Folk and Feudal Societies', *American Journal of Sociology*, 58 (November 1952), p.238.

[72] Ludwig Feuerbach, *Selected Works*, II, p.356.

[73] Marx and Engels assumed that a complete solution of this problem could be found only under socialism. The Soviet Union, however, not the first in extending the employment of women. What the State Planning Commission for the Second first-Year Plan undertook in increasing women's employment was simply an application of what was developed in capitalist countries during the period from 1880 to the earlier part of the 20th century. M. van Kleek, 'Women in Industry', *Op. cit.*, p. 452.

[74] 'British Wives in Jobs Increase, but Their Homes Come First', *The New York Times*, January 4, 1960. Also, 'Nearly a Third of Wives Have a Job', *The Times*, London, January 4, 1960. Nearly four millions wives in Great Britain have full-time or part-time jobs or nearly a third of the total, 1960.

[75] Figures quoted by Engels in 1844 showed that of the husbands of 10,721 married women to be employed in 412 factories, 5,314 were also employed in factories, 2,927 were otherwise employed; no information was given for 659. Only 821 were unemployed and presumably supported by their wives. *Manchester Guardian*, May 1, 1844, p.5, Cols. 4-5.

[76] Engels, *Op. cit.*, p. 148.

[77] Engels' view that women's place was in the home was shared by Peter Gaskell, "The Manufacturing Population of England (1833), pp.166-67.

[78] *Liverpool Mercury*, April 26, 1844, p. 139.

[79] Engels, *The Condition of the Working-Class in England in 1844*, p. 164.

[80] Ivy Pinchbeck, *Women Workers and the Industrial Revolution, 1750-1850*. London: George Routledge and Sons, Ltd., 1930, pp.166-67.

[81] J.C. Symons, *Arts and Artisans at Home and Abroad*. Edinburgh and London, 1839, pp. 154-55.

CHAPTER IV

The Development of the Soviet Family and Woman's Status

The change in a historical epoch can always be determined by the progress of women towards freedom, because in the relation of woman to man, of the weak to the strong, the victory of human nature over brutality is most evident; the degree of emancipation of women is the natural measure of general emancipation.

CHARLES FOURIER*

1. THE RUSSIAN FAMILY BEFORE 1917

In early Russian history, the matriarchal-matrilineal family was dominant, particularly among the Slavs. Elnett showed that women enjoyed full independence in holding large possessions, in being the heads of families and even of tribes, and in choosing their husbands and lovers.[1] Evidence to support an early Russian matriarchal-matrilineal system was not given root and branch. It was based on the linguistic roots of the early words for mother and father, and on reports of blood-revenge rights: those who traced descent to a common female had the right to avenge the murder of one another. Although the evidence, however scanty, may suggest a matriarchy, the form and struture of the earliest Russian family still remains an enigma for want of written evidence.

The family form has been intertwined with an economic organization. Since the Russian Slavs were an agricultural people, they developed the patriarchal extended family. In the Russian Tratsvo, the South Slavic zadruga, the family consisted of the elder or the surviving brothers, together with their wives, married sons with their wives, unmarried daughters, and so on, down to the great grand-children. Such large groups could sometimes include several dozen persons living and working under a common authority.

This form of the extended family served to accomplish the physical work involved in agriculture. Also the ownership of the land and of the

---

* Charles Fourier, *Théories des Quatre Mouvements* in *Oeuvres Complètes*, 1841, I,p. 195.

homestead, parental authority, and economic leadership were vested in the eldest ascendant or in the community of brothers descendant from the same ascendant. Although there was considerable cultural diversity among the Russian peasants, the economically self-sufficient extended family system was prevalent.

Towards the end of the tenth century the Russian princes were converted to Christianity and espoused the Greek orthodox religion. Elnett held that the introduction of Christianity in Russia was one of the main factors in bringing about a state of shameful subjection for the Russian woman. As a matter of fact, the teachings of the Greek orthodox Church acknowledged the superiority of males, who headed their families in secular and spiritual affairs. In the thirteenth century the Mongols from the East conquered Russia; and the intermingling and intermarriage with the Mongols led to cultural change. With regard to the family, the Mongol invasion reinforced and developed the strong patriarchal family. When the Mongols were driven out under the leadership of Ivan III, he declared himself the first Czar of Russia. Then more severe demands were made on the peasantry in that they found themselves bound to the land. As a result, there developed the two hereditary classes of landowners and workers, thus paving the way for true serfdom.

At the peak of serfdom in the seventeenth and eighteenth centuries, misery, hardships and oppression fell to the lot of the serf. Landowners had the right not only to order the serfs beaten but also to increase the amount of their work. Moreover, they allocated land not to individuals or families, but to village communes within which the extended Russian family was found to consist of a male head, his wife, their unmarried children, and married sons with their spouses. The dominance of the male and the subordination of the wife and children enlisted the support of the Russian Church, which likened the father's authority over his children to that of the Almighty. The father exercised his authority over his children in various ways. For instance, disinheritance, which was within the right of the bolshak, the head of the household, could be resorted to in controlling a contumacious son.

The Demostroy, a code of Russian family practices drawn up in the sixteenth century, upholds the corporal punishment of sons:

Beat your son in his youth, and he will comfort you in your old age. . . . And do not weaken in beating the child. Beating with a rod will not kill him, but will make him healthier. . . . Loving your son, inflict more wounds on him and you will rejoice afterward.[2]

Wives fared little better than children when the extended patriarchal family was developing under serfdom.The folk proverb says: 'the husband is father to his wife'.

Such were family systems and the conditions among the peasants under serfdom; but family conditions among the working classes of the cities were not very different. In fact, the Demostroy was originally drawn up as a code for the urban families when the wives and children were found to have resisted fulfilling the approved family roles. Although serfdom was officially abolished in 1861 under Czar Alexander II, the emancipation provisions were made for the interest of the landowner, and the peasant still continued to be bound to his village commune and to be subordinated to oppressive authority of the head of the household. Peasants were subjected to long arduous hours of work, poor working conditions, and low wages. Women suffered under many social and legal disabilities and lacked political rights. A wife was in the power of her husband and divoce was not easy; at any rate not without active help from her own family. The institution of marriage constituted above all else an important element of the system under which property was held. This state of affairs was promoted by the women's unemancipated state.

Peter the Great undertook a drastic reform of Russian womanhood, by his edict of 1704, which was the first step towards the liberation of women from slavery. He abrogated the term 'slavery' and ordered that parents and relatives must not, under oath, force their children into matrimony. The courts, he added, would prosecute in any case of forcible seizure of women for marriage. It was Peter the Great who inaugurated equal rights for women even in the matter of divorce. In 1898 revolutionary parties formed the Social and Democratic Parties which drew its inspiration and doctrines largely from the writings of Karl Marx. Furthermore, in the nineteenth century there had developed in Russia a strong feminist movement; the women who joined it were largely recruited from among the bourgeoisie and ardently advocated full equality of the sexes in political, economic, and social spheres.

There were two main classes in the pre-Revoltionary period: the well-to-do family which was organized on a paternalistic basis and held sufficient land, and that of the poor peasant who had to work on another's land to live. In the first type of family married sons customarily remained in the household under the authority of the father; but new laws in 1907 allowed adult sons to escape the control of the father by claiming their shares of land upon marriage. On the other hand, the poor farmer, being constantly confronted with his small land holding and a growing number of children, found it impossible to enjoy this type of family life under the patriarchal system. To support the family, even the mother was often forced to seek some outside earnings.

The intelligentsia took the initiative in moulding the Russian family system as a non-class matter.[3] They deviated from the prescribed political, social, and religious order, and in an effort to endorse new functions in society and to reject both property and convention, the Intelligentsia dismissed the authoritarian and property basis of the husband-wife and father-child relationship. The ideal image of family, conceived and approved by the pre-Revolutionary intellegentsia, demanded that a marriage should be a complete union of ideas and emotions. In other words, marriage should be based on a free and equal choice of both partners, uninfluenced by considerations of social class or property.[4]

This idea that woman is endowed with equal rights to emotional satisfaction in love and marriage is exemplified in Tatiana's love letter in Pushkin's 'Eugene Onegin' and Nekrassov's 'Russian Women'.[5] Further, if one attempts to seek a social forerunner to the revolution of 1917, the significant event was the emancipation of the serfs by Czar Alexander II in 1861. Emancipation was an effort to disrupt the feudal structure of Russian society and to introduce a modern economy.[6]

2. THE COMMUNIST REVOLUTION AND THE RUSSIAN FAMILY

Engels clearly stated that the individual family would be abolished when it ceased to be an economic unit. In accord with Marxist theory and Bolshevik planning Alexandria Kollontai wrote an essay in 1932 which stands for a characteristic pronouncement on the family question. To answer the question : 'What is the family?' Kollontai said:

The family is no more than an economic institution, the form of which has varied throughout history with the dominant economic forms of society. The family is not a permanent but a fluctuating concept. Its moral content and external form are always changing, since every class gives to the family its content and to a certain extent even its outward form, and every age has a different conception of the 'family'.[7]

Here again in taking issue with the development of family Kollontai stated:

But the family is an economic unit which is cut off from the collective. Its main functions, such as production, house-keeping, consumption, the education of children etc. are taken over by the community, so the necessity for its existence will disappear.[8]

The development in this connection within the Soviet Union she described as follows:

In the Soviet state, this tendency-the suppression of the role of the family by the state -is particularly noticeable. Of course, the old family form continues-the mutual relationship of the married couple and the relationship of parents to children are regulated by the laws . . . The social education of the children is one of the important functions of the Soviet state. The woman is treated by the law as a labour unit on exactly the same footing as the man. The new houses, especially those being constructed in the new industrial areas, are designed less and less for family requirements and more and more to suit the convenience of individual men and women. They have, for instance, central kitchens, single rooms etc. . . . [9]

On December 19 and 20, 1917 after the October Revolution, the Soviets issued two decrees which deal with dissolution of marriages, civil marriages, children, and the introduction of Registry Books for marriages.[10] These decrees moulded Soviet family legislation and provided the basis for most fundamental principles of family and marriage.

There are drastic changes in marriage and the family. The terms were as follows:

(1) *Secularization of marriage.* In accordance with the 1917 decree, Church marriage was considered a private affair, but a later 1918 decree declared that religious marriage conferred no rights or obligations upon the individual entering it. Only civil or secular marriage registered in the Bureau of ZAGS (Civil Registry Authorities) was valid and legally recognized.

(2) *Monogamy as the basic form of Soviet marriage.* In a socialist society the pseudo-monogamy of the bourgeois must disappear in conformity with Engels' contention that "within monogamous marriage at the side of the husband who enhanced his existence with hetaerism stands the neglected wife."[11] Again, Engels emphasized that a marriage based on sexual love must, by its nature, be monogamous. This does not mean, however, that within monogamy modern sexual love developed exclusively, or even chiefly, as the love of husband and wife for each other.[12] In Soviet Russia, monogamy has been instituted as the most suitable form of marriage; and bigamy and polygamy were stigmatized as remnants of old religious or tribal customs.[13]

(3) *Full equality of the spouses.* Under the Family Code of 1918 divorce could be applied to the Civil Registry Bureau[14] or to the People's courts.[15] The Communist International laid down as one of the main tasks the social equalization of men and women. They made a fundamental revision of marriage and family law and recognized motherhood as a social function, and the protection of mothers and children a necessity.[16] In full compliance with these demands of the Comintern, the programme of the All-Union Communist (Bolshevik) Party declared that the Party aimed at freeing women from the material burdens of the obsolete household.[17] The Constitution[18] allowed women an equal wage for equal work. According to the 1918 Family Code (art. 105), each spouse owned separately what was acquired by him or her. Inheritance, since it is related to private property, loses its *raison d'être* when private property

has been abolished. Thus, no later than four months after the Soviet regime was established, the abolition of inheritance was boldly declared.[19]

(4) *Protection of mother and child.* Early Soviet legislation was codified on the hypothesis that, with the appearance of the final stage of communism, the family would cease to be an individual unit, but would be collectivized, with children raised in public institutions. The protection of mother and child which constituted the primary objectives of Soviet family legislation was to be accomplished by releasing them from the material as well as moral domination of the father, and by establishing crèches and kindergartens.[20]

It is easy to see from the study of the preceding Soviet legislative acts that there were several implications of state policy towards the family. Marriage legislation implements state endeavours to influence and control the family. Once marriage has been contracted, the Soviet interest turns to the development of large families viewed as the fulfilment of individual instinct, and beneficial to society as well. The state intends to increase the population, and this can be assured when a stable, happy and normal family life is maintained.

3. THE CODE OF THE FAMILY LAW OF THE R.S.F.S.R. (RUSSIAN SOCIALIST FEDERATIVE SOVIET REPUBLIC)

The 1918 Family Code was based on two decrees issued by the Soviet government, the December decree on divorce, and that on the registration of births,deaths, and marriages. Amendments in 1925 enabled the Soviet government to remove certain inequalities and injustice which were inherited from Tsarist rule and were inherent in all bourgeois countries. The central theme on which many 19th century bourgeois family systems were based granted all privileges and all rights in property ownership to a man at the woman's expense. The state-enacted pattern of legal marriage strengthens this bourgeois system and refuses to ratify any relations existing outside such marriage. Moreover Church marriage occupies a predominant position in bourgeois societies, in France and the United States for example, where Church and State are separate entities.

The 1918 Soviet Family Code deprived Church marriage of any significance and recognized only civil marriage, and replaced the clergy's parish register of births, deaths, and marriages. As a result, for large centers such as Moscow we estimate that only one-third of the marriage are contracted through the Church and two-thirds are purely civil Soviet marriages.

The following are the main points which the new Code presents to the

All-Russian Central Executive Committee for study in which it differs from the old one.

1. Registration has changed its role and its significance.
2. Registered and non-registered marriages have been decreed as equal in their material consequences.
3. Protection for the children has been increased where a marriage has been dissolved either by divorce or by the unilateral rescinding of one of the spouses.
4. Certain guarantees have been required before a marriage is registered as a safeguard against ill-considered unions.
5. The property relations between the married parties have been differently construed and enjoined.

Before presenting the debate on these five points, we should bear in mind that they were discussed at length in two separate meetings. During the first meeting of October 17th, 1925, the All-Russian Central Executive Committee expatiated upon only the first three points; during the meeting of October 19th, 1925 the Committee put forward and debated the last two points, that is, required a guarantee before marriage and property relations between the married parties.

(1) *Change in the role of Marriage Registration* The 1918 Code was enacted when Church marriage was still prevalent. To counteract the Church ceremony, the new Code provided for the setting up of Registrar's Offices and ratified only those marriages which had been registered according to its requirements. This was laid down in article 52 which decrees: "Only those civil marriages which have been registered at the Office of Registration of Births, Deaths, and Marriages, shall involve the rights and obligations of married parties as set out in this section". By such limitations *de facto* marriages would be deprived of absolutely all rights and the State's protection, except in regard to children.

(2) *Equal Rights for Registered and de facto Marriages* In the old family Code children's rights were inherent in parenthood and thus safeguarded regardless of whether marriage was registered or not. But in a *de facto* marriage the wife was granted no rights. This clause of the family code is basically amended as follows: "registered marriages and *de facto* marriages are now to have equal rights before the law." This of necessity leads us to re-define *de facto* marriage.

The definition of marriage which is given in the amendment reads: "Marriage is a voluntary association, without time limit, which is accompanied by all the legal consequences implied in a free contract between a man and a woman". In this definition a great threat to women's rights is concealed in the sense that any legal protection of these rights is obliterated as soon as one of the parties refuses to acknowledge the presence of a voluntary agreement. That is the reason why both the Commissions and the Soviet of People's Commissars discarded the amendment, and the subsequent sections of the enactment refer to both registered and *de facto* marriages.

It should be made clear that under the old Code there was no possibility of antedating the registering of a marriage which had existed as a *de facto* relationship for some time before being registered. Marriage was not regarded as having been concluded except from the moment of its registration at the Registrar's Office in accordance with Article 62 of the old Code. This is amended in the proposal for the new Code, which reads: "Persons maintaining *de facto* marital relations not registered under the established order may formalize their relations at any time by registration, taking the period of *de facto* association into account. It is for these reasons that the material consequences of *de facto* marriage are rendered the same as those of registered marriages.[21] And it is in this point that the fundamental reason for the new project rests.

(3) *Protection of Women and Children* With regard to the rights of women and children the most urgent and essential point is the question of 'alimony', the right to support and maintenance in case of a marriage dissolved for any reason. Groucho Marx defined alimony as 'feeding oats to a dead horse.' Alimony is abolished unless one partner is disabled. In tackling this problem Article 11 says: 'A destitute spouse who is unable to work has the right to receive support from other spouse if the court decides that the latter is able to provide such support. The spouse who is able to work may claim the right to receive support during unemployment'. This article means that persons maintaining *de facto* marriage relations, even though they have not registered the fact, may equally avail themselves of the right to receive support. Alimony is rather rare in the U.S.S.R. Comrade Kursky argued that Article 11 applies equally to men, since the word 'spouse' means either husband or wife. Nevertheless the article is primarily intended to safeguard or protect the woman.

In Article 11 there are two points: firstly, that apart from being needy, a destitute spouse is incapable of working because of sickness and is entitled to support; and secondly, that the Soviet of People's Commissars added the provision that support was also claimable.[22] A clear and distinct definition of the term 'unemployment' must be provided, so that it should prevent any attempt by a spouse to live at someone else's expense and labour. Soviet society does not tolerate unemployment. In the Land Code there is a rider to the basic Article 66 which reads: "Persons joining a Dvor by marriage or adoption acquire a right to use the land and the communal property which constitutes the Dvor in question in accordance with common law; at the same time they lose their rights in any other

Dvor".[23] If the wife returns to her own, original Dvor and her material conditions presumably become no worse than before, she is not entitled to alimony.

In the new project the Soviet of People's Commissars came to the decision that all cohabitants with the woman are responsible for her support, but she has the right to demand alimony from only one of them. There remains the problem of registration of marriage in the National Republic. The fact is that in the centre of R.S.F.S.R. (Russian Socialist Federative Soviet Republic) registration of marriage has been widely carried out and the rights of women are protected by the law; but in the distant National Republics such as Auls (villages in he Caucasus) and far-away Nomad Camps there has been found the firmly entrenched custom of contracting marriage and organizing the family under the auspices of the clergy.[24]

In the provision for alimony the Soviet of People's Commissars made registered and non-registered marriages equal, that is, they abandoned the legal effect of contracted marriage by allowing the same rights to the *de facto* relationships. There is no need to reformulate the law on account of *de facto* relationships. For *de facto* relations which approach the relations regulated and prescribed by the law must be protected or safeguarded in the same way as registered marriages. It is maintained that Article 11 and its annotations make real progress as regards *de facto* marriages. The new law or Code will deviate or differ from bourgeois law and alter certain bourgeois elements in that it may be adapted to apply to the whole population of the Soviet Union. If a certain number of people even now dislike Soviet marriage, that does not mean that it should not have been introduced in 1917. Again, there is no sense in condemning registered marriage and destroying the conception of marriage. "If we reject," said Kursky, "the definition of marriage, that is, the criteria by which certain persons can be judged to be in a state of marital relations, we shall have to rely on the practice and ruling of the law courts which characterize the American system".

Party Meeting of October 19, 1925

Extracts from the Speech given by Comrade Brandenburgsky are appended.

Brandenburgsky stated that on the basis of the project of the Code of Marriage, Family and Guardianship Law there are two important ideas which the two critics of the project, Comrade Krassikov and Beloborodov, omitted. The first one is that under Soviet Law, family and its relationships are founded on *de facto* parentage or on common blood, and not on the formality of registered marriage. The second idea rests in the fact that legal consequences of marriage result not from the registration, but from the very fact of living together. Bearing these two ideas in mind, we shall dismiss the main objections levelled against the project. We shall not distinguish between 'legal' and illegal' marriage, just as we made no distinction between legitimate and illegitimate children. This lays down the foundation of the Matrimonial Code.

Beloborodov expatiated upon the theme that continuous and stable marriages are essential and necessary. Comrade Popova, a new woman, said that the possibility of frequent divorce should be curbed and drastic measures should be taken to prevent married parties from changing their 'partner' so often. Comrade Brandenburgsky put the question: if you object to a frequent change of spouse, what proposal do you make for fighting it? If we write down a law restraining divorce, it would not be a new one, but an old one. The whole bourgeois law in this issue is aimed at achieving and preserving a stable and enduring family as an absolute essential for a bourgeois society. However, experience attests the fact that it is precisely in these countries, such as France, where the impediments to divorce and the preconditions for marriage are most rigid that the family disintegrates. The law formulates the fundamental factors of life, whereas the functions in the point at issue spring from life itself, i.e., from the way in which the new life and morals emerge. It has been argued that by introducing this new Code we shall rule out marriage registration and afford support to Church marriages. This, however, has not proved to be the case. Our problem is to formalize those relationship rather than to forbid 'nonmarriage' relationships.

Property relations between married parties have been differently construed. Article 11[25] declares that the property acquired by the married parties should be shared, since they acquired it together. The clause clarifies the statement in the old family Code in 1918. This sharing affects the peasant and working women who have divorced their husbands. This point is not difficult to settle for a worker's family, since there is no great property. But in the villages the problem is much more complex. For instance, a married peasant girl lives and works in the the family for over three years, and when she divorces her husband she may obtain no more than two or three pounds of flour and a few sacks of potatoes. Hence Article 11 should provide for greater fairness and satisfaction to all parties sharing property in divorces in villages. Further, it should take another point into consideration, that where one of the spouses has lived with his or her partner for only one month, or two or three, neither of them is entitled to share the property; on the other hand, when he has contributed to the household for several years he has every right to be allotted a certain proportion of the property.

In respect to the emphasis upon registration of marriages, Comrade

Krylenko made the following statement: "There was a suggestion that a norm of divorces, or a norm of husbands, and a norm of wives sanctioned by the law should be enacted". Similarly it was suggested that we should interfere in the private relations of some people or compel them, in the old fashion, to continue their cohabitation when one of the parties declares his unwillingness. In other words, compulsory Soviet marriages must be established.

There is the problem of polygamy and polyandry. Comrade Krassikov lodged a proposal that a legal norm must be established and criminal legislation introduced for punishing polygamy. Comrades Krassikov and Beloborodo were afraid that our attitude towards the question of optional registration of marriages will lead to polygamy. Under the new family Code, *de facto* relations are granted protection, including a right to alimony if they lead to pregnancy, separation and the birth of a child.

Some speakers raised the question: What measures should be taken against polygamy? The new Code in 1925 serves as a potent implement against it. Under the previous Code in 1918 there was no full protection of *de facto* relationships, while under the new Code we protect them. We confront the spouse who attempts to evade his or her duties, towards wife or husband, with a threat of material and other sacrifices. For every spouse will have to face the problem of regulating his relationship. Apart from the preceding problem there exists the irresponsibility and vagueness of relations with one's first spouse. The new Code opposes these vague relationships by imposing responsibility for *de facto* marriages and pressing non-registered couples to clarify their relations.

(1) Safeguards to be observed before Registration of Marriage. In Article 5 it is stated:[26] "It is unlawful to register marriages between persons one or both of whom is or are already married either with or without registration or between persons one or both of whom has or have been adjudged weak-minded or insane". The decree demands that, before marriage is concluded, not only should a signed statement be produced to the effect that there is no infection with venereal disease, tuberculosis or any other contagious diseases, but that a doctor's certificate of health should be submitted".

In regard to Article 7 of document 7-relating to surnames in marriage-attention should be called to the fact that whereas under the former family Code in 1918 a common surname was obligatory for the spouses, either the husband's or the wife's or a combination of the two, a law was passed in 1924 under which a common surname was not obligatory. Under the present Code the original surname is resumed after divorce. By making the maintenance of the common surname optional each party preserves the apparent independence which is inherent in all the articles.

(2) Property Relations between Spouses. Article 10[27] affirms that mar-

ried parties may come to all kinds of agreements in connection with their property. But the Soviet of People's Commissars bring the addendum in an effort to protect the interests of the weaker party where these agreements are ineffectual. Article 10 is of the utmost importance, seeing that it introduces something new. At first there was 'segregation of property', but now 'community of property' is being put forward, that is to say, property acquired by common effort becomes common property and in case of divorce it is to be shared equally. Such community of property is apparently a quite sound principle. As for the peasants the Land Code provides that everything acquired by the Dvor, i.e., by every member of the Dvor, should be regarded as common property.

Regarding alimony on dissolution of marriage there should be aid and assistance for spouse and child, but we propose one basic modification: only a destitute spouse *unable to work* is entitled to claim alimony. At any rate we cannot deny a peasant woman the basic right to alimony; otherwise we should have these women unprotected and be placing at a disadvantage an innocent woman who has been divorced by her husband.

The Meeting of November 15, 1926

Report given by Comrade Kursky

(1) Comrade Platov, a member of the All-Russian Executive Committee, declared that the project of the People's Commissariat of Justice was a project of no marriage or polygamy, and that the villages obstinately hold fast to Church marriage and to the patriarchal, i.e., the old family. Comrade Kursky avowed that "we must completely abolish the reactionary Utopian idea of preserving the patriarchal family and preventing the division of peasant family into small units. Also in reviewing the whole development of marriage "we are obliged to declare that the registration of marriage has become a custom and is now the normal way of formalizing marital relations".

2) Another trend of opinion expressed at the village meetings advocates the registration of marriage, that is, the preservation of the law as it exists at present. For example, at the meeting of the citizens of the Ukhtobtrovsk Commune of the Kholmogor region in the Archangel district the resolution was adopted as follows: (a) The need for registration of marriage should be realized; otherwise both men and women in the villages will lead lives of greater profligacy and debauchery; (b) The reason for the division of agricultural Dvors must in all circumstances be stated and property will be allotted or withheld from persons demanding it with a view to the preservation of existing Dvors.

3) A further contention of the advocates of this point of view is that

registered marriage implies both property rights and a number of other rights including the right to vote and regarding military service.

The actual text of the project for the Code of Laws relating to Marriage, Family and Guardianship was approved by the Soviet of People's Commissars and differs from the earlier project in that it sets out with greater precision a number of norms. For we are confronted with a widespread incidence of marital relationships unformalized by registration existing alongside registered marriages.The 1923 Census showed that for every 10,000 inhabitants there were 7 more marriages than were registered.[28] This means that for every 100,000 inhabitants 70 marriages had been entered, but they remained unregistered though they were still considered marriages. We must note that the cases in which alimony was claimed for the upkeep of children were reviewed, i.e., the *de facto* marriages include only those in which there were children. With regard to the property, the earlier project laid down that the property of persons who in fact are in a state of marital relations even though unregistered is subject to the provision of the same articles as apply to registered marriages, and that such persons are entitled to claim maintenance and support. The present project clearly defines what is meant by registration as well as by *de facto* marital relations. The idea of registration is defined in articles 1 and 2 of this project as follows: "The registration of marriages is established with the aim of facilitating the protection of personal and property rights and the interests of spouses and children. A marriage is formalized by registration at a public Registrar's Office as laid down in part IV of this Code". This clearly indicates the significance of registration and the advantages over non-registered marriages for property relations. The time will come when we shall equalize registered and *de facto* marriages in all respects and abolish their difference; but for the present registration always has the advantage of providing an indispensable title to all the rights arising out of marriage.

The Evening Meeting of November 15, 1926

Comrade Krassikov, a member of the Supreme Court of the U.S.S.R. delivered a speech as follows: "The new law which is submitted to the present session of the All-Russian Executive Committee for approval has nothing communist in it. The State is bound to enact laws enjoining the care of women and children. In a communist society this care is committed to society itself without imposing these responsibilities on individual members. In fact during the period of transition we are forced to follow the ways of the bourgeois societies. But our project missed the most essential aspect, that the society be informed a marriage has been concluded between two people with all the attendant consequences. Marriage should be declared to society. It is much more beneficial for a child if his mother's marriage is a registered, not a *de facto* one. We must assert that only registered marriage is marriage. Such a law is purely bourgeois: Comrade Lenin has said that we shall have to make use of bourgeois law for a long time to come. I suggest therefore that to the new Code of Laws on Marriage, Family and Guardianship an article should be added providing that only the marriage of two people who have undertaken definite duties both towards each other and towards their children and who have registered their marriage before society, shall be considered as marriage. Comrade Kutuzov declared that in view of article 4, which says that for the registration of marriage the mutual consent of the marrying parties is necessary, proof should be presented to show that neither of the parties is already married. Similarly Comrade Larkin insisted that marriage must be registered and that alimony should be exacted only from a father whose paternity can be proved by registration. Comrade Kostenko says that the villages required a law providing for registration.[29] Since we can enact only a single law, it should take care of the interests of both town and country. The project declares that a marriage is formalized by registration: Do we recognize only registered marriages? *De facto* marriages also exist. Now the problem is what we understand by *de facto* marriage.

Comrade Kiselev asserted that the question of marriage should be tackled in such a fashion that the Proletariat State would create a stable family. Since the family is the small unit of Soviet society, and therefore organized on Socialist lines, the problem of the family is not an individual one. Thus the state must play its part in the process of the family being formed. As to the question of alimony in the towns and the villages, Comrade Kursky suggested that alimony suits occur more frequently in the towns than in the country. The partly landed character of rural economy constitutes the main obstacle to any solution of the alimony problem in the villages. For instance, a Kulak registers his marriage with a farm-hand girl and divorces her in the autumn. Hence the power of the law must be exercised for protection of the so-called 'wife for a season.'

Closing Speech given by Comrade Kursky

We understand that Comrades from the villages propose compulsory registration. But we must bear in mind that at the village meeting 40 per cent opposed compulsory registration. They were led by the new school of thought. Comrade Krassikov's speech was inconsistent, in that he first stressed the fact that registration is an act sanctioned by the State, and then raised the need of an article in the law defending the rights of a *de facto* wife. The consistent argument would run as follows: only registered marriages are valid, and no other relations are to be regarded as marriages or taken into legal consideration. When the project is examined in the Commission we shall not only succeed in making our Code conform to those conditions that will exist in the Communist society, but also take fully into account the peripheral phenomena which demand the protection of the law.

The Constitution of 1936

The Revolution of 1917 removed all the laws that had placed women in an inferior position and put them on an equal footing with men. These changes are made in article 122 of the Constitution of 1936:

Women in the USSR are accorded all equal rights on an equal footing with men in all spheres of economic, government, political and other social and cultural activity.

The possibility of exercising these rights is ensured by women being accorded the same rights with men to work, payment for work, rest and leisure, social insurance and education, and also by state protection of the interests of mother and child, state aid to mothers of large families and to unmarried mothers, maternity leave with full pay, and the provision of a wide network of maternity homes, nurseries, and kindergartens.[30]

The equality granted to women under Article 122 amounts to equality of rights and obligations; yet under present conditions inequality remains, since women must carry on their domestic duties together with their participation in work outside the home.

From 1936 onwards, apprehension of war grew and the attention of the state, which had hitherto been concentrated on women in professional employment, was turned to the mother and housewife. This tendency towards strengthening the socialist family acted against the matrimonial legislation of the first period as regards the emancipation of women. It was this point of view that made the decree of June 27, 1936 a turning-point in the Soviet attitude towards the family and woman's status.

On May 26, 1936, the draft of a law amending some important aspects of matrimonial law was published. While the prohibition of abortion was the central issue, the measures to discourage a reckless approach to marriage and divorce and to increase the prestige of mothers of many children were expressed in public utterances. The prohibition of abortion entailed the provision of large investments for the care of mothers and child as well as the improvement of the existing procedure for collecting alimony. The legislative establishment of minimum sums which the father of a child must pay for its upkeep when husband and wife live apart, on the one hand, and prohibition of abortion on the other, was coupled with an increase in the penalty for failure to pay maintenance of the children awarded by a court; there was also the introduction of certain changes in the legislation on divorce combatting a light-minded attitude towards the family and family obligations. To increase the fees for registration of divorce 50 roubles are required for the first divorce, 150 roubles for the second, and 300 roubles for each of the third and subsequent divorce. (Document No. 13)

With regard to alimony one fourth of the wages of the defendant is allotted for the maintenance of two children; and 50 per cent of the wages of the defendant for the maintenance of three or more children. (Document No. 13).[31]

The Family Law of July 8, 1944

The legislation of 1944 (Document No. 17 a) deprived *de facto* marriage of its legal recognition and put considerable obstacles in the way of divorce. The same legislation took also into account huge losses of adult male population as the aftermath of WWII.

A Decree of the Presidium of the USSR Supreme Soviet enacted an increase of state aid to pregnant women, mothers with many children and unmarried mothers; strengthened measures for the protection of motherhood and childhood; established the title 'Heroine Mother'; the Order 'Motherhood Glory', and the 'Motherhood Medal'.

1. On the increase of state aid to mothers with many children and unmarried mothers it was decreed that in place of the existing regulation which gives state aid to six children at the birth of the seventh and of each subsequent child, state assistance was given to mothers who had two children, on the birth of the third and of each subsequent child. (Article 1).

2. The following amounts were decreed for state assistance to unmarried mothers for support and upbringing of children born after the publication of said Decree.
100 roubles monthly for 1 child
150 roubles monthly for 2 children
200 roubles monthly for 3 or more children. (Article 3)

3. On the institution of 'Motherhood Medal', Article 12 decrees 1st and 2nd class of 'Motherhood Medal', an award to mothers who have given birth to and brought up:
5 children ..... 2nd class medal
6 children ..... 1st class medal

Article 3 decrees the Order 'Motherhood Glory' 1st, 2nd and 3rd class
—for award to mothers who have given birth to and brought up:

7 children ..... 3rd class
8 children ..... 2nd class
9 children ..... 1st class.

Article 19 stipulated that only registered marriage produces the rights and obligations of husband and wife. On Marriage Family and Guardianship of the Union Republics persons having *de facto* matrimonial relations before the publication of the present Decree might officially establish their relationship by registering their marriage.

As for the dissolution of a marriage Article 24 laid down the following compulsory conditions:

(a) Presentation to the People's Court of a notice of the desire to dissolve the marriage, indicating the motives for the dissolution, and also the surname, name, patronymic, year of birth, and place of residence of the husband and wife . . .

(b) The husband or wife to be summoned into court to become acquainted with the divorce statement of the spouse, and to hear evidence of the grounds for dissolution, and also for the identification of witnesses to be summoned to court for examination.

(c) Publication in the local newspaper of the notice of a court action for dissolution of marriage, the cost of publishing such notice to be borne by the husband or wife as plaintiff.

In accordance with Article 33 of the Code on Marriage and the Family, a court might grant a suit a dissolution of marriage only in cases which prove that further co-habitation of the spouses and preservation of the family are impossible.

In February 1972, the Presidium of the RSFSR Supreme Court discussed the question of practices in enforcing of the legislation on marriage and the family in the Russian Federation. It was noted that the new legislation on marriage and the family strengthens the Soviet family and socialist legality in the sphere of marital relationships.

Summary

The consequences of early Soviet matrimonial legislation and of the predominant public opinion both in towns and villages can be learned from studying the discussion of the new family code by the Soviet Parliament. During the New Economic Policy (N.E.P.) in 1925, revolutionary power was still of recent date. In the village the 'kulak' was firmly entrenched, and took whatever profit he could from the dissolution or separation from the traditional household. The reported discussion initiated from rural conditions focused on the fear lest mistakes in progressive family legislation should have put young women at the mercy of exploiters. In the discussion there were some learned arguments on the basic attitude of Marxism towards the family in the period of transition. But one is not told that the impact of matrimonial legislation on the peasant 'Dvor' would become a second-rate issue once agriculture had become collectivized. In brief, after the 1918 Family Code had been approved, juridical issues were brought before the session of the All-Union Central Executive Committee -issues of the Family, Marriage and Guardianship. Certain amendments were adopted. For example, there was the change in the function and importance of the fact of registration. The previous Code was enacted when Church marriage was still prevalent, and there was no other way of formalizing marriages. The new Code in 1925 provided for the setting up of the Registrar's Office and granted the protection of the law only to those marriages which had been registered under the order of the new Code.

1) Soviet Russia introduced a new Matrimonial Code based on complete equality of rights between husband and wife, and between legitimate and illegitimate children.[32]

2) Divorce was still decided by Courts. However, neither partner obtained, until 1926, an unrestricted right to divorce, which was shifted from the courts to the Registrar's Office. The Registrar's Office made an entry of the divorce and at the request of the married parties delivered to them a certificate of divorce.

3) The Family Code of 1926, while restricting the divorced spouse's right of support to one year, granted to the housewife the right to remuneration for her work during the marriage and provided that all property acquired during the marriage was to be regarded as jointly held.

4) Designed to be a support for the wife's right to divorce the 'jointly held' property rule of the 1926 Code provoked protests from the peasants fearing the dispersal of their property; the more so because the Code made provision against the circumvention of the rules by granting to women living in *de facto* marriage the same rights as to 'registered' wives. What was required to be safeguarded by the new obstacles in the case of divorce was not so much the personal interests of either partner as those of the community, particularly those of minor children.[33]

5) In 1926 the great majority, at least in rural areas, were opposed to *de facto* marriage and admitted facilities for divorce only if it was petitioned by both parties. By rejection not only of the legal recognition of *de facto* marriage, but also of the legal procedure for the determination of paternity, the elements of Soviet Matrimonial Law have been changed.

6) In 1936 the village had been collectivized and the stabilization of family relations simply represented stabilizing the new society. The legislation of 1936, while retaining divorce as an institution accessible to

anyone who demands it, expresses such disapproval even in relation to the ordinary citizen, let alone a member of the Party.

The law of 1944 (Article 23 ff) renders divorce difficult and empowers the courts to refuse divorce even after all attempts at reconciliation have failed. Legal family relationships exist only on the basis of a registered marriage. Moreover, fatherhood outside wedlock constitutes no rights or obligations either for the father himself or for his children.

From the materials collected and Code of laws on the family we have been able to answer the questions: what are the functions of the family in a socialist society and how has the Soviet Union challenged Marxist theory on the family? We should bear in mind that we are concerned with the application of Marxist theory in a country where the tasks of emancipation had still to be carried on, a country confronted with losing fifteen millions of its young generation in WW II. Shortage of labour was considered to be a favourable condition for the realization of actual equality of the sexes and the emancipation of women. Nevertheless, it is difficult to promote actual equality for women in employment once motherhood is demanded and the encouragement of large families of ten or more children. In view of the family system in Russia it is unlikely that Marxist theories can be held true.

4. MARXIST DOCTRINE ON WOMAN AND FAMILY IN RUSSIA

In this section we shall examine the basic propositions of the Marxist doctrine on family in the light of past and present social phenomena, in Soviet Russia. Attempts will be made to determine the validity and limitations of the doctrine, and to compare it with the actual conditions of Soviet family life. Inasmuch as the characteristics of Marxist doctrine are hypothetical, it must be possible to test their consistency by this means.

THE FAMILY INSTITUTION

The first question to be considered relates to the nature of the family in Soviet Socialist society. In *The Communist Manifesto* Marx and Engels said: 'The bourgeois family will vanish as a matter of course when its complement—private property—vanishes, and both will vanish with vanishing of capital'.[34] In the *Origin of the Family, Private Property and the State* Engels held that with the transfer of the means of production into common ownership, the single family ceases to be an economic unit of society. Elsewhere he wrote that 'the first condition for the liberation of the wife is to bring the whole female sex back into public industry, and this in fact demands the abolition of the monogamous family as the economic unit of society.'[35]

Two leading Marxist adherents in Soviet Russia, Kollontai and Wolffson have offered lengthy interpretations of the Marxist theory. Kollontai
contended that once the family ceases to be the economic unit, the working state of the comrades will conquer the family.[36] It means that the
family under socialism becomes extinct and care of the children will pass
completely into the hands of the State. Wolffson wrote on page 450 of
his book *Sociology of Marriage and the Family:*
> In a socialist society this natural category, i.e., the family will meet with
> the same end that Engels predicted for the State: it will be sent to the
> museum of antiquities'.[37]

Wolffson thought that during the transition period the withering away of
the family begins already with the introduction of communal education
of the children, the participation of communal education, the organization of communal living and feeding. Since the State is for time being
unable to take upon itself these family functions, it is forced to postpone
this disintegration of the family, to keep this institution in existence for
a time. The flaw of the Marxist theory is that it has not specified whether
the family ceases to be an institution or its functions have undergone
considerable modifications in a socialist society.[38]

Engels' theory of the 'withering away of the family' was generally
accepted in the first decade of the Russian Revolution, but abandoned
when the State was in great need of stabilization and integration. In other
words, the institution of the family and monogamous marriage which
early Marxist theorists thought of as 'opiate' and certainly destined to
wither away has been entirely reclaimed and reasserted for socialism. The
moot question in this matter is the need for registering marriage,
together with difficult procedure of divorce and the abolition of legal
recognition of *de facto* marriages. All this leads, ideologies apart, to a nice,
stable modern family. The Supreme Court of USSR codified their family
and marriage legislation on the methods of bourgeois law. Lenin said that
we shall still have to make use of bourgeois law for a long time to come.
To advocate compulsory registration of marriage the society must be
informed that a marriage has been contracted between two individuals
with all the consequences. It was not only the conviction of Lenin, but of
Marx, Engels, Trotsky, Bukharin, and Kollontai that bourgeois elements
of the family and monogamy could not be eliminated without disrupting
the form of the family.

The crucial difference is that there is not the slightest suggestion that
the Soviet family is ever likely to 'wither away'. On the contrary, all Soviet
statements since 1936 have emphasized the principle that a new kind of
family, the firm, stable and socialist family has appeared throughout
Soviet society.[39] In other words, there has been a restoration of the
bourgeois form of family on a new 'socialist' basis; this represents a

transitional stage. Moreover, a reversal of the Marxist hypothesis apropos of the disappearance of the family came into existence in 1936.[40] Under the new family law of May 31, 1935, the police were authorized to fine parents up to 200 roubles for any disorderly conduct or public hooliganism on the part of their children.[41] In a survey of 1000 pupils in classes 1 and 2 in Moscow, 50 per cent thought that responsibility for their misbehaviour lay with parents and teachers rather than themselves.[42] It is also interesting to note that the parental role and its responsibility are now being re-emphasized. A woman writing an article entitled *Bringing up Parents* in *Soviet Weekly* in 1962 said that parents must be exemplary:

> Every parent really needs to be something of a teacher, but some feel that if they feed and clothe a child, prevent it from becoming ill and punish it for every bit of mischief, they are doing their duty.[43]

Thus it may be said that parental responsibility in shaping the personality of children represents a deviation from the Marxist hypothesis of the ultimate disappearance of the family. On the other hand, there is patent evidence that the family is now regarded as the basic unit of society; that a strong family system brings about a strong society. The State regards the family as the actual foundation upon which it can be built, though its functions have been markedly taken away by the State. During the years of the Eighth Five-Year Plan between 1966-1967, the number of children reared in day nursery-kindergartens and kindergartens increased from 7.7 million, that is, approximately 32 per cent of youngsters in the pre-school age groups were accommodated by children's institutions.

Further, the determined effort which has been made to solve housing problems reflects the aim of the Communist Party and of present Soviet policy. This is illustrated by the following statements of Lenin and Khrushchev.[44]

Lenin	*Khrushchev*
The aim of the Communist Party is to exert its greatest effort for the improvement of the housing conditions of the toiling masses without infringing on the interests of non-capitalist house ownership.	The Communist Party of the Soviet Union undertakes the task of solving the most acute problem in the improvement of the well-being of the Soviet people —the housing problem. At the end of the second decade, every family, including newlyweds will have a comfortable flat conforming to the requirements of hygiene and cultural living. In the course of the second decade, housing will be gradually provided for all citizens rent free.

Housing laws encourage the private construction of single family dwellings; local government encouraged the idea of building one's own house. Building loans were allotted for a minimum of 10,000 roubles and seven year amortization; the interest was as low as two per cent. Loans totalled 7,000,000 roubles in 1942, 35,000,000 in 1943; 260,000,000 in 1944; 325,000,000 in 1945.[45] There is no doubt that encouragement to build permanent houses was a significant trend in shifting from the big apartment buildings. One or two-storey flats, with two or four apartments on each floor, appeared as a common type.[46] Nevertheless, *Tass* reported that it would take six or seven years before every Soviet family would have its own apartment. The official press agency said that 7,700 apartments were being completed daily.[47] At the same time, a Communist Party and Government decree calls for a halt to grants of land, and credit for private building in fifteen Republics. This decree indicates the gradual transition from the construction of one-family homes to the construction of modern co-operative houses.[48] Because of various abuses of the right to private house ownership, such as bribery, the decree has been put into effect. However, in spite of Marxist overtures, the new decree does not adversely affect the ownership of houses already built, many of which are summer houses used by city residents for week-end holidays. After the adoption of the Basic Principles of Civil Law in the USSR in 1961, the 'dwelling house' has replaced all other legal definitions of housing space; some republics have statistically fixed the maximum and minimum living space in such houses (RSFSR: 65m^2 and 25m^2). In Lithuania the space of the outhouses is stipulated at 40m^2. Many people own a 'dacha' in addition to the one dwelling house to which they are legally entitled. The present law regulating personal ownership of house seems inequitable; the same living space is allowed for a single person as for a family, and no account is taken of the possibility that the family may grow after a house has been acquired.[49] Nevertheless the co-operative houses are dictated too as they foster a communal spirit, because Soviet socialists contend that a separate, isolated apartment encourages an individualistic, bourgeois attitude in families.[50]

In 1962 and 1963, housing construction in town and country was proceeding on an unprecedented scale: 8.8 million new flats have been built in the past four years in towns and workers' communities, and 2.4 million homes in the countryside. In these years practically one out of every four people in the Soviet Union has been given better housing conditions.[51] Most of the construction is of large-scale apartment buildings, owned by the state or state-owned factories. Rents usually average from 2 to 5 per cent of income, depending on the size of the family and the floor area. For example, an apartment for four people providing kitchen, bedrooms, sitting room, bathrooms, lavatory and hall would cost approximately £3 to £4 ($8.4 to $11.2) a month, including heat and

water. Non-official citizens, however, admit that the rooms are small.[52]
The United Nations Economic Commission for Europe reports that the U.S.S.R. showed the highest rate of housing construction with 11.7 dwellings per 1,000 inhabitants. Switzerland occupied second place (10.-5), West Germany the third (10.1), Belgium (4.9), Poland (4.6) Portugal (4.3). The lowest rate was in Ireland (2.4).[53] In May 1964 the Soviet government poured more and more building materials and labour into co-operative projects and the number of apartments to be constructed about 20,000 a tenfold increase on the previous year.[54] In the last ten years the Soviet people have provided about 100 million people with new or better flats.[55] The State has envisaged 580,000,000 square meters of new living accommodation in the course of the 9th Five-Year Plan (1971-75). About 23,000,000 people have already lived in their renovated housing; so far 215,000 square meters of housing has been built. Another 117,600,000 square meters have been put up in the third year of the Five-Year Plan. Working people who are allotted a flat make no down-payments, but they pay only a nominal amount for its maintenance. The rent they pay for their flats is 13.2 kopeks per square meter, and it has not changed since 1928. A family rent for its flat does not exceed 4-5 per cent of its total budget, and this includes heating, electricity, gas and water.[56] What is more, since the Soviet Economic Reform which has entered its ninth year, the country has built between 2.2 and 2.4 million apartment units annually. In 1976, 2,000,000 flats and individual homes were built with a total living space of 108.5 million square metres, providing better living conditions for about 11 million people.[57]

Under the new provisions, pensioners employed in mines, or in agriculture will be entitled to keep their full pensions, in addition to their regular wages. In other categories, unskilled workers, postmen, restaurant employees, teachers and physicians, pensioners will be paid from 50 per cent of their regular pension to 75 per cent in harder living areas in Siberia, in addition to wages. Again the government grants benefits for disablement, loss of a breadwinner, and other social insurance cases. In 1963 a total of 25 million persons were provided with pensions.[58] This is reaffirmed in the Constitution of the USSR 'Citizens of the USSR have the right to maintenance in old age and also in case of sickness and disability. Nowadays pensionable age in the Soviet Union is 55 years for women and 60 for men. A woman may retire at 50 if she has given birth to five or more children and brought them up to the age of eight. If one of the five is an adopted child, the normal retirement age of 55 will apply. There is a discrepancy between this stipulation and that of the family code which specifically defined adoption as a strictly confidential matter, and the adopting parent need divulge it to no one.[59] Further old-age pensions for industrial and office workers amount to 50-100 per cent of their wages. It was the 9th Five-Year Plan that had completed, in its 1971-1972 programme, an increase in minimum old-age pensions for all industrial and office workes and collective farmers, and Soviet legislation grants increasing privileges to the working pensioner. Since January 1970 the law has been that all factory workers, foremen, junior service personnel, and some other workers in the services, industry, public education, and health services are entitled to their old-age pension in full, along with their wages. Engineers and technicians and some other fields are entitled to 50 per cent of their pension as well as their wages. A working pensioner has a right to sick benefits of up to 100 per cent of his wages.[60] Again maternity grants have been paid for all women equal to their full wage; an expectant mother as long as she nurses her baby is assigned easier work but at no cut in her pay. She gets 56 full pay days off before birth and 56 more after birth. As a result of all these benefits the state's spending on social insurance has risen considerably and amounted to 21,400 million roubles in 1973.[61]

To summarize, one may say that the current trend may serve as a general index of the present Soviet attitude towards the family. It is worth noting that the drastic shift of Soviet policy since 1936 indicated a reaffirmation of the importance of the family institution as a basic functioning unit in the social system at large, and invalidated the Marxist prophecy of the disappearance of the family.[62] Indeed, the revival of the family institution shows a rapprochement with the Western conception of the family. This proves true despite a noticeable transfer of major traditional family functions, educational and political, for example, to other social institutions. Obviously, in response to expanding industrialization[63] an appropriation of family functions by other institutions should be expected. The same phenomenon appears in the United States, though the early care and upbringing of the child still take place within the family.

The drastic reversal of the initial policy[64] towards the family leads one to believe that the Marxist vision of the disappearance of the family has not been empirically proved. The U.S.S.R. Supreme Soviet adopted the Fundamental Law on marriage and the family in the summer of 1968. The present marriage and family code defends with more rigour the rights of women, mothers, children, old people and disabled wives and husbands. It also improves the status of the single mother and her child. In the past, the place for filling the father's name was left blank on the birth certificate of a child born out of wedlock; now the document can legally include the name of a man given by the mother. Again if the father and mother of a small child are not legally married but have been living together for several months, the child has a right to claim support. Moreover the new code forbids managers to insist that women and young workers work overtime, night shifts or days off. Women with children under eight are under no obligation to go on business trips unless they choose to do so.[65]

It may be argued that there is an inevitable conflict between the family and the State; conflict between the requirements of the Party and the expectations of the family. In training children to be loyal to the Party at all times,[66] there seems to be an undermining of family loyalties, and a conflict between attachment to the family and to the Party.[67] In addition, since the new family policy is rationalized in Bolshevik ideology as the cultural-educational implement of the socialist state, family functions tend to weaken. The Twenty-third Congress of the CPSU (Communist Party Soviet Union) enacts the following basic tasks of the school: improving the quality of upbringing and education so that young people will leave school as highly educated young people and ardent champions of Communism transmitting Communist ideas and lofty culture, and bring about true and young builders of Communism.[68] On the other hand, because of the tendency of the Party to interfere in family affairs, the family members are compelled to withdraw into themselves in order to keep outside contacts to a safe minimum. But despite the reduction of the functions of the family, it continues to exist.

The current Soviet policy tends to emphasize family functions. In controlling juvenile delinquency, for example, the family is allotted an important part to play, and parents are ordered to exert continuous influence on their children and to control many aspects of their lives. Since a child spends most of his life in the family circle, as Soviets admit, he derives most of his opinions and moral attitudes from his parents. Every parent really needs to be something of a teacher.

Marriage and Divorce

(1) Marriage.

In the book the *Origin of the Family, Private Property, and the State* Engels wrote: 'Full freedom of marriage can only be established in the absence of all the economic considerations which exert a powerful influence on the choice of a marriage partner'. With class barriers eradicated in the Soviet Union, a free choice of a marriage partner has been significantly practised, though young people seem to prefer their intellectual equals. A girl, for instance, marries a journalist after finishing a 10-year school; her girl friend from a specialized secondary school marries a scientist; a student contracts marriage with a girl who is a home painter; a bus driver enters into marriage with a translator; a violinist's wife is a hairdresser. These marriages between people of widely different occupational categories have been rather common as a result of class barriers being loosened.[69] Again in contrast to the concept of marriage advocated by Marx and Engels, new principles altering earlier legislation were published in the Soviet press. *Pravada* wrote in 1936:

So-called free love and loose sexual life are altogether bourgeois and have nothing in common either with socialist principles and ethics or with the rules of behavior of a Soviet citizen. Marriage is the most serious affair in life. Fatherhood and motherhood become virtues in the Soviet land.[70]

Engels also wrote:

. . . That will be settled after a new generation has grown up; a generation of men who never in all their lives have had occasion to purchase a woman's surrender whether with money or with any other means of social power, and of women who have never been obliged to surrender to any men out of any consideration other than that of real love, or to refrain from giving themselves to their beloved for fear of the economic consequences.[71]

Lenin expressed himself in the same spirit and said that the forms of marriage and sexual relations in the bourgeois sense no longer give satisfaction. In the realm of marriage and sexual relations a revolution is approaching that will be consonant with the proletarian revolution. Again Engels commented that because the care and upbringing of children becomes a public matter, the worry about consequences which prevents a girl from giving herself to the man she loves without apprehension and fear will disappear. Engels noted the extinction of the double standard that men may have premarital and extramarital sexual relations, but that women must be chaste before marriage and faithful after it. In socialism the normative morality implies that the sexual relations of men and women will be evaluated not from the standpoint of the institution of marriage, but from that of integrated and harmoniously developed personality and its spiritual and emotional needs. Increasingly cultivated emotions directly influence the spiritual enrichment of personality and develop its needs; and it must be noted that individual freedom in sexual life by no means abolishes social control of man's sexual behavior, but makes it more effective. This control is based on internal conviction, on social and moral values such as conscience, duty and dignity in association with social progress in general and with the building of a socialist society in particular. In love, by contrast with alienated sexual relationships, the man and woman act not merely as sex partners, but above all as personalities.[72]

In interpreting these statements, Boshko, a Soviet professor of law asserted in the official periodical of the *Attorney General:*

Marriage, basically and in the spirit of Soviet law, is in principle essentially a lifelong union. . . . . However, marriage achieves its full life-blood and value for the Soviet State only if there is birth of children, proper upbringing, and if the spouses experience the highest happiness of motherhood and fatherhood.[73]

A question may be readily raised: do Russian women know about the 'intimate' sexual side of marriage? Most of them are unaware what sex pleasure is, and do not think it is a part of family life. Many women say sex does not give them anything but at least they know that their husbands love them. Recently the magazine *Health* has brought, in a diffuse way, the need of subtlety in a man's behaviour to his wife's psychology, her moods and her need for patience. If a woman is bold enough to complain to her doctor of frigidity, he will diagnose fibroids or some other physical source of her malaise. A few people avowed that more often discussion in this matter should be broached, but the populace of extreme puritanism is not in an enthusiastic vein.

Regardless of whether her sex life is satisfactory or not, a wife has not much worry about her straying husband. If the husband is giddy, all his wife has to do is to report him to the Party Committee. An erring husband, be he adulterous, alcoholic or a wife-beater, will be hauled into his trade union to explain himself and to be duly reprimanded. Can cuckolds do the same? They do not, though they can, because they are too proud of their virility.[74]

Again the idea of the family within the Soviet Union is formulated in the article 'Familienrecht' in the Encyclopedia of the U.S.S.R. as follows:

The law relating to the family regulates marriage, the legal position of the family and of guardians. . . . Soviet family law is based upon the principle of the equality of men and women before the law, which is firmly fixed in the constitution of the U.S.S.R. and in the constitution of the Republics of the Union. . . . Among the sources of the family code the most important is the decree of the presidium of the Supreme Soviet and the U.S.S.R. of the 8th July, 1944, relative to the increase in the state allowance for pregnant women, for mothers with many children and mothers without husbands, and dealing with the conferring of the honourable title 'Mother-heroine' and the creation of the Order 'Mother-Glory' and the 'Motherhood Medal'. . . . This distinction has made considerable changes in the previous legislation of relating to marriage and the family; henceforth registered marriage alone will ensure the rights and obligations of a married woman.[75]

Thus Soviet women have been awarded 1.5 million government Orders and medals. The honorary title 'Mother Heroine' has been conferred to 138,000 women who have brought up 10 children. The Order of Motherhood Glory has been offered to approximately three million mothers who have raised seven, eight or nine children, whereas the

Motherhood Medal has been awarded to nine million mothers raising five or six children.[76]

This declaration sounds like the inauguration of a programme to strengthen traditional family ties. In fact, current Soviet legislation on marriage and divorce is the implementation of such a programme. Moreover, not only has recent Soviet policy restored the family, but it has also obstructed common-law marriage and illegitimate proceedings, and relieved the father of the duty of supporting an illegitimate child. Further, upon the re-affirmation of the importance of the family in 1935 and 1936 the courts and the legislators became more emphatic in their disapproval of bigamy. The registration of the second marriage was in fact made illegal and subject to annulment. It was only the registered marriage that could legitimately constitute the rights and duties of spouses prescribed in the present code.[77] Similar provisions were enacted in relation to alimony and the rights of inheritance. For a child born prior to July 8, 1944 outside a registered marriage, his mother was in a legal position to claim alimony from the natural father provided that the latter had been recorded as such at the Civil Registry Office. Such children had rights of succession to the property of the person so entered. If born after July 8, 1944, children had no such succession rights, nor was such a father liable for maintenance and support of these children. Whether or not children are socially stigmatized for their illegitimacy is a matter of law.[78]

According to current Soviet legislation and policy, children are first placed in nurseries, kindergartens and boarding schools, and are entirely supported by the State. Some unmarried mothers can lodge a valid claim of paternity and child maintenance provided that the following conditions can be proven, such as cohabitation with alleged father, participation of both parents in the child's upbringing, actual maintenance or support by the alleged father, and acknowledgement of paternity by the alleged father. But the mere fact of sexual intercourse does not constitute grounds for a paternity suit.[79] This suggests that the state acknowledges the status of illegimate children.[80] However, the fact that children born out of wedlock have no claim on their fathers, creates material and moral disadvantages.[81]

The actual situation of 'fatherless' children has been described by Nikolin who wrote:

> . . . There are cases of babies born out of wedlock, and in those cases the State and our society as a whole try to give the unmarried mother and her child every help, material as well as moral. The rights of mother and child are protected by Soviet law. Special homes have been established for unmarried expectant mothers, where they are under good medical observation and are taught how to take care of their infants.[82]

The programme adopted by the 22nd Party Congress emphasizes that a happy childhood is one of the noblest and most important aspects of the building of Communism. In this connection, a lawyer has recently stressed in the magazine *Soviet Justice* that this task cannot be fulfilled until children born out of wedlock receive absolutely equal rights with children born in wedlock. Again, a lawyer wrote in *Izvestia:*

> We are not advocates of extramarital relations, but one cannot close one's eyes to the fact that such relations do exist. . . . And the children should not suffer because their parents could not, or did not want to, register their marriage.[83]

(2) Divorce.

The change of divorce legislation was no less radical. Under the law of June 27, 1936, three major alterations were introduced in the regulations governing such separations. First, divorce had to be referred to the courts, and an inquiry into the motives of parties involved had to be made. The petition had to be accompanied by witnesses and other evidence presented.

To avoid divorce, Peoples' courts attempted reconciliation first, although they were authorized to grant separations or to hand the case to the next highest court. This court tended to take a liberal view of grounds for divorce, and, having conducted a complete hearing, could use its discretion without regard to existing law. Fees for a registered divorce increased. The cost of a first divorce was 50 roubles, of a second 150, and of a third and subsequent divorces 300 roubles.[84] Still higher amounts ranging from 500 to 2,000 roubles[85] were to be paid for a certificate of divorce. The results of these anti-divorce measures are illustrated by the fact that during the second half of 1936 the number of divorces in the Ukraine was 10,992, while in the same period of the preceding years the number had been 35,458.[86]

The unlimited discretion of Soviet courts to grant or refuse divorce represents a modification of the Marxian theory of the family,[87] and a sharp departure from original Soviet ideology. The extent of the deviation appears striking when one compares the statements of Lenin:

> Reactionaries are against the freedom of divorce. . . . The reactionaries are in fact defending the omnipotence of the police and the bureaucracy, the privilege of the one sex. . . . The recognition of freedom of divorce to leave one's husband is not an invitation for all wives to leave their husbands.[88]

This policy on divorce was also reflected in the two divergent declarations of 1938 and 1945. In 1938 the Soviet jurists insisted that the Soviets do not have what the capitalist countries understand as divorce proceedings. But the Soviets were compelled, after 1945, to adhere to their own di-

vorce proceedings, which were far stricter and provided less privacy and
~~certainty of the final outcome than those in many capitalist countries.~~

It is significant that divorces are less common in the Soviet Union than
in capitalist countries.[89] S. Strumilin said in 1960:

As many as 12.5 marriages were registered for every 1,000 of the
population in the USSR in 1958 as compared with 8.3 in the United
States, 7.6 in Great Britain, and 7 in France. The number of divorces
in the USSR has never exceeded 8.5 for every 100 marriages, while in
the United States it has reached 26.3, i.e., more than three times the
number in the USSR.[90]

According to a recent report, divorce still remains a problem even though
it is discouraged by the Soviet government. This is based on the people's
dissatisfaction with divorce procedure. When reconciliation seems impossible, the couple must pay about £15 to publish a newspaper announcement. This being done, they return to court for the divorce
petition. The procedure takes about six months, whereas formerly the
cost was only about £1 for the announcement, and there was no delay.[91] These two requirements theoretically tend to prevent frivolous
marriages and, accordingly, reinforce family stability.[92] Nevertheless
there is a widespread demand for simpler procedure and for a reduction
of the functions of the civil registry authorities (ZAGS). Professor Sverdlov, however, believes that divorce should be granted only by the courts;
otherwise, the State would act merely as an impassive registrar of the
break-up of a family. Others propose, as a compromise, that the courts
should handle only those divorce cases in which husband and wife are in
disagreement about the future of their children. There are in fact no
grounds for divorce in Soviet law; the only 'ground' is the fact that the
family has been disrupted and that normal matrimonial relations cannot
be restored. Only after careful investigation of all the circumstances and
of the relations between the parties will the court be in a position to
decide whether the family can be preserved or a divorce granted.[93]

In the Soviet Union today a marriage is dissolved by the court; if the
court of law after a thorough investigation of all facts decides that the
further joint life of the partners has become impossible, it will dissolve
the marriage. For the fundamentals of legislation of the USSR and the
Union Republics on Marriage and Family do not lay down formal reasons
for the dissolution of a marriage. Documents certifying to the dissolution
of the marriage are issued to the husband and wife three months after
they apply for a divorce.[94] No doubt, it is the children who suffer from
divorce. Many Soviet social scientists feel that a divorced father should
visit regularly his child even though the child becomes part of a new
family group.

As for children, when one parent has custody of the child or children, the other must pay as an alimony a quarter of his income to provide for one child; a third, if they have two children; half of his income for three or more children; with rare exceptions, the courts give custody of children to their mother.[95] Soviet law does not require alimony payments to an able-bodied wife who has no children. Difficulties in tracing alimony may arise in a case when a man opts for his wife's surname after their marriage ends. Eventually they are always brought to justice, but considerable delay may occur.[96] For persistent non-payment of alimony the Turkmen Criminal Code decrees prison for up to two years, banishment for up to three years, or corrective labour for up to one year. Unfortunately, the tracking down of these miscreants is often delayed which causes their families material privation.[97]

(3) *The Rate of divorce.*

A handbook issued by the Central Statistical Bureau records that divorces numbered 0.4 per 1,000 population in 1950, 1.3 in 1960, and 2.6 in 1969. In 1967, the number of persons marrying a second time was somewhat larger than half the number of those divorced. Those who were remarried numbered 17% of men and 15% of women. An increased number of divorces also partly multiplies marriages. Hence while for the country as a whole there were 2.7 divorces and 9.0 marriages per 1,000 in 1967, in urban areas the figures were 4.2 and 10.3 respectively.

| Group | Per thousand persons | | Divorces per |
	Divorces	Marriages	hundred marriages
I	3.4	10.0	34
II	4.7	11.8	40
III	5.8	12.3	47

In this table we examine marriages and divorces in terms of a group of the country's 33 largest cities, those with more than half a million each in 1967. Now we divide them into three equal groups in order of raising number of divorces.[98] Here again in 1967 one new marriage was concluded after 10 divorces. Seventy per cent of the women who divorced remained single, and 30 per cent who remarried had no children. According to a Soviet Handbook, the ratio of divorces had risen to a permissible 27% by 1973 as compared with 24% in Britain and 40% in the United States.[99]

The Soviet government favours as a matter of course a stable family with women at home bringing up the children to the age of seven and taking charge of the household; yet broken families have not been averted. Although the divorce rate is growing fast, it is still difficult to conclude why it is so. It seems that the main reasons are: (a) inadequate help for women who work both at home and outside; (b) marriage at an early age; (c) the growing desire for independence of the individuals; (d) lack of knowledge regarding sex and married life; (f) a weakening of moral principles; (g) insufficient scientific knowledge about a family.[100]

(4) *Inheritance.*

Engels wrote:

By transforming by far the greater portions, at any rate, of permanent heritable wealth—the means of production—into social property, the coming social revolution will reduce to a minimum all this anxiety about bequeathing and inheriting.[101]

Similarly, one of the leading ideas of the *Communist Manifesto* is the abolition of the inheritance of property, which has become the foundation of the socialist programme. With this programme in mind, the first Soviet decree concerning inheritance proclaimed on April 27, 1918 bore the title 'Testable and Intestate succession are abolished'. It must be pointed out that despite a complete elimination of private enterprise and of all the basic instruments of production under the First Five-Year Plan (1929-33) the inheritance of property was legalized in the Constitution, and succession rights were extended. Greater freedom in bequeathing individual property was officially acknowledged.

With the advent of the New Economic Policy in 1922, production of property rights and inheritance was recognized, and, though with some limitations, inheritance was introduced by the Soviet Civil Code, which came into effect on January 1, 1923 (Section 416). In limiting inheritance, the Civil Code first set a fixed amount of 10,000 roubles as the maximum legal net value of an estate (Section 416); it also restricted the kin to whom the estate might descend by interstate succession or by will (Section 418). If the net value of an estate exceeds 10,000 gold roubles, it now becomes the property of the state. A similar restriction was applied to certain insurance premiums in accordance with the amendment of June 1, 1925 (Section 375 of the Civil Code). However, the limitation on the size of estates gave rise to practical difficulties. There is no doubt that the limitation discouraged to some extent the entry of material and resources into the country.

Another limitation on inheritance under the Civil Code takes the form of restrictions on succession rights. Until March 15, 1945, persons who could inherit were: direct descendants, children, grandchildren and great-grandchildren, the surviving spouse, and disabled and destitute relatives or strangers who were dependents of the deceased for at least one year before his death.[102] The limitations on succession were gradually eliminated by Soviet legislation. First, in 1930 and 1935 some specific types of property were made legally inheritable; later in 1945, the number of eligible heirs was changed. In 1930 the category of specific types of property inheritance included insurance premiums, government loans, stocks and bonds, and, in 1935, other deposits besides money with government banks. As a result of the removal of inheritance restrictions, there is sound reason to believe that certain groups, such as the ruling élite, the superior intelligentsia, the highly skilled workers, and some kolkhoz members, found it possible and profitable to accumulate large sums of money.[103] The accumulation of money presumably has the effect of reinforcing the stratification system.[104] As a result, large income differentiations may be protected during the lifetime of the earners, and families are provided with the means of maintaining their socio-economic position for protracted periods after the death of the head of the household.[105] The Constitution of USSR declares the right of citizens to own, as their personal property, income and savings from work; and to own a dwelling-house, a supplementary farm, household articles, articles for personal use and convenience; there is also the right of citizens to inherit personal property.[106]

This analysis shows that current Soviet laws of inheritance contradict the Marxist doctrine of abolishing private property and inheritance. According to Mitchel Wilson's report of his tour of the Soviet Union, private property has not been abolished as Marxist doctrine predicted. He said that the people he met were either very well-to-do or rich. It is not professional political people who receive the highest incomes, but those in the arts and sciences. According to his account, many aristocrats and wealthy members of the middle class may have come back; they and their children have reappeared now that their background is no longer a disgrace to them.[107] The Soviet Constitution of 1936 officially recognized socialism as the new order in Soviet Union, but inheritance under such a system involves all the essential elements of inheritance found in a capitalist country.

It may be argued that the words 'private property' do not refer to all private ownership of productive goods. Marxists declared this ownership to be the key to both economic and political power.[108] This argument is vitiated when one considers that in Soviet Russia one may command such assets as insurance premium, government loans, stocks, bonds, money deposits, and securities. These assets are considered to be capital in any capitalist country, and are deposited either with government or private banks. Recent works[109] relegate this disappearance of such things to the remote future beyond human prediction, when, according to the expectation of Marx, the productive forces will grow, and individuals will develop their full potential and all the sources of collective wealth.[110]

At present, Soviet jurists emphasize that the transmission of property is a pertinent matter, and that succession appears to be one stimulus for the development of personal ownership, for increasing the productivity of labour, and for fortifying the socialist family. It follows that the earlier legal theorists who characterized inheritance as a capitalist institution are at present branded as 'subversive'. The contradiction between early and present policy on inheritance has been expressed by Gsovski:

Paradoxically in 1926 the removal of the limitation of inheritance was officially motivated by the intention of securing 'continued existence' of private enterprise, but in 1938 and 1944 the abolition of this very private enterprise in Soviet Russia is given as the reason for the inheritance of property as a sound institution of Soviet socialist law.[111]

Another view which helps to explain away the 'abolition of inheritance' by the decree of 1918 was expressed by the Soviet professor Serebrovski who said that 'abolition of inheritance' was not abolition but merely a transformation of it. Under the present system, Soviet jurists argue that restoration of inheritance of property could not result in the re-emergence of private enterprise and of capitalism. However, wage differentials among executive and technical personnel in various fields permit the accumulation of money and property. As an illustration, workers in medium-income brackets receive from 100 to 160 roubles monthly, while some highly skilled workers in coal mines and steel mills are said to receive up to 400 roubles a month.

At its 24th congress the Central Committee of the Communist Party of Soviet Union, with the participation of the All-Union Central Council of Trade Union decided the sequence and schedule of the 1971 5 year plan.

(a) In accordance with this programme the minimum wage is to be raised to 70 roubles in 1971 (p. 190)

(b) As from July 1, 1971, it is envisaged to raise the minimum pension for collective farmer and fix pensions that apply to workers and office employees. (p.191)

(c) As from September 1, 1972 it is planned to raise the salaries of school teachers and doctors simultaneously throughout the country by an average of about 20 per cent.

(d) The pension of servicemen's families who have lost their breadwinner will also be increased. (p.191)

(e) The average monthly cash wage of workers and office employees is to rise by 20-22 per cent in the five years, and collective farmer's remuneration for working in the commonly-owned sector is to go up by 30-35 per cent. (p.193)

(f) In the new Five-Year Plan the market supply of products such as meat, fish, vegetable oil, eggs and vegetables will increase by 40-60 per cent. Refrigerators in the possession of the population will rise from 32 per 100 families in 1970 to 64 in 1975. TV sets from 51 to 72 and washing machines from 52 to 72. By the end of the five years, sales of motor cars to the population will increase more than six-fold as against 1970[112]

One of the best indices of living standards is real income. In the Eighth Five-Year Plan period (1966-70) real income grew by a third. In the Ninth Five-Year Plan period (1971-75) it will grow by another 30.8 per cent. In 1971-1972 the salaries of teachers in kindergartens and nurseries were raised by 29 per cent. The state pays 75 to 90 per cent of the cost of keeping 6.5 million children in nurseries and kindergartens. Temporary disability entitles a worker to from 80 to 100 per cent of his wages, depending on length of his service. All workers are granted annual paid vacations of 21 working days. In 1976 average monthly wages and salaries were more than 151 roubles as against 146 in 1975. Payments and other benefits from medical services, sanatoriums and holiday homes amounted to 94,500 million roubles, 4,400 million roubles more than in 1975.[113]

In fact, the stand taken by both Lenin and Khrushchev on disparity renders the Marxist contention of abolishing private property absolutely unrealistic. Here are the statements of Lenin and Khrushchev:[114]

Lenin	*Khrushchev*
While striving towards equal remuneration of labour and communism, the Soviet government does not regard the immediate realization of such equality possible at a moment when only the first steps are being taken towards replacing capitalism by communism.	The disparity between high and comparatively low incomes must gradually shrink . . . As the living standard of the entire population rises, low income levels will approach the higher, and the disparity between the income of peasants and workers, low-paid and high-paid personnel, and the population of different parts of the country will gradually shrink.

Pravda reported a long debate on ways and means of linking incentive payments with profits, which are regarded as a percentage on capital investment. The assumption that in a rapidly-developing economy, capital is itself particularly scarce and accordingly ought to be expensive would seem to most Soviet economists to be an anti-Marxist heresy.[115] After a long debate by the Central Committee of the Soviet Communist Party on the role of 'profits'[116] in stimulating more efficient industrial output, it was agreed that material incentives are necessary to increase efficiency. In socialist society where all enterprises are publicly owned, the productivity of each individual is determined on the basis of material as well as moral incentives. The present policy centers on the concept: 'from each according to his ability, to each according to his work'. Thus the diversity of people's abilities has been taken into account, and each individual has been encouraged through material and moral incentives to achieve his potential in the interests of society. Millions of the Soviet people offer obligingly to work overtime, without pay, and to raise production. This practice called 'emulation' refers to friendly competition between factories and between working people. Those emulators whose work has produced the best results will be rewarded by the government. Their names, photographs and work records are announced in the newspapers, or radio and television programmes.[117]

The plan is designed to reward the plants on the basis of 'profits' rather than on the old inefficient system of over-fulfilment of quantitative plans. Yevsey Liberman, a professor from Kharkov has presented the most complicated set of proposals for making the profitability of each enterprise the measure of fulfilling the task of socialist economy. According to Liberman's model, the more profit a plant can earn on a given production job, the larger should be the slice of wages and benefits for the factory managers and work force. Again the directors of industrial enterprises would no longer be thought to be fulfilling their plans by reaching merely an allotted level of gross output, but should also be required to work harder to produce the things that would be most profitable in the present state of market demand. Actually, although the professor's formula that profitability should be used as the sole guide line is criticized as 'un-Marxist', the central and regional planning organizations have been receptive to Liberman's ideas.

Now a question may be raised: where does profit go in the USSR? In answering this question we have to take the economic system of socialism into account. In a socialist society the basic means of production is the whole society, that is, they are not owned by an individual or a group of individuals. In a capitalist society, on the other hand, surplus value is the operating principle. What interests an employer in terms of production is the source of profit. As a matter of course, he attempts to accelerate production in a cheaper way and sell it at less than his competitors so that he can secure more profit. The operating principle under socialism on the contrary, is 'securing for every member of society, by means of socialized production - an existence guaranteeing to all the free development and exercise of their physical and mental faculties'.[118] This does not mean that under socialism profit is no longer an economic category. So long as money relations exist and operate, profit cannot be ruled out. Back in 1921 Lenin insisted that state-owned enterprises operate without loss, that they bring in a profit.[119] In the Soviet Union profit is made by the working people themselves in their own interests. Profit is not to be made through speed-up or price-rigging.[120] The only methods that are legally permitted in increasing profits are the application of advanced technology, automation and the rational organization of labour. It was the state that has owned all industry profit and distributed it for all kinds of social needs ever since January 1966. The economic reform in 1966 changed this. Today part of the factory's profit falls into three funds: one for bonuses for workers, another for social and cultural projects and housing construction, and the third for production expansion.

The state budget has not been adversely affected by the reform; instead, revenues have accumulated. In 1970 about 64 million roubles out of the total budget expenditure of 144.5 billion were spent for more industrial construction and expansion of city buildings, old age and disability, pensions, medical services and education.[121]

A second question may be posed: how do Soviet workers dispose of profit? As private ownership of the means of production is illegal under socialism, none of its members may invest money in production. For personal use people are allowed to buy a house, a car, a refrigerator even jewelry, and deposit money in a state savings bank or state bonds. Yet workers who gain profit from their work are forbidden to use it for making more profit. In the Soviet Union workers take part in distributing the national income. From the highest level of state power—the USSR Supreme Soviet which designs the plans and approves the budget of the national economic development—down the factory trade union, which decides on distributing the incentive funds, representatives of the Soviet working class have voice. Ultimately the working class together with the collective farmers and the intelligentsia are the owner of all the country's wealth.[122]

As regards the question of centralized controls over the allocation of materials in the Soviet Union, academician Nemchinov, one of Russia's leading economists argued that the present system of control over inputs for plants was out-dated and that this was excessively centralized, economically ineffective and highly inflexible.[123] Nemchinov held that the more production increased and the more diverse it became, the more scope must be given to direct and immediate economic relations between plants based on mutual agreement between the interested parties.[124]

In 1963 an elaborate system of material incentives, i.e., rising salary according to the difficulty of work and living conditions has been introduced. At Bratsk the monthly wage of a construction teacher averages 200 roubles, twice what a Moscow secondary school teacher earns. Farther north, the salary reaches 400 roubles a month. In the week 7-14 April 1963, *Izvestia* revealed that in the Mica mines north of Irkutsk miners working on officially approved private enterprise system had earned the sum of 8,000 roubles a month.[125] Khrushchev said:

> Giving the people material incentives is raising Soviet agricultural production. We must boldly and resolutely advance along the road of material remuneration for the quality and quantity of produce.[126]

Miller recounts the difficulties into which Soviet planning has run as a result of misplaced and often unfinished investment and bad distribution of components and stock. These economic difficulties arise from Gosplan's habit of trying to run the economy in a state of persistent inflation of demand. The economic experiments now really follow Keynesianism *à outrance* in the direction of full employment of resources and construction of productive power. In brief, the 'capitalist concept' of profit and full employment of resources as stimuli to production have been undertaken by Russian economic planners. If such is the case, Soviet economists would soon introduce the *laissez-faire* system and substitute Keynesian for Marxist ideology, however heretically the former may be applied. Socialism, once having destroyed capitalist *laissez-faire* in Russia, has found it again as the cry of the worker who does not want to be bothered with workers' control.[127]

More recently the *Economic Survey of Europe,* published by the United Nations Economic Commission for Europe describes an important shift of emphasis in Soviet official policies. Soviet economists have indicated that the high degree of centralization of planning and management tended more and more to de-stimulate the producing units and reduce their efficiency.[128] Thus much emphasis is being laid on the necessity for increasing the role of material incentives. The need to give greater autonomy to enterprises is frequently emphasized in major newspapers and publications. In addition, the wage reform is intended to stimulate higher output of crops and animal products. For example, under the present practice, members of the Soviet Union's 39,000 collective farms are paid for the number of the work-days put in during the year. On State farms, which are owned and operated by the Government, workers are paid fixed salaries as in industry.[129]

A feature of Soviet incomes policies in 1964 which were felt in 1965 was the planned raising, by 21% of salary scales for persons in the service sectors of the economy, including about 20 million wage-earners; the differential between them and their counterparts in the productive sector was therefore narrowed to about 10%. Personal savings, for example, amounting to 1,700m roubles, or 30% more than in 1963, were among the factors helping to maintain internal equilibrium.[130]

Also there was the shift in terms of price controls. The Soviet government announced that price controls on privately grown farm products sold in peasant markets had to be abolished. *Izvestia* said that from then on the sale of agricultural products on collective farm markets would be conducted exclusively according to prevailing market prices. Again *Izvestia* reported that local government authorities next year would begin building and equipping new market places for private trade in farm produce.[131]

The foregoing evidence seems quite adequate to show that private property has been more and more stressed and encouraged and thus the

Soviet leaders have been obliged to modify Marxist philosophy on private property and sacrifice many of their original socialist principles.

In addition, that private ownership has in fact re-appeared in the Soviet Union may also be clearly seen on the basis of a field study published by *Ekonomischeskaya Gazeta,* a weekly economic journal of the Soviet Council of Ministers. Evidence of appreciative profits made by self-employed vendors seems quite convincing. One individual is said to have retailed a ton of bay leaves (much in demand for borsch seasonings) at a profit of 20,000 roubles (£8,000). According to the same study all facilities are laid on for speculators. They have marked hotels, left-luggage depots, and other services at their disposal.[132] *Moscow Pravda* also reported that a man had been sentenced to death for organizing a racket in the illegal sale of knitted goods made by handicapped workers in Moscow.[133] These facts reflect, first, people's oblivion of the horrors of Stalinism and a reaction against the old regimentation; secondly, a Georgian University lecturer has attributed many of the defects and crimes to Khrushchev's relaxation of discipline. 'If Stalin had lived,' he said, 'we would have had communism today'.

THE EQUALITY OF THE SEXES

Engels asserted that the legal inequality of the two partners is not the cause but the effect of the economic oppression of woman. The necessity for creating real social equality between man and woman will only be realized when both possess complete legal equality of rights. Lenin wrote:

The Party's aim is not to limit itself to the formal proclamation of woman's equality, but to liberate woman from all the burdens of antiquated methods of house-keeping, replacing them by household communes, public kitchens, central laundries and nurseries.[134]

The Constitution of the USSR declares that 'women in the USSR are accorded all rights on equal footing with men in all spheres of economic, government, cultural, political, and other social activity. The possibility of exercising these rights is ensured by women being accorded the same rights as men to work, payment for work, rest and leisure, social insurance and education, and also by state protection of the interests of mother and child, state aid to mothers of large families and to unmarried mothers, maternity leave with full pay, and the provision of a wide network of maternity homes, nurseries and kindergartens."[135]

In the earlier years of the Revolution the tenet of the equality of rights of both sexes and of the unlimited access of women to all professions, was rigidly enforced. Women were encouraged to take any occupation for which they were physically competent.[136] However, some modifications occurred in 1936 when in accordance with official Soviet ideology, women were given full recognition for performing their civic duties, such as social welfare work or even the bearing of children. Today woman's place in the kitchen has been discarded forever from the Soviet mentality or belief. A third of all Soviet women are engaged in industry, not in traditional female occupations. More than 70% of Soviet doctors and teachers today are women, but they include midwives as 'doctors'. More than 400,000 women carry on scientific research. Every woman is paid exactly the same as every man who does the same work. This law has been implemented ever since the Revolution.[137] Again, when a girl marries, it is legal for her to maintain her maiden name, take her husband's name, or use both names if she so prefers to. After marriage, everything a couple buys is owned equally by both regardless of whether or not both share the cost. When their belongings are disposed of, money must be equally divided between husband and wife according to the law.

There were two contributory factors in this altered attitude. The first was the change in education which had marked repercussions on the equality of woman. Co-education of the sexes from elementary schools to university was instituted on May 31, 1918,[138] and intended equal access to the professions. In 1943[139] education at secondary schools was abolished. Official arguments in favour of this reform were based on the fact that there was a need to train boys to be the most efficient soldiers and girls in nursing and domestic science.[140] This argument may be summarized by the following statement:

> Education in our schools was formerly co-educational in order to over-
> come as quickly as possible the centuries-old social inequality of the
> sexes. But what we must have now is a system by which the school
> develops boys who will be good fathers and manly fighters for the
> socialist homeland, and girls who will be intelligent mothers compe-
> tent to rear the new generation.[141]

It must be recognized that, however legitimate and logical this standpoint may be, the change made in the organization of secondary schools was opposed to the position of Kollontai, the radical representative of Soviet feminism.[142]

The second factor was the official attitude to motherhood. The Marxists may argue that the reform of the educational system would not undermine the basic Marxian principle according to which equality is the equality of rights granted by progressive legislation. But, on assuming her duties towards the reproduction of children, the wife would be incapable of participating in social production on equal terms with men. Once the wife ceases to be employed and is considered par excellence to be the mother, it is inevitable that either the state will provide for annual allowances for large families or increase the income of the husband.[143] If the family income is to depend on the size of a man's family rather than on the quantity and quality of his work, the birth rate would be encouraged at the sacrifice of major incentives to production.

The Communist Party and government show much concern for women as mothers and for their children. The government's grant to mothers and services to children in 1969 was 8.9 times as great as in 1940. This includes an increase of 13.8 times for kindergartens and nurseries.

Number of Mothers of Large Families Receiving Monthly Government Grants (in Thousands)

	1945	1950	1960	1969
Total of mothers of large families receiving grants	844	3,079	3,455	3,377
With four children	287	1,449	1,660	1,289
With five children	181	839	899	833
With six children	100	440	484	570
With seven children or more	276	351	412	685

Source: 'Women in the USSR:' *Statistical Data in Vestnik Statistiki*, 1971, No. 1, pp.1-17. Cited in *the Soviet Review*, Vol.XIII, No.2, Summer 1972, pp.163-64.

Mothers with two children are entitled to fixed sum grants upon the birth of third and of each subsequent child, whereas those with three children receive a monthly grant upon the birth of a fourth and of each additional child. In 1969 mothers receiving monthly grants for their fourth and additional children numbered 3,377,000; mothers of two children receiving fixed sum grants upon the birth of a third were 386,000. Mothers of large families and single mothers received 438,000,000 roubles in grants.[144] Clearly, no state would be tempted to risk material loss simply because of its birth rate. Since the income differential in a socialist society depends upon the quantity and quality of the work performed, care of children and related expenses are major incentives to work. Thus it would appear more reasonable that the Soviet government considers the free distribution of bread preferable to a complete exclusion of incentives.

A recent report on women's status suggests that there should be an expansion of public catering for family needs by lightening of women's work in production and increasing child care center facilities. The text of Soviet Party Draft Program proclaims:[145]

(a) Women must be given relatively lighter and yet sufficiently well-paid jobs.
(b) Conditions must be provided which will reduce and lighten domestic work of women and later make possible the replacement of domestic work by public means of satisfying the daily needs of the family.
(c) Special attention must be paid to the extension of public catering, including canteens at factories, institutions and big dwelling houses, until it meets the demands of the population.

According to Abakov's survey, there are still families, young and old, where the man considers himself the head and forbids his wife to work or to study, and in reality treats her as a servant. Similarly Madam Vinogradova complained:

> . . . Husband and wife are not now equals. Many men believe that they can do exactly what they please. They are unfaithful, boorish, and inconsiderate to their wives . . . Care of children and their upbringing are in most cases completely on the wife's shoulders. . . . Too often our husbands are unwilling to lend a hand at home, so that we women carry a burden beyond our strength.[146]

As motherhood is known to be incompatible with participation in social production, it implies, to some extent, actual inequality of the sexes. In fact, in 1936 the Soviet government abandoned the idea that woman's natural function, like that of man, consists essentially in social production outside the home. It avowed that motherhood should be an accessory to the production, just as the defence of the state is contributory to economic production in man. This version of Soviet ideology demolishes the foundation upon which socialist feminists have laid their demand for equality of the sexes. Khrushchev said:

> The remnants of the unequal position of women in domestic life must be totally eliminated. . . . Up-to-date, inexpensive domestic machinery, appliances, and electrical devices will be made extensively available for this purpose.[147]

Vlasova reported that sometimes after marriage and motherhood the woman becomes absorbed in household matters, and she begins to lag behind her husband.[148] Nikolin replied to Batt and other readers that parents can place their children in nurseries and kindergartens where they receive loving care. Nevertheless the facilities here still do not fully meet the demand, but they are expanding at a remarkable rate.[149] The kindergarten is of late a large area of separate building. Every morning nine million children are taken to the kindergartens. The children are divided into age groups, each with its own bedroom and playroom; it is the first rung in the Soviet educational ladder, and prepares children for formal schooling. Children are taught to sing, dance and do gymnastics. Mothers were once afraid that the kindergartens would not lavish good care on their children with regard to food and affection. Experience, however, taught that the children are happier and develop faster in the company of playmates than at home.[150] All this goes to prove that Marxists' desire for putting women solely in social production has yet to be realized.

There is some indication that women who are now engaged in employment outside the home play an active part in state affairs and other fields of work. Bergson and Kuznets reported that Russia's labour force has grown more swiftly than its population owing to the increasing engagement of women in full-time jobs. That is, the normal housewives are employed full-time at the workbench as well as in the kitchen.[151] Yet women are beginning to raise a hue and cry in the press against inequities imposed on working women. Working wives lodged a complaint that they had been graded into bearing the unequal burden of two jobs, while their husbands take their ease. Soviet women are engaged in hard physical labour such as digging ditches, cleaning the streets, mowing public gardens, or putting up buildings. They also enter into such low paid fields as medical personnel, teaching and the telephone and telegraph system, whereas men undertake highly paid posts as engineering and mining.[152] Another complaint was that husbands had seldom helped raising children and had almost never attended meetings at school. It was said that 90% of the fathers did almost nothing in raising their children; at school there were only one or two men out of 40 parents. Palova said that 'our women have achieved equality; so all the doors have been open to them including the door upstairs!'. Nevertheless what underlay the relative failure of women to move upstairs in appreciable numbers was their double burden of work at home and on the job.[153]

The number of women with secondary or higher education increased from 90 to 500 per thousand in 1975. Women with higher education numbered 45 per thousand. Today half of the students in the Soviet Union are females and, what is more, in the technical higher schools approximately 40% of the students are girls against 8% in the United States and 1.5% in Britain.[154]

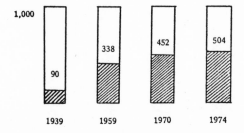

The Education of the Women in the USSR, the number per 1,000 women, with higher and specialized secondary education

In the political field women account for 40% of the deputies (471,276) in the local Soviets. Over 50% of all the deputies in Uzbekistan are women, and there are deputies to the Supreme Soviet of the USSR.[155] Two million women are Party members. In 1973 the Communist Party of USSR has 3 million woman members. Wadgar Nasriddinova, a Uzebek women is the Chairman of the Soviet 15 Republics, and 53 of 100 members are women. In the local city or municipal Soviets, 46% are now women. With regard to enforcing the law one out of three judges in Soviet courts is a woman.[156] In 1975, 475, that is, nearly a third of the elected deputies to the USSR Supreme Soviet, are women; so are 2,045 of deputies to the Supreme Soviets of the Union Republics and 1,039,000 (nearly half) the deputies to local Soviets.[157] Many women are in the top management of industry and administration, collective and state farms, research institutes and schools.

Soviet Life reported that women's participation in social and economic production has been increasing. Some 80% of the able-bodied Soviet women hold jobs. They make up 51% of the country's factory and office workers. Women comprise 58% of the workers in communication, 47% of those in science, 61% of those in administration, 75% of those in trade, some 60% of the annual increment in the labour force. As many as 72% of the physicians and 71% of the teachers are women.[158]

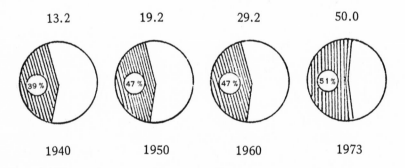

| 13.2 | 19.2 | 29.2 | 50.0 |

| 1940 | 1950 | 1960 | 1973 |

Women at work in the USSR—the millions and in per cent of whole labour force

In the light of the considerable role played by Soviet women in both political and economic activities, especially since Valentina Terehkova's space flight, Soviet propagantists have proclaimed the complete equality and freedom of Soviet women. There can be no doubt that this flight provided proof of female physical prowess and contributed significantly to space exploration. Article 122 of the Constitution of the USSR says: "Women in the USSR shall be accorded equal rights with men in economic, government, cultural, political and public activities."[159]

Today the emancipation of woman has changed from legal equality of woman and man to the sphere of inner family ethics and activity. Family diarchy has developed by leaps and bounds, but it requires of both husband and wife higher moral standards and greater understanding. The richer the spiritual world of the married couples, the stronger and more harmonious their union will be.[160]

5. THE MARXIST VIEW ON POPULATION

According to Malthus population tends to increase at a more rapid rate than the food supply can sustain. Marx scarcely tackled the population problem, though he severely criticized the Malthusian theory;[161] he asserted that every society has its own law of population which requires surplus labour for its development. It exists because there have been more workers than jobs.[162] In the *Communist Manifesto* and the *Origin of the Family, Private Property and the State,* the Marxists' view of the good society was expressed in the emancipation of woman from household drudgery as a main theme; but whether she should likewise be emancipated from bearing many children was not explicitly articulated.[163] In a letter to Kautsky, Engels answered the question of whether over-population could arise under communism and admitted 'the abstract possibility' of a necessity to impose limits on numbers, but added that if a regulation of human reproduction ever became necessary, only a communist society could carry out such regulation successfully.[164]

Adherence to the above Marxist view is understandable in the light of the Soviet Russian demographic history. Lorimer said that in the period of 1917 and 1926 a loss of 25,000,000 to 30,000,000 people was caused by war and postwar conditions.[165] An additional loss of approximately 5,000,000 lives[166] resulted during the period of the collectivization of agriculture, the settlement of the nomads, and the initial campaign towards the development of resources and rapid industrialization. It is estimated that about 45,000,000 people were lost during World War II, including actual deaths and decrease in births.[167] According to professor Nina Orlova, Doctor of Science and Law, the second World War took a toll of 20 million Soviet lives.[168] It is no wonder that in consequence of these losses the Soviet Union felt a pressing need for population increase and accordingly accepted the Marxist 'anti-Malthusian' theory with zest. It must be pointed, however, that, whereas Marx and Engels criticized the Malthusian theory on population, they never ruled out the possibility and even the necessity for population planning. Engels envisaged a situation in which population planning might be inevitable and necessary for certain socialist societies. Here it is worth mentioning that in spite of an enormous loss of population between 1917 and 1926, the population problem had begun to influence Soviet policy on the family before the last war; this problem arose largely from the pre-revolutionary condition of the Russian village. Modification of the Marxian theory on population in Soviet society was made for the following reasons:

(1) The land of the village was periodically re-distributed among its members according to the size of each family. A large family received a larger share of land, yet this incentive to fertility in rural areas necessarily ceased with the abolition of the periodical re-distribution of land. The cessation may be attributed to the following factors: (a) the re-establishment of private land ownership; (b) the transformation of the poor peasants into agricultural labourers as a result of the Stolypin reform[169] or by the collectivization of agriculture under which the incomes of peasants came to depend on their working achievement. Consequently, Soviet population policy, particularly with regard to the support granted to large families, was altered. Here anti-Malthusian Marxists would be inclined to argue that fear of unemployment leads the working class in capitalist countries to limit births. Such a problem would seem to be readily unravelled in Soviet socialist society.

(2) A positive population policy is necessary in the USSR for both urban and rural populations. True, the demand for such a programme arose not only because of the undeveloped land, but also because of national defence which had been threatened by neighbouring countries with the largest population in the world. Hence it is clear that population policy in the Soviet Union was adopted in response to geographical situation and national needs rather than to the immutable Marxist blueprint; and the experiences of the USSR marked a degree of tension between the original Marxist theory of the family, i.e., the ideology of emancipation of woman from traditional bondage, and the need for stabilizing and strengthening the new society with a higher birth rate. Soviet population policy has been therefore confronted with, on the one hand, the original issue, the emancipation of woman as anticipated by the Marx-

ist doctrine together with all the obstacles presented by tradition and, on the other hand, the necessity for a change of attitude towards this issue as a result of an expanding population.

(3) The Soviet government has continued its policy of increasing population in order to regain the estimated loss of 45,000,000 people during World War II.[170] The rate of natural increase in the Soviet Union during its history has been about 0.8 per cent annually.[171] Considering the small population in contrast to the colossal territory of this country, one can easily understand why Soviet planners prefer a larger, more rapidly growing population. The current growth rate is about 1.8 per cent annually, approximately the same as that for the world as a whole.[172] The following table presents a change in Soviet urban and rural populations.

Change in Numbers of Urban and Rural Populations

Years	Total population (in millions)	Urban	Rural	As percentage of total Population	
				Urban	Rural
1939	190.7	60.4	130.3	30%	68%
1959	208.8	100.0	108.8	48%	52%
1970	241.7	136.0	105.7	56%	44%
1974	270.0	150.0	120.0	59%	41%

Source: *Sovetskaia etnografiia*, 1971, No.4, pp.8-30. *USSR Questions and Answers*, Moscow: Progress, 1975, p.55. *Moscow News*, Feb. 5-12, 1977, p.14.

Percentage of men and women in population

Years	Women	Men
1959	55.0	45.0
1965	54.3	45.7
1970	53.9	46.1
1975	53.7	46.3

Sources: *Sovetskaia etnografiia*, 1971, No.4, pp.8-30. *Soviet Life*, March, 1975, p.12

The difference between the numbers of men and women changed considerably after WWII, which brought enormous losses among the male population. The 1959 census shows a greater gap between the number of men and women, women outnumbering men by 20,800,000 more than men. The 1970 census records a certain decrease in the disproportion between the numbers of men and women, women outnumbering men by 19,000,000 more than men.

Estimates of Mid-Year Soviet Population
(in millions)

1970	1971	1972	1973	1974	1975	1976	1977
142.76	245.09	247.46	249.74	252.06	254.38	256.07	257.09

Source: *United Nations Monthly Bulletin of Statistics* (New York), May 1973, Vol. XXVI, No.5, pp.1-5; *Population and Vital Statistics Report*, U.N. 1975, 1976, 1977 p. 26.

There are gaps in the age structure in USSR. In 1970 as many as 722 men per thousand are married, whereas for women the figure was 579. During the war the birth rate fell sharply so that the number of young women in the most favorable child-bearing age declined, and entailed a lower birth rate in recent years. The country's demographic policy aims at raising the birth rate. The Twenty-fourth Communist Party Soviet Union (CPSU) Congress Directives pass the legislation making grants-in-aid to families with many children and subsidizing working mothers. In spite of substantial damage done by the war, the natural increase of population is improving. The differential ratio (males per 100 females) is becoming smaller. In 1970 men and women struck a balance in the age groups up to 43 inclusive. With an aggregate population growth between 1959 and 1970 of 15.8%, the number of those married increased by 23.8%, and the number of married women has risen in all age brackets from 19 up. The age bracket of up to and including 15 grew by 11.2 million compared with 1959. More than half of the country's population is under 30. As a result of the higher average life span, now 70 years in the Soviet Union, the percentage of people in the higher age groups has risen.[173]

The Soviet policy of increasing birth rate would be confronted with a dilemma between the growing population and the attempted industrialization, a problem which exists as well in capitalist countries. Nonetheless on the grounds of the optimum population theory in the Soviet Union, this problem may be negligible. In the national interest, the higher birth rate which Marxist doctrine considers a hindrance to the emancipation of women has been supported by the state. For instance, childless women must pay a 5 per cent extra tax, whereas expectant mothers are allowed 56 days of paid maternity leave before confinement and 56 days after. In case of abnormal delivery the after-confinement leave is prolonged to 70 days.[174] The population increase in the postwar years varies with different living standard levels. The higher the living standard, the lower the birth rate is and vice versa. Yet if the Soviet state provides for child care and the necessities of life, mothers would not hesitate to have more children. Thus a higher living standard in the Soviet Union may not invert a high birth rate.

It may be concluded that the Marxist population theory and the Soviet policy are both consistent and divergent. The Communist Party has never discarded the institution of the family in spite of the Marxist prediction of its 'withering away'. In fact, what underlies Marxist theory bearing on the family is its attack on the superiority of man and its insistence on the emancipation of woman. It is this doctrine that led the state to make allowances for the mothers of large families.[175] On this issue Schlesinger wrote:

. . . The fact that Marxist criticism was directed against the traditional man-dominated family has saved the Soviets from any dispute about the mothers' right to get whatever public benefits are provided for families with children, and has helped it to look for possible solutions of the population problem and for suitable surroundings for the new generation without being limited by the family ideology.[176]

6. ABORTION

One may argue that in the light of the Marxist 'anti-Malthusian' theory Marxists would reservedly condemn abortion. This is in fact by no means the case. Since the size of a population is determined by many variables, the variable of abortion cannot be treated as unimportant. There are four distinct phases in the evolution of Soviet abortion laws. In 1917-1920, the pre-revolutionary anti-abortion law was still in force. In 1930 the first Soviet decree was issued, legalizing abortion by a surgeon and advocating contraception.[177] This was done in conformity with Marxist theory on the emancipation of woman. The first condition for this, according to Engels, is the re-entry of woman into industry on the largest possible scale; and to this end some limitation of the family whether by birth control or abortion, is obviously both necessary and desirable.[178] In 1975 there were in Moscow 200,000 abortions a year about twice the number of births.[179] But the official document reads:

> The legislation of all countries combats this evil by punishing the woman who chooses to have an abortion and the doctor who performs it . . . The Workers' and Peasants' Government is conscious of this serious evil to the community. It combats this evil by propaganda against abortion among working women.[180]

The reasons for the adoption of the practices was the forced collectivization of farms, and the insufficiency of crèches and similar institutions. The bearing of additional children would, it was felt, prevent the mother from remaining in employment. Other considerations were the shortage of housing, illness, large families, and the unavailability of contraceptives.[181]

In 1936 the legality of abortion was revoked by a law passed by the Council of People's Commissars of the Soviet Union, except in cases where continued pregnancy threatened life or health. In the discussions which culminated in the Law of Abortions and Aid to Mothers, no one defended abortion as an expression of a woman's right to her own body'.[182] Public opinion was clearly against it,[183] and the attitude of the ruling party was summed up by N.V. Krylenko, People's Commissar of Justice of the R.S.F.S.R. He said that 'a system of measures directed towards a single aim, that of protecting the health of more than half of the population of the USSR, that is to say, the women'.[184] As a result of this measure, the reported number of abortions in Moscow in the third quarter of 1936 decreased to only seven percent of the number performed within the same period a year earlier.[185] In the entire Soviet Union, therapeutic abortions declined by 97 per cent from the first half of 1936 to the second half of 1937,[186] and secret abortions reportedly dropped considerably as well.[187]

From 1936 onward, motherhood[188] was publicly regarded as a profession, incompatible with any other form of productive activity. It was in the point of view, rather than an abhorrence of abortion, that the decree of June 27, 1936 was enacted. This view can be taken as an indication of the discarding the theory of family's eventual 'withering away' in a socialist society.[189]

In 1955, after the legislation forbidding abortion took effect for almost twenty years, a 'Repeal of the Prohibition of Abortions' was enacted by the Presidium of the Supreme Soviet.[190] The text of the decree, however, includes the statement, 'The repeal of the prohibition on abortion will permit the limitation of the harm caused to the health of women. . . . by abortions carried on outside hospital'.[191] In his study of this problem, Dr. Shening-Parshina discovered that as a consequence of the revocation of the abortion law the number of uncertified cases of abortions was reported to have decreased sharply but still to remain considerable.[192] Reports from a Moscow hospital reveal that since November 1955, fifteen to twenty operations have been performed weekly,[193] amounting to about twenty per cent of the total number of births. The United States Public Health Mission to the Soviet Union reports that the number of abortions has ranged from thirty to eighty-five per cent of all births in those hospitals.[194] In one of the Frunze (Kirgizia) hospitals, in 1956 it was found that there were 1,425 abortions performed to 2,367 births delivered at, or assisted by, hospitals.[195]

A study of the causes and consequences of abortion among women in the *Aginsk National Okrung* was made between 1963 and 1966. During this period, 2008 Russians and 693 Buryat women resorted to termination of pregnancy at medical institutions. Of these 33.6 per cent of the Russians and 35.6 per cent of the Buryats were between the ages of 25 and 29. The authors found that among both Russians and Buryats, white collar workers were the most likely to abort, unmarried women were 2.59 per cent of those aborting among Russians, while 8.14 per cent among Buryats. The congent reasons for women of all ages and both nationalities were the aversion to having the child and the presence of many children. Desire to continue education also played an important role in the young age groups.[196]

Now a question may be posed: what is an ideal family size? Today in the Soviet Union the desirability of limiting the family size or postponing child bearing is virtually a social phenomenon of every married couple. The family planning by spouses to have a certain number of children is influenced, on the one hand, by the socio-economic conditions of the family's life and, on the other hand, by the individual notion about an ideal family size. Between January and May 1969 the Laboratory Demography of the Research Institute of the Central Statistical Administration of the USSR undertook a sample, mail survey of family opinion in regard to the ideal number of children. The opinion survey included 62,500 women in the whole Soviet Union. Of some 1,938 questionnaires sent to Belorussia 1,060 women had responded. This table shows that less than 1 percent of the children regarded one child as ideal. Seventy-eight per cent of women prefer two or three children. This coincides with the favorable attitude of women who had been previously surveyed in Moscow towards this number of children (80%). In Belorussia forty-five per cent of women regard a family with three children as optimal. In 1977, most Russian families regard one or two children as optimal. *Moscow News,* March 26-April 2, 1977, p.2

Distribution of Women of Capital Cities by Ideal Number of Children [197]

Ideal number of children:	0-1	2	3	4+	Total	Average ideal number
Percentage of women choosing their ideal number						
Moscow	19.5	72.9	7.6	——	100	1.9
Minsk	1.5	50.3	36.0	12.2	100	2.6

Among the women of the two capital cities, the greatest unanimity of opinion was found among Muscovites, that is, about three fourths preferred the family of two children, whereas women in Minsk and the Belorussian oblasts do not prefer the very small family. Instead, the percentage of women who held a family of three or more children to be ideal is significantly larger. Analysis of these data and information about an ideal family size help to increase the accuracy and validity of hypotheses in respect to future changes in number of births and population trends. Moreover, whereas birthrate is about the same in urban and rural areas, it is considerably lower in the cities. Particularly low birth rates are typical of large cities. In 1969 it was 11.2 in Moscow, 11.9 in Leningrad, and 13.1 in Riga.

Urban-Rural Birthrate [198]
Number born per 1,000 in population

Years	Total	In urban areas	in rural areas
1940	31.2	30.5	31.5
1950	26.7	26.0	27.1
1960	24.9	22.1	27.7
1969	17.0	15.9	18.3
1975	18.2	—	—

The different levels of fertility in urban and rural areas are associated with the different social traditions and attitudes towards marital and sexual relations, such as marriage and divorce, forms of marriage and family size, age at marriage, and limitations upon sexual relations. This variance is due to different levels of prosperity, education and urbanization. In urban areas women's concern with holding a job while doing a mother's duties at home, add to the burden of child-rearing prevents them from having many children.

In the Soviet Union as a whole, the birth rate within the past ten years has been relatively low, i.e., 17-18 babies per 1,000 persons in contrast to 45-47 people per 1,000 in the pre-revolutionary Russia. One of the facts that has caused the low birth rate is that women did not regard motherhood as their chief and sole calling. Work has been given much importance, as work is not only a source of income but also a source of psychological satisfaction. Today women are eager to raise their educational level, to engage in creative work, to improve their skills and to participate in public life. Looking after their babies has been thought by women to be an obstacle to their accomplishments in all spheres of professional and cultural life. For a working woman to have more than three children is incompatible with a development of professional skills.[199]

Secondly, the cultural and professional training of people for the national economy entails more money and time and thus deters women from bringing up more children. Today it is not at 12-14, as it was 60-70 years ago, but it is at the age of 19-20 that children embark on their independent life. This makes parents feel it an obligation to restrict the number of children to one or two. Thirdly, the policy that the State social insurance for all aged and invalids guarantees to all the citizens independence and security in old age affects birth rate decline. People no longer want more children for old age security as formerly. Finally, the birth rate decline is influenced by the decrease in child mortality. In 1977 child mortality per thousand people is ninth of what it was in 1913.[200]

Conclusion

So our analysis thus far would seem to indicate that, in the interest of family stability and of the nation as a whole, a profound modification of the Marxian philosophy and early Bolshevism has been effected by Soviet law. The Marxist position of marriage as based primarily on natural affection, and the notion of the family as historically relative and economically determined, are far from being satisfactory in support of enduring marriage and family solidarity. Therefore The Soviet State has reinstated the value of family life, not only for the fulfilment of the spiritual requirement of human personality, but also for preservation of sound public morals and the establishment of better social life. Present Soviet marriage owes much to its pre-revolutionary Russian heritage. However, recent Soviet legislation, though inconsistent with the laws of the earlier period of the Revolution, shows a steady policy of intervention in family life. At present, both *de facto* marriage and divorce are recognized, so much so that the spouses and children, be they divorcees or illegitimate, are granted rights of succession and maintenance. Divorce, irrespective of the grounds, is not a matter of right, but is subjected to the unlimited discretion of the Soviet courts, which, of course, faithfully implement government policy.

In brief, the legislation in respect of the family and marriage has not drastically changed ever since 1945. There is yet some indication that, in the national interests, ways have been found to reconcile Marxist revolutionary ideas with the traditional heritage of the Russian past.

NOTES

[1] Elaine Elnett, *Historic Origin and Social Development of Family Life in Russia*, New York: Columbia University Press, 1926, p. 1.
[2] Elaine Elnett, *Op. cit.,* pp.32-35.
[3] Daniel Kubat, 'Soviet Theory of Classes', *Social Forces,* 40 (October 1961) p. 7. Kubat holds that the Soviet Intelligentsia does not appear as a class; this group constitutes a kind of residual category.
[4] Philip E. Mosely, 'The Russian Family: Old Style and New', in *The Family,* ed. by Ruth Anshen, New York: Harper and Brothers, 1959, p. 108.
[5] Harold J. Berman, 'Soviet Family Law in the Light of Russian History and Marxist Theory', *The Yale Law Journal,* 56 November 1946, p. 32.
[6] The emancipation was, in Marxist terminology, the first stage of the Russian bourgeois revolution, a convulsive process akin to the French Revolution (1789) in Western Europe, and its economic concomitant, the Industrial Revolution in Great Britain roughly between 1730-1800. E.H. Carr, 'The Background of Revolution', *Current History,* 25, 1953, pp. 65-66.
[7] Alexandria Kollontai, What is the Family? Moscow, 1932.
[8] *Ibid.*
[9] *Ibid.*
[10] The first decree, without date, was published by Krestianskogo Pravitel'stvo in issue no. 38 of the Newspaper *Gazeta Vremennogo Rabochego.* Cited by G.M. Sverdlov, 'Milestones in the Development of Soviet Family Law', *American Review on the Soviet Union,* 9 (August 1948), p. 3. The second decree dated December 18, 1917 was published in issue no. 57 of the same newspaper on December 20, 1917.
[11] Engels, *Op. cit.,* p. 59
[12] *Ibid.,* p. 62.
[13] Bigamy and polygamy are categorized under Soviet Law as crimes. *Criminal Code,* R.S.F.S.R., art. 199.

[14] G.M. Sverdlov, "Milestones in the Development of Soviet Family Law", *Op. cit.*, 2n by Rose Maurer.

[15] These bureaux were established as bureaux of vital statistics. Their functions were performed in the past by the clergy.

[16] *Programme and Statute of the Communist International*, IV, 3.

[17] The removal of women's inequality refers to what Engels said: "The emancipation of women will only be possible when women can take part in production on a large, social scale". Engels, *Op. cit.*, p. 148.

[18] *Constitution of U.S.S.R.*, art. 122.

[19] This is reflected in the *Communist Manifesto* according to which abolition of bequeathing wealth to heirs is necessary for the socialist programme.

[20] In 1944 more than 7,000,000 children under seven years of age were in nurseries. Serebrennikos, *Women in the Soviet Union* (1944), p.12.

[21] R. Schlesinger, *Changing Attitudes in Soviet Russia—The Family*, p.91.

[22] *Ibid.*, p. 88.

[23] The 'other Dvor' refers to the Dvor of the woman before her marriage

[24] Schlesinger, *Op. cit.*, p. 91.

[25] Arts 10-11 of the final text (document 7).

[26] Art. 6 of the final text (document 7).

[27] Art. 13 of the final text (document 7).

[28] Schlesinger, *Op. cit.*, p. 128.

[29] R. Schlesinger, *Op. cit.*, p.146.

[30] *Constitution (Fundamental Law) of the Union of Soviet Socialist Republics* (Moscow: Foreign Languages Publishing House, 1962), p.100.

[31] *Collected Laws of the U.S.S.R.*, 1936, No.34, art. 309.

[32] *Document* 3 (a).

[33] G.M. Sverdlov, 'Some Problems of Judicial Divorce', *Sovetskoe Gosudarstvo i Pravo*, 1946, No.7.

[34] K. Marx and F. Engels, *The Communist Manifesto*, Chicago: Charles H. Kerr, 1947.

[35] Engels, *The Origin of the Family, Private Property, and the State*, p. 66.

[36] A. Kollontai, *The Family and the Communist State*, London: Workers' Socialist Federation, 19—?

[37] S. Wolffson, *Sociology of Marriage and the Family*, Moscow, 1929.

[38] Engels' thesis is that the monogamous family is the result of private property in the means of production. Now in spite of the so-called disappearance of private property in a socialist society the family has not altogether withered away.

[39] George L. Kline, 'The Withering Away of the State', *Survey—A Journal of Soviet and East European Studies*, No. 38, October 1961, p. 67.

[40] Collection of Laws or R.S.F.S.R., 1935, No. 32, Art. 522, Section 18.

[41] Yevgeni Boldyrev, 'The Study and Prevention of Juvenile Delinquency', *The Soviet Review*, May 1961, pp. 21-22.

[42] Uchitel 'Skaya Gazeta, August 10, 1971, p. 2. Cited in *Soviet and East European Abstracts Series*, Vol. 11, No.3(33), April 1972, p. 30.

[43] Ella Cherapakhova, "Bringing up Parents', *Soviet Weekly*, August 2, 1962, p. 11.

[44] 'Soviet programs compared-Lenin in 1919 and Khrushchev today', *The New York Times*, *August 6, 1961.*

[45] *Embassy of the USSR Information Bulletin*, No. 98, September 22, 1945 and No. 96, September 18, 1945.

[46] *Ibid.*

[47] *The New York Times*, October 3, 1962.

[48] *The Times*, August 8, 1962. Since Stalin's death, private house-building has been encouraged in the suburbs and countryside. The houses are limited in size to 650 square feet of living space and building with the help of loans of local authorities. 'Russia, A Home of One's Own?', *The Observer*, August 12, 1962.

[49] Pravovedenie, June, 1969, pp. 38-44. Cited in *Soviet and East European Abstracts Series*, No. 1 (27), July, 1970, pp. 34-35.

[50] 'Youth Has its Say on Love and Marriages', *The Soviet Review*, August, 1962, p. 32.

[51] Yakov Lombo, 'New Objectives—New Methods', *Moscow News*, No. 48, December 1, 1962.

[52] 'Moscow is now Building Plastic Flats', *The Sunday Times*, London, March 24, 1963.

[53] This is shown in the annual publication on housing and building statistics for Europe produced by the United Nations Economic Commission for Europe (E.C.E), *The Times* (London), November 6, 1964.

[54] A single person is allowed only the so-called one-room, with an alcove for sleeping space, kitchen, a small hall and a bathroom. A family of two or three would qualify for two rooms, i.e., a living room, a separate bedroom, a hall, a kitchen and a bathroom, and of more than three, for three rooms. The top sized would be no more than 80 square meters, that is, four rooms, plus kitchen and bathroom. Elena Korevevskaya, 'State-seeking Through the Co-op: A Russian Wife's View of New Soviet Social Patterns', *The Sunday Times*, London, May 24, 1964.

[55] 'Socialist Society-Incentives to Work', *Soviet Life*, July 1973, No.7, p.22.

[56] Stepan Shalayev, 'Housing, Health and Pensions in the USSR', *Moscow News*, June 17, 1973, p.10.

[57] 'The National Economy of the USSR in 1976', *Moscow News*, No. 5, 1974, p.14.

[58] 'Russia Eases Its Pension Rules', *The Times*, London, March 6, 1964.

[59] *Literaturnaya Gazeta*. July 14, 1971, p. 2. Cited in *Soviet and East European Abstracts Series*, Vol. II, No. 2 (32), October, 1971, p. 28.

[60] Stepan Shalayev, 'Housing Health and Pension in the USSR', *Moscow News*, June 17, 1973, p. 10.

[61] *Ibid.*

[62] In reversal of their earlier policy of antagonism between parents and children, the Soviets now envisage the role of the family as a training ground in discipline . . . Kinko Tomasic, 'Interrelations between Bolshevik Ideology and the Structure of Soviet Society', *American Sociological Review*, 16 (April 1951), p. 145.

[63] One half the entire population of the Soviet Union is already urban. B. Svetlichnyi, 'Some problems of the Long-Range Development of Cities', *Soviet Sociology*, Summer 1962, p.58.

[64] The Russian Revolution which attempted to annihilate the traditional family system has reasserted the pre-revolutionary Russian heritage. To preserve the new, it is essential to restore something of the old.

[65] 'In steps with the times', *Soviet Life*, July 1973, p.14.

[66] Yevgeni Permyak, 'Long engagements', *The Soviet Review*, April, 1962, p.35

[67] Markoosha Fischer, *My Lives in Russia* (New York, 1937), p.55ff.

[68] M.A. Prokof'iev, 'The School and its Problems', in *Sovetskaia pedagogika*, 1971, No.1. cited in *The Soviet Review*, 1972, Vo..XIII, No.22, p.116.

[69] Larisa Kuznetsova, 'Choosing a Partner in Marriage', *Soviet Life*, March 1974, no. 3 p. 13.

[70] *Pravda*, May 28, 1936, p. 76.

[71] Engels, *Origin of the Family, Private Property, and the State*, p.72-73.

[72] S.I. Golod, 'Sociological Problems of Sexual Morality', *Soviet Review*, Summer 1970, Vol.XI, No.2, p.145.

[73] Vladimir Gsovski, 'Family and Inheritance in Soviet Law', *The Russian Review*, 7 (Autumn 1947), p.76.

[74] Gill Tweedie, 'How Liberated Are Soviet Women?', *New Statesman*, 21 September, 1973, p.378.

[75] 'Familienrecht', *The Encyclopedia of the U.S.S.R.*, Vol.38 (Moscow 1955), pp. 460-61.

[76] Nina Orlova, 'Women in Soviet Society', *Soviet Life*, March 1973, No.3, p.26.

[77] *Family Code*, RSFSR, Art. 1, as amended in April 16, 1945.

[78] This provision does not preclude the mothers of children who were born outside a registered marriage after the above mentioned date—July 8, 1944, from receiving some government aid.

[79] Noŭkogude Kool, October 9, 1971, p.2. Cited in *Soviet and East European Abstracts Series*, Vol.II, No.3 (33), January 1972, pp.30-31 'Family Law'.

[80] S. Strumilin, 'Family and Community in the Soviet of the Future'. *The Soviet Review,* February, 1961, p.10.

[81] Nina Prudkova, 'Marriage and the Family', *Soviet Weekly,* May 16, 1963.

[82] Alexei Nikolin, 'Unmarried Mothers and Child Care', *Soviet Weekly,* November 1, 1962, p.13.

[83] Nina Prudkova, 'Marriage and the Family', *Loc. cit.*

[84] Law of June 27, 1936, *Collected Laws of USSR* (1936), I, No.34, Art.27, 309.

[85] *Family Code,* RSFSR, Art. 138, Document 13, Art. 28.

[86] *The New York Times,* November 18, 1936.

[87] Engels foretold the eventual disappearance of the alleged supremacy of man, and the indissolubility of marriage. Bebel said also that the status of husband and wife will disappear, and marriage in the future will be a private contract to be broken at will.

[88] Vladimir Gsovski, 'Family and Inheritance in Soviet Law', *Op. cit.,* p.71, (Lenin, *Sochineniya,* 2nd edition, Vol.XIX, p.232.) Cited by Alex Inkeles, 'Family and Church in the postwar, U.S.S.R.', *Op. cit.,* p.5.

[89] In England there was a one-in-four risk for the wife under 20 that her marriage would end in divorce. 'Cruel Pressure upon Wives', *The Observer,* April 7, 1963, p.1.

[90] Strumilin, "Family and Community in the Soviet of the Future', *Loc. cit.,* p.5.

[91] Audrey R. Topping, 'Soviet Women Approach Equality with Men' *The New York Times,* (International edition), June 19, 1963.

[92] 'Youth has its say on love and marriage', *Loc. cit.,* p.24.

[93] Nina Prudkova, 'Marriage and the Family', *Loc. cit.*

[94] Mikhail Buloshnikov, 'Who's the Head of the Family', *Soviet Life,* No. 3, March 1975, p. 24.

[95] 'Soviet Women Are Overtaking their Men', *Northern Neighbours,* June 1973, p. 7.

[96] Zvyazda, September 13, 1970, p. 4. Cited in *Soviet and East European Abstracts Series,* No. 3 (29), January 1971, p. 29, 'Family Law'.

[97] Turkmenskaya iskra, 12 October 1971, p. 4, Cited in *Soviet and East European Abstracts Series,* Vol. II, No. 3 (33), January 1972, p. 31 'Family Law'.

[98] V.I. Perevedentsev, 'Time to Get Married', *Literaturnaya Gazeta,* April 21, 1971. Cited in *Soviet Sociology,* Spring 1972, Vol. X, No. 4, p. 379.

[99] 'Divorce Russian-Style', *Economist,* September 20, 1975, p.63. About one-third of Russian divorces occur in marriages less than three months' duration.

[100] *Literaturnaya Gazeta,* July 1, 1970, p. 11. Cited in *Soviet and East European Abstracts Series,* No. 2 (28), October 1970, p. 46 'Family'.

[101] F. Engels, *The Origin of the Family, Private Property, and the State,* p. 67.

[102] Money deposits and securities are viewed in any capitalist country as *prima facie* capital, and were confiscated by the Soviet regime thirty years ago. At present, however, accumulation of private wealth in money and securities is possible in Soviet Russia. Gsovski, 'Family and Inheritance in Soviet Law', *Loc. cit.,* p.83. 'Principles on Civil Legislation for the USSR and Union Republics', *The Soviet Review,* August 1962, pp.50-51.

[103] Large numbers of the peasantry accumulated very large sums of cash during the war from the sale of extremely scarce food products. To prevent this money from flooding the consumer goods market, the monetary reform of 1947 was undertaken. B. Alexandrov, 'The Soviet Currency Reform', *The Russian Review,* 8 (January 1949), pp. 56-61.

[104] The government claimed that the large number of savings bank accounts proves that wealth is evenly distributed; in fact, it is common practice for the wealthy to avoid conspicuousness by operating separate accounts. 'Changing Russia', *The Economist,* June 1, 1963, p. 878.

[105] Alex Inkeles, 'Stratification and Mobility in the Soviet Union', *American Sociological Review,* 15 (August 1950), p. 472.

[106] Constitution—the Fundamental Law—of the USSR as amended by the Sixth Session of the Seventh Supreme Soviet of the U.S.S.R., Article 10, Moscow: Progress Publishers, 1969.

[107] Mitchel Wilson, 'How Rich are the Richest Russians', *The Observer,* August 12, 1962.

[108] John N. Hazard, 'Soviet Property Law: A Case Study Approach', *British Journal of Sociology,* 4 (1953), p.1

109 *Textbook on Civil Law of 1944.*
110 Marx and Engels, *Collected Works* (Russian edition), Vol.5, 1921, p.275.
111 Vladimir Gsovski, 'Family and Inheritance in Soviet Law', *The Russian Review,* 7 (1947 Autumn), p.86.
112 Twenty-fourth Congress of the Communist Party Soviet Union (Moscow: Novosti Press Agencies Publishing House, 1971), pp. 190-194.
113 'The National Economy of the USSR in 1976', *Moscow News,* No.5, 1977, p.14.
114 'Soviet Programs compared-Lenin in 1919 and Khruschev today', *The New York Times,* August 6, 1961.
115 'Changing Russia', *The Economist,* June 1, 1963.
116 Khrushchev said that in capitalist countries profit is the aim of production, the main stimulus for its development, while in the socialist system of economy, profit aims to satisfy the requirements of society. Without consideration of profit it was impossible to determine the level on which it was working or the contribution it was making to the country. *Soviet Weekly,* November 22, 1962. 'Profit hint for Soviet Farms', *Daily Telegraph,* January 23, 1965.
117 'Socialist society-Incentives to work', *Soviet Life,* July 1973, No.7,p.22.
118 *Ibid.*
119 Yevgeni Bolotin, 'Profit in the USSR', *Soviet Life,* March 1972, No.3, p.32.
120 *Ibid.*
121 *Ibid.*
122 *Ibid.*
123 The system was set at a time when communism seemed around the corner, and it was thought that monetary and value categories would disappear during the first stage of building or forming socialism.
124 'Time to Relax Controls in Russia-Economist's Plea', *The Times,* March 21, 1964.
125 Mark Frankland's Report on Siberia 'The Land of the Long Rouble', *The Observer,* April 14, 1963, p.4.
126 'Farm Incentives Urged in Russia', *The Times,* February 29, 1964.
127 'The Stern Morality of Communism' extract from the book *The Rationalization of Russia* by Bernard Shaw who explains the class basis of the Marxist creed and the Russian Revolution. *The Times,* April 28, 1964, Part II, p.13. cf. Shaw, Op. Cit. p. 111.
128 'Material Incentives for Russians', *The Times,* March 24, 1965.
129 *Ibid.*
130 'Price Freedom for Soviet Peasants', *The Times,* May 14, 1965.
131 It is interesting to note that Soviet economists had begun to realize that, as their country grows richer, consumer's choice is likely to become much more a dictator of economic trends. This is a sort of dictatorship of the proletariat with which Communist economic planners are not yet prepared to deal. 'Changing Russia', *The Economist,* June 1, 1963.
132 'China indicts Russians as Bourgeois', *The Times,* July 31, 1963.
133 '21 Russians Sentenced for Factory Fraud', *The Times,* April 6, 1965.
134 'Soviet Programms compared-Lenin in 1919 and Khrushchev Today', *Loc. cit.*
135 *Constitution (Fundamental Law) of the Union of Soviet Socialist Republics* (Moscow: Progress Publishers, 1969), Art.100.
136 Schlesinger, *Op. cit.,* p.47.
137 'Soviet Women are overtaking their Men', *Northern Neighbours,* June, 1973, p.7.
138 *Collected Laws and Decrees of the RSFSR,* 1918, No.38, Art.499.
139 *Document 16:* 'Abolition of Co-education in Soviet Schools'.
140 The number of hours devoted to military training for boys increased from 596 in 1938 to 1,048 in 1943 or from 6 per cent to 11 per cent of the total number of hours of the ten-year course of secondary education. Nicolas Hans, 'Recent Trends in Soviet Education', *The Annals of the American Academy of Political and Social Science,* 263 (May 1949), p.118.
141 M. Tzusmer, *Soviet War News,* November 6, 1943.
142 Kollontai intimated in 1919 that the care, upbringing and instruction of children would have to be transferred to the community. A. Kollontai, *Communism and the Family* (London: Workers' Socialist Federation, 19—?), p.6.

[143] Monthly allowances range from 40 roubles for four children to a maximum of 150 roubles for ten or more children. *Decree of the Presidium of the USSR, Supreme Soviet,* July 8, 1944 as amended, November 25, 1947.

[144] 'Women in the USSR:' *Statistical Data in Vestnik Statistiki,* 1971, No. 1, pp.1-17.

[145] 'Solution of Housing Problems and Improvement of Labor Conditions Pledged', *The New York Times,* August 1, 1961.

[146] *Decree of the Presidium of the USSR, Supreme Soviet,* July 8, 1944 as amended, November 25, 1947.

[147] 'Soviet Program compared-Lenin in 1919 and Khrushchev today', *The New York Times,* August 6, 1961.

[148] 'Youth has its say on love and marriage', *Loc. cit.,* p.30.

[149] In 1963 alone places were provided for 30,000 and in the past five years the figure of additional places has totalled 120,000. Maria Kovaleva, 'Three in Five', *Soviet Weekly,* January 9, 1964, No. I, p.145.

[150] 'Kindergarten', *Soviet Life,* June 1973, p.60.

[151] *Economic Trends in the Soviet Union,* ed., by Abram Bergson and Simon Kuznets, Harvard University Press, 1963, pp.48, 56.

[152] Hedreck Smith, 'Soviet Feminists are Beginning to Speak out against Sexual Inequality', *The New York Times,* November 1, 1971.

[153] *Ibid.*

[154] *Moscow News,* No. 9 (1260), March 8-15, 1975, p.10.

[155] 'Did you know that?' *Soviet Weekly,* January 9, 1964.

[156] 'Soviet Women are Overtaking their Men', *Northern Neighbours,* June 1973.

[157] Yelena Novikova, 'An Equal Member of Society', *Moscow News,* No. 9 (1260), March 8-15, 1975, p.3.

[158] Zoya Yankova, 'Women in the Soviet Society', *Soviet Life,* No.3, March 1974, p. 6.

[159] 'Women in Soviet Society', *Moscow News,* No. 9 (1260), March 8-15, 1975, p. 10.

[160] Mikhai Buloshnikov, 'Who's the Head of the Family?' *Loc. cit.,* p. 24.

[161] Thomas Malthus, *An Essay on Population,* 1798 London: L.M. Dent and Sons, Ltd., Vol. I, pp. 18-19.

[162] Ronald L. Meek, 'Malthus-Yesterday and Today', *Science and Society,* N.Y. 13, Winter 1954, p. 32.

[163] William Petersen, 'Marx versus Malthus: the Man and the Symbols', *Population Review,* I, July 1957, p. 31, Madras, India.

[164] Letter of Engels to Kautsky, February 1, 1881. Cited by Meek in *Marx and Engels on Malthus,* p. 109. August Bebel, *Die Frau und der Sozialismus,* 1894, pp. 372-76. K. Kautsky, *Vermehrung und Entwicklung in Natur und Gesellschaft,* Stuttgart, 1920, ch. XVI. Kautsky argued that every effort to improve the conditions of the lower classes would result in a great increase in population; with increased welfare, the birth rate rises, and with increased intelligence, mortality declines. Thus 'birth control' was necessary to counteract the threat of absolute over-population.

[165] Frank Lorimer, *The Population of the Soviet Union: History and Prospects,* Ch. 3 (League of Nations Publications, 1946), A.3.

[166] *Ibid.*

[167] Warren W. Eason, 'The Soviet Population Today', *Foreign Affairs,* 37, (July 1959), pp. 598-600.

[168] *Soviet Life,* March 1973, No.3, p. 26.

[169] Stolypin was Prime Minister, 1906-1911.

[170] Warren W. Eason, 'The Soviet Population Today', *Foreign Affairs,* 37 (July 1959), pp.598, 599-600.

[171] *The New York Times,* February 4, 1960, p.5, Col.2.

[172] 'United Nations Department of Economic and Social Affairs', *Demographic Yearbook,* Tables 8, 25 (U.N. Publications Sales No.1959), XIII.

[173] Yevgeni Georgiyev, 'The Census Findings', *Soviet Life,* September 1972, No.9, p. 34.

[174] Nina Orlova, 'Women in Soviet Society', *Soviet Life,* March 1973, No. 3, p. 26.

[175] The state provides substantial family allowance for mothers of large families and children of unmarried mothers. No distinction is made between widows, deserted wives or

unmarried mothers. Alexei Nikolin, 'Unmarried Mothers and Child Care', *Soviet Weekly*, No. 1, 1962, p. 13.

[176] Schlesinger, *Op. cit.*, p. 7.

[177] Ministry of Health, *Decrees of the Communist Theory of the Soviet Union and of the Soviet Government on the Protection of Health of the Population* (1958), p.63.

[178] Here it should be noted that after the first decree legalizing the abortion, the legal position of the family came close to Engels' description of the 'pairing marriage'. Just as man reserved in this stage the right of being polygamous, the Communist Party has claimed its right to interfere in family affairs, as when the performance of abortion has been permitted on the decision of a commission if there are already three children.

[179] By 1934 the number of abortions almost equalled the number of births in many areas. In Moscow the number of abortions was 2.7 times the number of births in 1934. Lorimer, Loc. cit., pp.127-30. N. Robertson, 'Abortion Argued Around the World', *The New York Times*, March 23, 1975.

[180] *Document*, No.3

[181] Document, No.9.

[182] Schlesinger, *Op. cit.*, pp.399-400.

[183] *Documents* 9 (a) and 9 (b).

[184] N.V. Krylenko, *Love, Family Life, Career* (No date).

[185] Frank Lorimer, *Loc. Cit.*, p.127

[186] Granat, 'Report from the First Session of the Commission on Obstetrics', July 4-5, *Akusherstvo iginekologiya*, Nos. 2-3, 1939.

[187] Shening-Parshina, 'Medical-Explanatory Work on the Problem of Abortion', *Fel'dsherᵈ akusherka*, No.2 1957. p.49.

[188] *Document*, 13, Art.10.

[189] *Documents* 4-6.

[190] A. Marus, 'National Attitudes on Abortions', *The Observer*, August, 26, 1962, p.21

[191] V. Parker Maulin, 'Population Policies in the Sino-Soviet Bloc, *Law and Contemporary Problems*-Population Control XXV(Summer 1960), No.3, p.407.

[192] Shening-Parshina, 'Medical-Explanatory Work on the Problem of Abortion', *Loc. cit.*, p.50.

[193] Herschel and E. Alt, *Russia's Children* (N.Y. Bookman Associates, 1959), p.146.

[194] W. Sullivan, 'Soviet Surgery advances found by visiting American Scientists', *The New York Times*, July 21, 1959.

[195] U.S. Public Health Service, Department of Health, Education and Welfare, *The Report of the United States Public Health Mission to Union of Soviet Socialist Republics*, 30 (1959).

[196] *Zdravookhranenie Rossiiskoe federatsie*, February 1971, pp.22-25. Cited in *Soviet and East European Abstracts Series*, Vol.II, No.2 (32), October 1971, p.46 'Family'.

[197] V.A. Belova, 'Family Size and Public Opinion', *The Soviet Review*, Winter 1972-1973, vol. XIII, No. 4, p. 387.

[198] S.I. Bruk, 'Ethnodemographic Processes in the USSR', *The Soviet Review*, Fall, 1972, Vol. XIII, No.3, p. 208.

[199] Galina Kiselyova, 'Birth Rate', *Soviet Women*, No. 12, 1974, pp. 22-23.

[200] The Institute of Obstetrics and Gynecology of the USSR Ministry of Health prescribed special formulas of helio-oxygen mixtures to treat such conditions as birth trauma and severe oxygen insufficiency, so that half of the mortality of infants born in a condition of asphyxia has been greatly diminished. Leonid Staroselsky, 'Every Day 12,000 New Babies', *Soviet Life*, March 1974, No. 3, pp.48-49. *Moscow News*, March 26- April 2, 1977, p.4.

CHAPTER V

Change in the Chinese Family and Woman's Status

1. THE TRADITIONAL CHINESE FAMILY

> *Once mated with her husband all her life she (the wife) will not change, and hence, when her husband dies, she will not marry again. . . . The woman follows the man:- in her youth, she follows her father and elder brother; when married, she follows her husband; when her husband is dead, she follows her son.*
>
> Li Ki*

The traditional Chinese family persisted without substantial change for almost two thousand years. In the early part of the twentieth century, however, this age-old institution began to disintegrate among modern, educated intellectuals in the large cities and trade ports, and the elementary family emerged. With the coming of the Communist Revolution the changes in the family were common to all of Chinese society. As our interest centres on the change of the family under the impact of Communist principles, the traditional Chinese family will only be touched on.

The Clan System

The term 'clan' may be identified with 'unilateral descent group', either matrilineal or patrilineal; in the Chinese social structure, the framework of the clan consisted of the age hierarchy and the proximity of kinship. These two principles, especially the age hierarchy, laid the foundation of the family organization of authority in the clan, and for performing many of its functions, particularly in the joint family,[1] which was the ideal of the Chinese. The clan was of great importance to the gentry[2] as a mechanism for achieving social solidarity and power. The illusion that the Chinese family was organized on the basis of the clan was fostered by Chinese literati and Western researchers, who relied upon documents supplied by the educated Chinese to convey their own ideas. Hence the behaviour of the upper class has been extrapolated to represent that of the lower or even of the middle class. Here again, the clan

---

* *Li Ki*, Vol. XI 'Chiao Teh Shing' pp.13b and 14a in *Ssu pu pei yao* edition.

or 'tsu' is the largest corporate kin group; its functions may be listed as follows: lending money to 'tsu' members; the helping an individual family to pay an extravagant wedding and funeral; establishing schools; exercising judicial authority within the clan; acting as executive body for the misbehaviour and transgression of tsu members; acting as a government agent in collecting taxes; the clan serves to maintain ancestral graves and 'tsu' property. We refrain ourselves from expatiating upon the structure and function of the clan or 'tsu' as it falls outside the focus of our interest and exploration.

Filial Piety

The father-son relationship traditionally was the purpose of the family in China; the principle of this relationship is expressed in the concept of filial piety. It was a son's duty to cultivate filial piety, even on a strictly business basis, because he has benefited so much from his parents. As the Chinese proverb says: 'Men rear sons to provide for old age; they plant trees because they want shade'.[3] In terms of Confucian ritual the mourning period of three years for each parent is explained by the fact that 'a son, three years after his birth, ceases to be carried in the arms of his parents'.[4] Relating filial piety to 'group insurance' another Chinese scholar says:

> Among the concrete benefits which come to the individual from the system of filial piety is that of 'group insurance'. Each child has his birth-right, the right to whatever assets the family possesses. Each aged person counts on as much comfort in his declining years as the family can possibly give.[5]

In reference to the function of filial piety, it has been characterized as the major force of formal and informal social control. The sociologist Lee Shu-ching points to an important truth when she writes that it is the virtue of filial piety, with its binding force and its far-reaching effects that has reduced juvenile delinquency to a minimum in the Chinese family.[6] Nevertheless a realistic inquiry into Chinese society, which is to say, the Chinese family, reveals the fallacy of some of the conclusions with regard to filial piety. For instance, the strict observance of true Confucian ethics is something which is characteristic of only the exceptionally wealthy.[7] Again, in view of the fact that there have been numerous eras of unrest, turmoil, and disorganization, it cannot be assumed that the family is 'happy, content, stable, and cohesive'.[8] There is no doubt that both rural and urban families encountered an era of social change even before the establishment of the Communist government.

Other Personal Relationships

According to Confucian doctrine, two principles underlie the roles of the father and the mother: that of 'esteem' and that of 'affection' respectively. The father's duty is to discipline and arrange for the education of his children, while his wife is expected to procreate male children. Failure to fulfil this duty would lead to her repudiation. The first of the seven grounds on which a wife may be repudiated is infecundity. If a barren wife is tolerated, her husband is obliged to take a concubine.[9] A wife should obey three persons - her father before marriage, her husband after marriage, and her son after her husband dies. The mother-in-law is a potential enemy of daughters-in-law. The latter, however, peacefully endure harsh treatment until they, in turn, become mothers-in-law.[10] However, Hu Shih maintained that woman's position in the family is not so inferior as is commonly believed.

The care of the aged was the responsibility of the Chinese family, because there was little in the way of social security or assistance for old people.[11] Since China is predominantly agrarian, economic sufficiency and individual security depend upon the property of the family in the last resort. In China, unlike Western societies, where families have lost most of their strict authoritarian control, the family, along with its complex structure and functions, has always been the center of authority, the promoter of private and public economic enterprise, and the last refuge for individuals in crises. In recent times, however, a change of attitude towards family control has become evident, particularly among students, who vigorously criticized traditional controls and customs, and tried to introduce national ideologies and beliefs to supersede parental and familial authority.

The Selection of Marriage Partners

Since marriage in traditional China means receiving a new member into the family, not simply securing a wife for a husband, it is defined as a union between two persons of different families. Young people have been able to marry only on the condition that they belonged to different families.[12] Since marriage serves to draw two families together, its arrangement must be done not by two individuals, but by two families.[13] A young sociologist P'ang Yu-mei, who in 1932 carried out a survey of a village not far from Peking, wrote that 'the command of the parents, the assurance of the match-maker are, as of old, the most important preliminaries to marriage',[14] The match-maker serves not only to carry on negotiations between the two families, but also to transmit messages between the boy and girl who are engaged, thus giving each some knowledge of the other.

The arrangement of marriages by parents through match-makers is not regarded as depriving their children completely of choice and will, especially, in cities. The younger generation has increasingly rebelled against parental interference in selecting a mate. In urban areas there appear three deviations from the traditional patterns: before 1919 parents arranged marriage and asked their children's consent; after 1919 children chose their mates and asked the parents' approval; and children married without asking their parents' approval.

Another factor which influences parental arrangement is that an unhappy and unsuccessful marriage often causes a son to leave the family and choose a concubine. Similarly, the bride-to-be can express her disapproval by complaining and quarrelling. As a result of WW II, which separated parents and children, the tendency towards individual selection of mates was increasing, while the function of match-makers or go-between was declining.

2. THE INFLUENCE OF MARXIST DOCTRINE ON THE CHINESE FAMILY

Because Engels' ideas on marriage and the family provided the basis for the formulation of family policy in China, it is appropriate to recall what he wrote on the subject. Any policy of marriage and the family can be related to his ideal type, and can help us to understand the processes through which the family system has been modified. We note Engels' principle that as private property emerges, man's status prevails over that of woman. He wrote:

> In proportion as wealth increased, it made the man's position in the family more important than the woman's. . . . The overthrow of mother-right was the world's historical defeat of the female sex. The man took command in the home also; the woman was degraded and reduced to servitude. She became the slave of his lust and a mere instrument for the production of children.[15]

Elsewhere he wrote:

> The institution of family property elevated man's position, and the institution of the monogamous form of marriage determined the enslavement of the female sex, but monogamy was instituted for the woman only.[16]

Engels described the deteriorating position of woman in marriage in the following fashion:

> The married woman differs from the ordinary courtesan in that she does not lend her body on piece work as a wage worker, but sells it once and for all into slavery.[17]

The wife became the head servant, excluded from all participation in social production. . . . The modern individual family is founded on the open or concealed domestic slavery of the wife, and modern society is a mass composed of these individual families as its molecules.[18] In order to guarantee the fidelity of the wife, that is, the paternity of the children, the wife is placed unconditionally in the man's power; if he kills her, he is but exercising his right.[19]

In Engels' rationale it is thought that the oppression of one sex in 'civilized' monogamy by the other emerged at the same time as the first class oppression, that of slaves by their masters. Thus through the successive stages of civilization as conceived by the Marxists, the family has served to protect the ruling class in its control of property. Obviously, since the system of family property and the concept of traditional family solidarity are incompatible with the Communist ideas, efforts were made to change the traditional attitude towards them. Marriage was secularized, and made a private matter with state approval through legal instruments rather than a religious matter with a church ceremony. Furthermore early in the Russian Revolution the Soviets attempted to destroy the family by encouraging easy divorce and legalizing abortion. [20] Kollontai proposed a state-controlled nursery for children, communal living, and public mess halls, in order to free women from the slavery and drudgery of the household. As we have seen, such was the general Communistic attitude towards marriage and the family in the early years of the Russian Revolution.

The traditional family system was attacked by Chinese Communists. The low status of women, the traditional maltreatment of wives, daughters-in-law, and domestic maids were branded as vestiges of the evils of this family system. The attempt of the Communist government to bring about a fundamental, drastic revolution in the family system was implemented by means of the marriage law, whose effect was to implant in the minds of people, especially of youth, new ideas regarding marriage and the family, and to dismiss the Confucian virtue and ethics of the family. The attack on the traditional family institution was expressed in Mao Tse-tung's Report to the Executive Committee published at the Second National Congress of Representatives of the Soviets held in March 1934, and reads as follows:

This democratic marriage system destroys the feudal shackles which have fettered humanity and in particular the women and it establishes new norms in accordance with human nature. It is one of the greatest victories in human history, however this victory depends on the victory of democratic dictatorship. Only when, after the overthrow of the dictatorship of the landlords and capitalists, the toiling masses of men and women - in particular the women -have acquired political freedom in the first place, and economic freedom in the second, can freedom of marriage obtain its final guarantee.[21]

These first marriage Regulations of the Chinese Soviet Republic appeared to be applied, but one of the obstacles for their application was economic. . . . The economic position of the woman was still precarious, so that she encountered difficulties in practice to enjoy all those rights she had been granted in theory. On the other hand, Article 1 of the Marriage Regulations declares: 'The principle of freedom of marriage between man and woman is established and the entire feudal system of marriage arranged by parents other than the parties themselves, forced upon the parties and contracted by purchase and sale is abolished. The attack is frontal and fierce; the traditional family is to be eliminated'.[22]

Again, in Quotations from Chairman Mao, he said; 'Protect interests of the youth, women and children, provide assistance to young student refugees, help the youth and women to organize in order to participate on an equal footing in all works useful to the war effort and to social progress, ensure freedom of marriage and equality as between men and women, and give young people and children a useful education. . . . [23] Speaking about woman's labour Mao said: 'Enable every woman who can work to take her place on the labour front, under the principle of equal pay for equal work'.[24]

3. THE MARRIAGE LAW OF CHINESE PEOPLE'S REPUBLIC AND ITS IMPACT ON THE FAMILY[25]

> *In order to build a great socialist society, it is of the utmost importance to arouse the broad masses of women to join in productive activity. Men and women must receive equal pay for equal work in production. Genuine equality between the sexes can only be realized in the process of the socialist transformation of society as a whole.*
>
> MAO TSE-TUNG

To understand the Marriage Law of Chinese People's Republic, the Family Law of the National Government has to be presented, since both of them bear some resemblances. Promulgated by the National Government, the Family Law became effective on May 5, 1931. Its provisions are contained in the Civil Code, Books IV and V with titles 'Family and Succession'.

(1) Marriage was concluded by the parties of their own accord (Art.

981) in the presence of two or more witnesses, so that marriages concluded in contravention of the articles 982 and 983 were void. The minumum age for the man was 18 and for the woman 16 (Art. 980).

(2) As regards matrimonial property the statutory scheme provides for union of property, each spouse retaining the ownership of his and her contributed property, but the man has the right of management and the right to the fruits of woman's contributed property. (Arts. 1003-1048).

(3) Divorce by mutual consent was possible, the only required formality being a written document signed by two witnesses. (Arts. 1049-1050). The children were brought up by the father unless it was provided otherwise by agreement. (Art. 1051). On divorce the wife recovered her own property. (Art. 1058).

(4) Adoption was free, but it had to be effected in writing, and the adoptor had to be at least 20 years of age. (Arts. 1078-1073). An adopted child had the right to half a portion of the inheritance of a child of the marriage. (Art. 1142). Full provision was made for the recognition of illegitimate children. (Arts. 1064-1070).

(5) The parents had both the right and the duty to protect and educate their children; they also had the right to punish them within the limits of necessity. The children on their side had the duty to support their parents. This mutual duty of support was limited to ascendants, descendants, the spouse and parents of the spouse, brothers and sisters, and members of the *chia* (the family).

(6). With regard to succession, the law provided for an order of succession of four categories: (a) linear descendants; (b) parents; (c) brothers and sisters; (d) grandparents (Arts. 1138-1139).

(7). The surviving spouse ranked equally with a child, but if there were no children, he or she would inherit half the estate with the heirs of the second and the third categories or two-thirds in a case whether there were only heirs of the fourth category. (Art. 1144).

The new law to all intents and purposes prescribed the principle of equality between the sexes, saving that the man as head of the conjugal family was empowered with managerial rights over matrimonial property and, in the event of conflict with his wife, with rights overriding those of his wife. There was provision for maintenance and for guardianship of the children, but certain guarantees were given against the abuse of parental powers. Ancestor worship was eliminated from the law. It was policy to loosen the ties of the traditional family, but to preserve the family as an independent unit in the interests both of its members and of the nation. In short, the Code of 1931 is not aimed to destroy some of the fundamental principles of solidarity and cohesion in the family and relatives.

The presentation of the Family Law of the National Government serves as a contrast between this Family Law and the Marriage Law of the People's Republic of China promulgated on May 1, 1950 at Peking, China. There are some differences between these two laws, but their essential principles are not poles apart. Whereas the National Government expected that such a fundamental change could not be brought about through the law alone and that the people would be aware of their rights in the course of time and ready to assert them, the Communist Government has enforced the Marriage Law with rigour. When we look at the new State established in mainland China in 1949, we may assume that the family is to be abolished. In fact, imbued with the ideology of Marx, Engels, and Lenin, the Chinese Communists determined to make a drastic change in the family system. They accused the old family system of 'barbarism', including as it did the maltreatment and oppression of women by their husbands and mothers-in-law, and faithfully adopted Lenin's slogan that the success of a revolution depends on the extent to which women take part in it. This was the basis of the New Marriage Law, which was officially promulgated by the Chinese Communist Central Government at Peking on May 1, 1950. It was the first civil code announced by the Communist Party after the establishment of the People's Republic of China. Teng Ying-ch'ao, the wife of the former premier, Chou En-lai, acclaimed the Marriage Law as one of the achievements of the Communist Revolution and a reflection of the class consciousness of the oppressed workers, particularly women. She said:

The Marriage Law of the People's Republic of China is something China has never had in her past several thousand years . . . The law is a product resulting from our having driven out imperialism, overthrown the rule of the Kuomintang reaction, established a nation-wide scale the people's democratic dictatorship, and completed agrarian reform in areas inhabited by one-fourth of the country's poupulation. It represents the universal demand of the broad masses of our working people, especially our working women, with respect to the question of marriage.[26]

The cardinal principles of the Marriage Law are:

(1) The arbitrary and compulsory feudal marriage system which is based upon the superiority of man over woman and which ignores the children's interests shall be abolished.

(2) The new democratic marriage system, which is based on the free choice of partners, on monogamy, on equal rights for both sexes, and on

protection of the lawful interests of women and children, shall be put into effect. (Art. 1).

(3) Husband and wife are in duty bound to love, respect, assist, and support each other, to form a harmonious union, to perform labour and be productive, to raise children and to struggle for the happiness of the family and the building of the new society. (Art. 8).

The main provisions of the Marriage Law are as follows: bigamy, concubinage, child betrothal, and the exaction of gifts at marriage are forbidden. Widows are encouraged to remarry. (Art. 2). Since marriage is a completely individual affair, the intervention of a match-maker and the interference of parents are outlawed. (Art. 3). The required age for marriage is 20 for men and 18 for women. (Art. 4)[27] The article 5 decrees the prohibition against marriage with ascendants, descendants, brothers and sisters, and half-brothers and half-sisters (Art. 5). The restrictions on marriage pertain to sexual impotence, venereal disease, mental illness, leprosy, and similar physical disabilities. (Art. 5).

The other articles of the first chapter emphasize the quality in the choice of profession and participation in social and political activities. (Art. 9), and equal rights of ownership and management of the family property. (Art. 10). Each can retain his and/or her own surname. (Art. 11).

Article 13 stipulates the mutual duty of support between parents and children. This article also includes the prohibition against infanticide. (Art. 13).

No discrimination may be made between children of the present and those of a former marriage. (Art. 16). Divorce shall be granted when both partners consent. When the *ch'ü* registrar verifies whether divorce is petitioned by their own free will, whether the property of the spouses has been settled and whether proper arrangements have been made for the children, it issues a certificate of divorce without delay. After divorce the property the woman possesses before her marriage returns to her. Other family property is divided by agreement, or failing this, by decision of the Court. (Art. 23). If after divorce one of the parties who has not remarried plunges into financial difficulties the other is bound to support her or him. (Art. 25)

Article 12 and 14 recognize the right of spouses, parents and children to inherit from each other. (Arts. 12 and 14)

Article 15 in the fourth chapter provides clearly that illegitimate children shall have the same rights as those born in wedlock, that is, they are entitled to be brought up and be educated, and have the corresponding duty to support the parents. (Art. 15)

On the strength of the Marriage Law the family is conceived as a socialist cell, the first effort in China to forge the link between marriage, family and socialist society. The Marriage Law does not merely regulate the relations between husband and wife in material aspects; it is actually concerned with what role would the marriage and the family play.[28]

Looking at the legal provisions of the Marriage Law, it is ready to see that the family has undergone changes. The marriage system lays the foundation of the family system, while the families are component parts of society. The marriage system being also a constituent part of society, changes according as society itself changes. Likewise the family system built on society constitutes a system of socio-economic units, and it significantly influences the development of productive forces in society. The new-born society is in dire need of all the help it can get in political, economic and educational fields, and eventually it will transform China from poor, agrarian society into an affluent industrial society. By means and enforcement of the Marriage Law we shall accelerate the destruction of the old, feudal marriage system, establish a new family, and develop a new society. It is in this import that the new Marriage Law of the People's Republic of China is drafted and enacted.

Changes in the Family as a Result of the Marriage Law

The Communist Party took the view that marriage arranged by parents[29] is a bourgeois form and relegates woman to slavery. The features that the Communist government found most vicious in the old family system were lack of love in marriage, lack of freedom of marital choice, over-emphasis of masculine rights, and the subjugation of woman.[30] It encourages marriage for love so that the youth of China has enthusiastically adopted this new concept of romantic love.[31]

The Communist government maintains that love should not be personal or only ego-centered, but a social affair inseparable from politics. Accordingly, love between the sexes is to be oriented towards a common ideological and political interest. . . . The members of the Communist party are supposed to devote themselves completely to the Party rather than to their lovers.[32] It is written in *China Youth:*

Love is one part of life, and a constituent of happiness and must be built in mutual companionship and common interest. We revolutionary youth should frown upon a self-indulgent approach.[33]

Thus in the interest of the State young people are expected to be highly class conscious and should not permit personal love to interfere with revolutionary work and activities. Further in a state-centered or communal family system the state may meet no trammel in indoctrinating the youth with its totalitarian philosophy. We should bear in mind that Marxist historical materialism is resorted to as a justification for rapid industrialization and economic development. This underlies the efforts of the Communist government to undermine the traditional family system and thus weaken the authority of parents over children. As a result, industrialization may accelerate.

(a) Freedom to Select Marriage Partners. In accordance with the Marriage Law[34] women have equal rights with men in choosing marriage partners.[35] The Marriage Law attempts to revise the basis of the family system, to eliminate the feudal concept of women and to promote their economic, political, and marital freedom.[36] To implement these ideas, divorces have been made easy for those whose marriages are found to be feudalistic.[37] Today women's increasing participation in social production means that more women have more opportunity of meeting eligible men. Nevertheless, shy women still depend upon unofficial match-makers[38] who may be older relatives, neighbors, or friends of the family. In the earlier period of the Marriage Law, young people were not prepared for the new freedom in choosing marriage partners, and this sometimes made for a combination of the traditional and modern approach.

(b) The Liberation of Oppressed Women. The Communist Party has bitterly attacked the old marriage and family system which reduced women to slavery. [39] Taking a concubine was an economic status-symbol for men. Thus, wealthy men, businessmen as well as government officials, were found to possess as many concubines as they could afford. While highly-educated girls refused to tolerate concubinage, old-fashioned wives preferred to be left alone without divorce. This obviously reflects Engels' assertion that men never really practiced monogamy, but concocted social institutions to keep women in subjection.[40] Again, according to Engels, the legal inequality of the partners is not the cause, but the effect of the economic oppression of women.[41] In this connection, the Marriage Law prohibits concubinage and polygamy,[42] institutes monogamy as the only legal form of marriage.[43] In the past there was a widespread system of child marriage;[44] a young boy's family would take in a girl of about 10 years of age as a bond-maid. The girl would work in the family until she was old enough to be married formally. This custom served two purposes: the girl's family would be economically relieved, the boy's family was assured of a future daughter-in-law; the Marriage Law decrees that child bethrothal and the exaction of money in connection with it shall be prohibited, and offenders prosecuted.[45]

With regard to prostitution, Engels attributed it to the inequality of property under which wage labour appears side by side with slave labour, and, as its natural correlate, the professional prostitution of free women side by side with the forced surrender of the slave.[46] There is some evidence of the determination of the Chinese Communists to abolish prostitution.[47]

In 1951 when the government launched a campaign against prostitution there were about 60,000 prostitutes in Shanghai officially registered,[48] and there were still more unregistered prostitutes. In such cities, as Shanghai and Peking, houses of prostitution were raided, the owners and exploiters or pimps were punished or killed, and the girls set free or taught respectable trades and skills.[49] For prostitutes were not engaged in economic production but were social parasites. Foreign visitors to China said that there were neither night clubs nor striptease. Whereas in Western world venereal diseases are widespread, they have been wiped out in China. Dr. Ronald Ma said that from an early period until now, the prostitution in China was totally eradicated. The prostitutes left their profession either by the Communist persuasion or force. Yet instead of branding the prostitutes with infamy the Communist Party sympathized with them as being a victim of capitalism.[50] It was the Mao's thought that put an end to these social evils; and prostitution was abhorred as social evils in capitalist societies where prostitutes make venereal diseases rampant in large cities. In New York City, for instance, there are 4,000 prostitutes.[51] In Hong Kong there are 20,180 prostitutes according to the report of Chen Fei.[52]

(c) Abolition of Filial Piety. Filial piety, or respect for and assistance to the parents, fraternal love and devotion to one's spouse and children were considered essential elements of Chinese family solidarity. The incompatibility between family loyalty and the Communistic ideology led the Communists to take steps to eliminate these family virtues. The success of these measures was amply illustrated by the forced denunciation of persons by members of their own family, in the interests of the state which were a feature of the early years of revolution. The members of the Youth League exposed events happened despite the provision in the Marriage Law that the 'children have the duty to look after and to assist their parents'.[53] In late years this policy was mitigated, as it became clear that mutual surveillance had inevitably created mutual distrust and that the Communist Party's exploitation of youth had only served to broaden the gap between generations.

(d) Divorce. The Marriage Law provides that divorce shall be granted when both husband and wife desire it.[54] The enactment of this code justifies Engels' charge of man's supremacy when he wrote:

As a rule, it is n w only the man who can dissolve it, and put away his wife. The right of conjugal infidelity also remains secured to him at any rate by custom, and as social life develops he exercises his right more and more.[55]

In legalizing divorce by mutual consent, this article 17 aims at abrogating the inequalities of the sexes and introduces a drastic change in traditional Chinese society and the family. So great is the emphasis on divorce that there is an inclination to equate the Marriage Law with a divorce law. It was reported that in the years before the introduction of this law, the Peking court handled 887 family cases in a period of six months, 736 of which were divorce cases initiated by women.[56]

With regard to the increase in divorce cases, two points are of interest. First, the Communist authorities view such figures to demonstrate how women had suffered and how urgently they had struggled to liberate themselves from the family yoke. Second, since the Marriage Law grants divorce whenever requested, it seems deliberately to encourage men and women to seek new partners. This of course no longer applies in present day China. The actual situation will be described later.

The Communist Party contends that the underlying motive of the divorce petition is the struggle between progressive thinking and the conservative point of view. And the ideological cleavage between husband and wife tends to increase the rate of divorce. Further, the root problem of divorce is the belief that the Marriage Law undermines the traditional value of family chastity and the concept of mutual faithfulness of man and woman. Nevertheless this same family solidarity is at variance with the Communist ideology of 'collectivism'.

The preceding analysis demonstrates that the Marriage Law did affect the divorce rate; but it is the view of the Communist Party that the Marriage Law has been mistakenly equated with the legalization of divorce, and has not encouraged to seek divorce on trivial grounds.

4. THE COMMUNE AND THE FAMILY

> *With the completion of agricultural co-operation, many co-operatives are finding themselves short of labour. It has become necessary to arouse the great mass of women who did not work in the fields before to take their place on the labour front. . . . China's women are a vast reserve of labour power. This reserve should be tapped in the struggle to build a great socialist country.*
>
> MAO TSE-TUNG

Rural Commune

The rural people's commune is an organization which integrates government administration and economic management (Art 7 the Constitution); it is also a form of socialist collective ownership. Some people contend that communes should be called ' collective farms ' because they are simply enlarged agricultural co-operatives. Others refer to communes as ' state farms ' because, in the commune system, collective ownership is superseded by ownership by the whole people.[57] It must be noted that a commune is much larger in scope than an agricultural co-operative; it has large size and a higher degree of public ownership - these are two distinguishing characteristics of the people's communes. The commune system has been greatly modified and its size reduced for the sake of efficiency. Shukuang brigade has 707 households, comprising 2,769 people of whom 1,115 are able to work; the whole brigade is divided into 12 production teams, each of which has an average of 59 households.[58]

Marx held that the special features of the commune were government of the people by the people and expropriation of the expropriation; and this form of social organization would have paved the way for communism. Marx wrote:

The commune was a thoroughly expansive political form, while all previous forms of government had been emphatically repressive. It was essentially a working class government, the product of the struggle of the producers against the consumers, the definitive formula for working out the economic emancipation of labour.[59]

The nature of the people's commune is described in *Red Flag:*

The people's commune is a product of China's political and economic development, a product of the Communist Party's general life for building socialism and the big leap forward of socialist construction. The emergence of this new social organization marks a change of great historical significance in our society: its influence is felt in every sphere of the political, economic, and cultural life of our society.[60]

From the economic point of view, the people's commune has emerged as a result of both the success and failure of the advanced agricultural co-operatives;[61] the high production rates of these co-operatives created problem of handling and distribution of production.[62] The people commune established the system of distribution 'from each according to his ability and to each according to his work'.[63] For example, in the mess hall a worker may have plain rice and 50 per cent of his wages deducted, or rice with side-dishes and 60 per cent of his wages deducted. With regard to handling, the small agricultural co-operative has neither the means nor the manpower to control the development of productive power. Water conservation projects and the mechanization of agriculture cannot be achieved without the concentration of manpower and the accumulation of financial resources. The rural communes have, in short, introduced egalitarian distribution, collectivized all means of production, and provided the most effecient unit for managing small-scale industry, for mobilizing manpower for irrigation, and for procuring the internal savings necessary for financial investment.[64]

From the political point of view, each hsiang (township) has a commune, but in some cases an entire hsien (county) is organized into a large commune or a federation of communes. In Liaoning province, the entire 2,845 hsiang are merged into 1,226 hsien.[65] In Hopei province, the original 147 hsiang are to be merged into 70 to 80 counties.[66] Towards the end of 1958, over 26000 people's communes were established, representing 120 million households, over 99 per cent of the total household.[67]

Social organization of the Rural Commune

The general principle of commune is more or less the same. Here we present **the Chiliying People's Commune** as an illustration.[68]

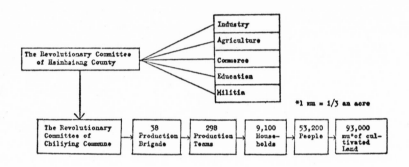

The Revolutionary Committee of the Chiliying People's Commune corresponds to the former Chiliying Township People's government and comes directly under the Revolutionary Committee of Hsinhsiang County; this oversees all activities within the commune, embodying industry, agriculture, commerce, education and military work. The industries of Chiliying Commune include its farm machinery repair and building plant, phosphate and fertilizer plant. A trade network supplies farm tools and machinery, chemical fertilizer and insecticide as well as quantities of consumer goods. Rural education is concerned with establishing schools and removing illiteracy of the peasants. The Chiliying militia regiment carries on its functions and training with productive labour.

Generally speaking, each production brigade of the Chiliying Commune comprises one village; every brigade is divided into production teams. Thus the commune, production brigade and production team are three levels of a people's commune. For ownership, the commune has also three levels: commune, brigade and production team each owning part of the means of production; but the production team is the basic. For the land belongs to the team and the distribution of income takes place chiefly within the team which is the basic accounting unit.

The brigade owns some larger and more expensive means of production, such as tractors, larger irrigation and drainage equipment; all are used in helping teams with their production. The Chiliying brigade, the largest in the Chiliying Commune, owns several tractors, a flour mill, brick and tile work, farm tool repair workshop and pig breeding farm. It has six tractors ploughing the land of its 34 production teams. The Chiliying Commune has a separate plant which repairs other farm machinery and manufactures some types, such as threshers and crushers. Other commune undertakings include a phosphate fertilizer plant and a spinning mill, some large scale irrigation and drainage facilities serving the whole commune and high voltage power lines with transformers and other accessories.

Blue-print of the Rural Commune

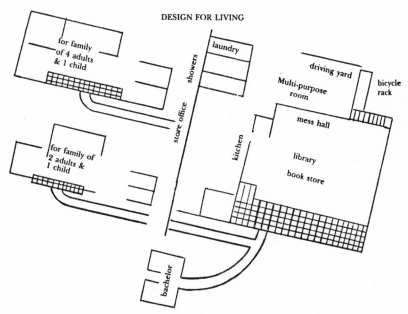

DESIGN FOR LIVING

Some houses in the Chinese living group are built for one family; others are for 2, 3, or 4 families. The public canteen is close at hand.

A commune near Shanghai with 70,000 to 100,000 people is reported to be the guinea-pig for the creation of this new Utopia, and a description of the plan was published in Shanghai 'Science Pictorial' The picture given is of an agricultural commune with little or no industry, forming an agro-town of up to 100,000 persons. At the bottom level are the living quarters or households of various sizes with varying numbers of rooms, grouped in single units or in terraces with three or four quarters in each. The living quarters have an independent entrance and all are provided with bright rooms facing south, light, water, and sanitary installations.

About a hundred households (500 persons), group round a mess hall, for the 'basic living group'. The mess hall can be used for eating or for drawing meals to be eaten in the living quarters. It also contains a boiling water service, a laundry with drying space, and showers or baths. The mess hall doubles as a recreation room and for other public purposes.

The next group up is the 'work team' of four 'living groups' or two thousand people. It has a crèche and a parade ground or assembly ground where the work team assemble to go off to work. This open space serves as a sports ground.

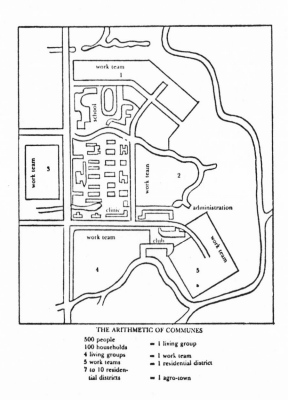

THE ARITHMETIC OF COMMUNES

500 people 100 households	= 1 living group
4 living groups	= 1 work team
5 work teams	= 1 residential district
7 to 10 residential districts	= 1 agro-town

Five work teams form the residential district, which provides the next layer of communal services. The plan lays down that each residential district should have a supply store, barber's shop, post office, bank, book store, tailor's shop, shoemaker, club houses, primary and secondary schools, an administration building, a broadcasting station, and a cinema.

Residential districts up to ten in number are to be grouped round a sort of civic centre to form the agro-town of 100,000 people. In this agro-town are to be established a cultural and educational centre, including a technical school, a cultural palace, an exhibition hall, opera house, sports stadium, science institution and library. There will also be a hospital and a large department store, together with the necessary administrative building which together will form the business centre of the town. The whole area will be turned into a garden city with the planting of fruit trees.[69]

Urban Communes

Economically, urban communes[70] are for the most part self-supporting. Capital is raised through savings, bank loans, reduction of distribution, the allocation of resources, the supervision of work, the creation of new products, the increase of capital accumulation, and contribution of means of production at cost price. Payments may be determined either by a fixed wage plus a productivity bonus, or by piece rates. It is required that the workers in state factories and schools and other agencies be members of the commune, even though they may not work in commune enterprises. For the most part they participate in repairs, service work, and ancillary production for state or other large factories. For example, the small work shops and many enterprises run in the past by the municipalities, until it comes through transition to 'ownership by the whole people'.[71] In brief, the urban communes, like the rural ones, serve to make the most intensive use of China's immense manpower, by engaging it in social production which requires little capital or equipment.

Experiments had shown that politically the urban communes could serve a useful purpose by the beginning of 1960.[72] On March 30, 1960, leading officials asserted that the urban communes had to be developed on a large scale, and the urban communes are of three types: those organized on the level of one or more big state factories, those formed around government organizations, or schools, and those composed of local residents. The urban communes which were made contiguous to the existing hsiang (township) governments encroached on many of their functions. Also the administration of the urban communes seemed to cut across existing administrative divisions.[73]

Socially, the people's communes, both rural and urban, were not only a system of collective ownership and a political instrument, but also a centre of community life. The Communist Party intended, by the establishment of people's communes in 1958, to break the system of the patriarchal family. They claimed not to have eliminated the family altogether, but to have replaced the old family with a new and rational small family in which true equality of the sexes, and marriage based on mutual admiration and love without regard to property and status have come true.[74]

Although the commune system was found at fault particularly in its administration and amended in 1959, its basic functions have remained unaltered. All people's communes have established community mass halls, kindergartens and nurseries.[75] With all the adults completely occupied in their own jobs, babies and young children have to be cared for in nurseries and kindergartens, so much so that parents have been deprived of their association as in the past with their children. As a result,the children may feel more at home in nurseries and kindergartens than in their own home. Since older women are incapable of doing whatever is beyond their physical strength, they have been assigned to look after the children in nurseries and kindergartens. Young children in schools were also compelled to join half work, half study program in which the hours of study dovetail to productive needs. The workers who lodged in dormitories could easily be observed in what they could with their leisure and how they spent their money. It was also much easier to bring pressure on families to send their children to nurseries and thus to limit their birth rate. With one day off a week and five days holiday a year, the rest for the workers was enjoyed to the full.

In the third textile mill in Peking, 70 per cent of their workers were women and most of them mothers, who, while working, committed their babies and young children to the nurseries and kindergartens of the mill, which built flats, dining-halls for their workers and the two storied buildings serving as nurseries. More than 490 infants and young children were accommodated. Infants from two months to three years of age entered the nursery, while young children three to six years of age are put in kindergartens.[76] The salary and other miscellaneous expenses of such workers as nurses, cooks and teachers, have been subsidized by the welfare department. Fifty-six days after the birth of a baby the mother was entitled to take her infant to the nursery.[77] The mother was permitted to take half an hour off twice a day in the morning and afternoon to nurse the baby at the crèche. In the day crèche the mother paid six yuan (Chinese dollars) a month for both care and food including milk and fruit; the low fee of the nursery was subsidized by workers' welfare fund.[78]

Likewise in the Flower Mountain Commune near Wu-han in Hupeh province there have also been commune hospital and brigade clinics; the hospital was staffed with a qualified full-time doctor who could perform stomach operations with acupuncture. Each brigade had its own primary school as well as collective health centre-simple clinic. Three of the 10 brigades also had junior middle schools. One school for the whole commune afforded education above junior middle school level.[79] As a result, housework has been gradually socialized, and women have been freed from their domestic chores; their emancipation has enabled them to participate in social production on a large scale,[80] and to attain equality with men. While there is equality of the sexes in that women have the same economic and political rights as men, there is also the separation of husband and wife at work for a considerable time; their engagement in work outside the home makes inroads upon their household work.[81]

In both rural and urban communes elderly people without families either live alone under the care of other families in their village, or live in government-subsidized nursing homes. In urban communes, special Neighborhood Committees assume responsiblity for their older residents. For a very elderly city resident whose children work in the daytime and often attend meetings at night one neighbor has done his cooking, young students wash his clothes, and other neighbors take charge of his housekeeping and cleaning chores. In rural communes, a special welfare fund is set up to meet the needs of members who are ill, retired, or incapable of working. These members are provided with food, lodging, pocket money and free medical care.[82]

Some comments may not be out of place about the value of emancipating women and their extensive participation in social production. The commune system has undoubtedly freed women from domestic labour and extended the field for their involvement in social labour. Their economic and social status is on the increase accordingly. On the other hand, the emancipation of women from household work may also influence their domestic happiness; nonetheless some women would react favourably to emancipation because having been imbued with Mao's thought they have been prepared to join social production. Again they can enjoy more freedom under Communism than in the past.

Within twenty-six years the emancipation of women occurs in three phases: one, the adoption of the new Marriage Law in 1950 emancipated women from the century-old feudal system of bondage; two, the Great Leap Forward of 1958 put a new face on women's emancipation; three, women's emancipation gained momentum during the Cultural Revolution in 1966. In the last phase women played a militant role together with men. The workers, cadres and technicians in their spinning and weaving shops remodelled equipment and increased the roving output in shifts by 30 percent.

Because the existence of the clan and its functions are incompatible with the Communist ideology, they became the object or target of Communist attack. Ancestral graves have been converted into farm lands, and economic life has been controlled by the state rather than by the clan. The clan has been deprived of its political power which has been surrendered to the state. The Communists have attacked the clan as the mechanism of the rich and puppet of the former corrupt government, and as the stronghold for the dominance by the older generations and by males. Thus the clan has been supplanted in its functions by the communes.

5. THE MODIFICATION OF THE COMMUNE

Marx and Engels intended to substitute for the bourgeois society another organizational form,[83] though their writings omitted any explicit statement regarding what it was to be. However, it is stated in the *Communist Manifesto* that 'in place of the old bourgeois society we shall have an association in which the free development of each is the condition for the free development of all.'[84] Again, the *Communist Manifesto* states explicitly that the proletariat will use its political supremacy to centralize all instruments of production in the hands of the state, i.e., of the proletariat organized as a ruling class, and that state factories will be extended according to a 'common plan.'[85] The same idea is expressed in the section on political economy in *Anti-Dühring* where Marx says that the colossal productive forces developed within the capitalist system . . . are merely waiting to be taken possession of by a society organized for cooperative working on a planned basis.[86] Moreover, at the end of the first chapter of *Capital*, Marx asserts that the life of society, which is based on the process of material production, is not stripped of its mystical veil until it is treated as production by freely associated men, and is consciously regulated by them in accordance with a settled plan.[87] This is a clear indication that the means of production will be held in common, and the 'settled plan' will establish the proper proportion between the different kinds of work in the planned society and the various needs of the community.

The Amendment of the Commune System

In this section our central interest focuses on the degree to which the Communist Party has instituted and modified the commune system. In Communist China, in applying the works of Marx, Engels, Lenin, and other socialists,[88] the Communist Party in 1958 introduced the system of the commune which was claimed to represent a stage in the development of the ultimate Communist form of common ownership and equal distribution according to *need*. In September and October 1958, various Chinese spokesmen looked not to contemporary Soviet writings but to the works of Marx and Engels to justify their path to ultimate Communism through the commune.[89] They contended that the Russians had forsaken classical Marxist ideological goals and were interested merely in building a modern, powerful economy. The emphasis of Chinese Communists on incessant struggle and experimentation is apparent in Mao's development of the Marxist-Leninist theory of uninterrupted revolution.[90] The transition to Communism is to be achieved by continuous struggle, by 'leap' forward, and by continuous experiments. The Marxist insistence, therefore, on ceaseless struggle seems to mark an unshakable adherence to the Marxist doctrine of ultimate Communism. However, inadequacies in the commune system and in the introduction of amendments to the system, indicate dysfunction in the commune and reflect the apathy of the masses.

Not only once, but three times, the people's communes have been amended and readjusted. The first modification occurred towards the end of 1958 and in the beginning of 1959, the second in early 1960. The first two were somewhat limited to readjustment in commune organization and method, whereas the amendment of the commune in August 1960 was accompanied by a political purge. The reasons for the adjustment are as follows:

(1) Recurring natural disasters resulted in a low yield of grain. In 1958 the peasants were compelled to adopt a three-year plan trying to reverse the downward trend in agricultural production. Yet when the three-year period was over, Peking's *Hsin hua News Agency* make it known that the country's agriculture in 1960 had suffered from 'serious natural calamities unparallelled in the past 100 years'.[91] In his speech, Chou En-lai acknowledged the shortcomings and mistakes in the organization of the communes.[92] Considering that agricultural output had failed to reach the targets first, a readjustment of the commune became inevitable [93]

(2) The modification was necessitated by the go-slow tactics adopted by the peasants. Many fields, for example, remained uncultivated in the autumn ploughing. According to the *New York Times*, articles published in Chinese magazines also uncovered mistakes made in forcing pastoral areas to concentrate on grain production at the sacrifice of traditional livestock breeding.[94] This naturally gave rise to bucolic discontent.

(3) Many Party officials became dissatisfied with the commune, and numbers of them conspired with the peasants to hide their products and engage in black market business; and in fact, they joined with the peasants in their resistance to Communist rule. The pronouncement of Secretary Chang vividly described this situation. From November 28 to December

10, in 1961 in order to vitiate internal crisis and external resistance the 6th Plenary Session of the Eight Communist Party Central Committee was held. Four decisions were in the end reached.

(a) Collective ownership still performed its positive function in terms of the development of production in rural areas. The transition from collective to private ownership by the people was determined by both productivity and the level of the people's political understanding. The Communist Party no longer approved of the free supply system which was praised in the past, but it took the view that, even after the transition, the people's commune would retain the differentiation of distribution system of 'to each according to his work' instead of 'to each according to his needs'. This system is at variance with the warning to workers by Marx and Engels that they would not receive the full value of the work they perform.[95] It can further be argued that if distribution varies with the amount of work one accomplishes, the Marxist theory of equality is open to debate. So we may deduce that China is still under socialism rather than communism. Marxist theory postulates that socialism pre-dates communism; under socialism it is necessary to apply certain incentives, and the doctrine remains still 'to each according to his work'. There is still the question how great the material incentives should be and of what kind. Chinese workers are paid on the basis of their ability and labour, but the Chinese view links them with a worker's political attitudes. Over the past years there has been an increasing emphasis on paying workers piece rates. In a commune those who have contributed more labour and more value have been paid higher wages than those who have offered less labour. A semi-skilled worker at a factory is earning more than a highly skilled needlewoman doing intricate embroidery. When the woman is asked if she thinks it is fair, she says it is, because the factory worker has contributed more to production. In industrial plants the workers of light industries are paid monthly in a range from thirty to one hundred and four dollars of people's money. Heavy industrial workers in Northeast China have received monthly wages ranging from sixty-two to one hundred and forty dollars.[96] But in Chinese social theory this would not deviate from socialism but would be merely a variation on it. Socialism is a philosophy which assumes that human beings will work hard in the interest of society, and not only to gain benefits for themselves as individuals.[97] In America the incentive for people to work hard is private profit, and although profit is excluded in China, people still work terribly hard. Expecting no high financial rewards, the people associate their work with political progress. The principle 'to each according to his work' is not limited to material reward-money. Chinese officials decisively reject the term 'material incentive'; they insist that people should and do work for the good of the community and not for personal gain. What is more valued than money is a government's reward of the 'model' worker. In a commune near 'Tachai', Shensi province people devoted their time and energy to cultivate their allotted plot of land at the negligence of commune land; although the total produce is higher than that of other communes, the people have been criticized as revisionists.[98]

(b) The Communist Party temporarily abandoned its original aim of putting an end to private ownership. This is revealed in an editorial in the Peking *People's Daily* of August 17, 1959,[99] which proclaimed that items owned by members of a commune, such as houses, clothing, bedding, furniture, and even bank deposits would always remain personal property after they had joined the commune.[100] Ownership of most of the production means was shifted from the commune to the 'productive brigades', that is, the former collectives composed of 20 to 30 families.[101] Free markets were allowed to re-open. André Piettre wrote:

> In order to give this peasant back his taste for effort, his village was first given back to him, this village forming the unit of the co-operative or production brigade about 50 to 3,000 persons who enjoy a fairly large autonomy. In the same way, a part or least of his patch of ground was given back to the peasant for his personal farming comparable to the 'dvor' for the peasant of the Kolkhozes (collective farms).[102]

Chou En-lai put forward 'Ten Tasks' for the adjustment of the National Economy in 1962. Among these he stressed the increase of agriculture production of grain, cotton, and family necessities, such as food, clothing, pots, pans and even pins.[103] Each household was permitted to keep its private cooking stove. Small plots of land were returned to individual households for private cultivation. The private plot that a peasant belonging to a commune retains as his own property is limited to one twenty-fourth of an acre. Private plots took up some 5 per cent of the land, but probably accounted for 10 per cent of total national production, especially of vegetables, pigs, poultry and eggs.[104] The Constitution stipulated that ' . . . people's commune members may form small plots for their personal needs, engage in limited household side-line production. . . . '(Art. 7).[105]

(c) The duties of the brigade officials have been diminished. Production teams bore responsibility for basic accounting and power to decide on production and distribution.[106] This inevitably reduced the duties of brigade officials. But their primary function would be to stimulate the initiative of every party member, and to strengthen Party leadership within the whole brigade.[107]

The main purpose of the preceding adjustment of the communes was to re-affirm the 'three-level ownership with production brigades as the basis', which was drafted earlier in the *Liberation Magazine* as follows:

> The amount of production contracted by the production teams should be handed over to the production brigade for unified distribution; with the exception of a certain proportion which should be handed over to the brigade, all the surplus production and the extra income of the production teams are to be kept by the teams themselves.[108]

This suggests that the communes were maintained only in name and that the main ownership, administrative management, and authority were definitely returned to the production brigades. The tendency towards economic autonomy becomes even more striking in the current situation in the Chinese mainland. Here, although a continued emphasis was placed on people's communes in all governmental pronouncements, it was quite clear that these large collective farms or communes existed in name only. From the beginning of 1962, the fundamental productive unit had reverted to the 'productive team', consisting of 20 to 30 peasant families. These teams resemble the cooperative, established in 1955. Unlike communes, which are usually directed by Communist Party officials, these teams are mostly managed by a working farmer who has better knowledge of local conditions and resources.[109]

Once the production team became the basic accounting unit, the principal means of production was given to these teams, They then had the power to decide their production and distribution.[110] This assuredly reduced both nature and scope of brigade officials' duties. Thus the problems between the brigades and the production teams could be dealt with by the method of democratic centralization, but compulsory means could not and should not be adopted. Although ninety per cent of China's farms were said to be organized into communes, the liberal economy within this system did not decrease, nay, it loomed even larger. The Communist Party was anxious about the dangers of deviation from the socialist road. Journal after journal scrutinized the economy to identify danger points such as 'abuse' of private plots and rural free trade, the reluctance of individuals to operate through cooperatives and manipulation and speculation in the socialist sector. This reflects Peking's uneasiness with the 'capitalist' character of the small agricultural production teams that have helped to increase production, whereas simultaneously reducing central control and discipline over the peasantry.[111]

Tao Chu, a prominent Communist official brought to the public the importance of the commune system which was to be introduced when the level of agricultural production was raised.[112] Undeniably the state controls production and distribution under central planning,[113] but it is equally true that private ownership of certain means of livelihood belongs to individual households.

(d) To amend the commune system, the Communists decreed that 8 hours for sleep each day and half a day's rest each week had to be guaranteed to peasants. This serves to discount the alleged picture of a commune as a place where regimented 'blue ants' work till they drop, building dams by day and forging steel by night.[114] The 'Mar Chiao' commune which covers an area of 3,224 hectares, about 15 miles north-west of Shanghai is a show case selected for visits by Western journalists, and more than 6,700 families and 28,000 individuals live and work there. Their average working day is said to be nine hours, though it varies with the season: women have six days leave a month and men four days; the average earnings of each employee is about 240 dollars (some $140) a year. In addition, each worker is entitled to a private plot land measuring 66 square metres. The crops from these plots, if sold, can augment the peasant's earnings by about 20 per cent.[115] Production costs range about 33 per cent of the commune's total income. Apart from paying seven per cent of the aggregate income to the government the remainder is divided among the members.

This 'Mar Chiao' commune is headed by a director and is organized into 26 big production brigades, each averaging 200 to 300 families, and 22 smaller production brigades, each made up of 30 to 40 families. Each big production brigade has its own administrative board or committee democratically elected by the members.[116]

The commune system has plunged a mass of peasants into the gigantic organization which turns over the principal role to the production teams; the production team is the collective owner of the land they cultivate, and of the draught animals and agricultural implements; it is incumbent upon the team to decide the cultivation of crops and the distribution of work; and being salaried persons, the peasants report to the team directors who assess their work and pay them their wages either in cash or in kind.[117]

The 'Lu Ku Chiao' (The Marco Polo Bridge) commune was used by the Communist Party as another showcase. About 6 per cent of the land was divided into private plots, tiny but enough to grow more for consumption or sale. Its land was fully used for vegetables as well as for piggeries and young orchids; this particular commune portrayed, ordered contented and successful communal farming. New houses were constructed on the site; simple structures about 40 ft. long were divided into two or three rooms, which, it is said, were built by the production teams, working under a skilled builder in five days.[118]

In a commune near Sian, Shensi province, there are 11 administrative units or brigades: a brigade consists of 5 villages, 7 production teams, and 356 households with 1,812 members; and 2,750 mou of land (about 460 acres) are cultivated by the members. Each commune is a self-sufficient unit; the families work together, and even the leaders take part in the field; members are provided with adequate food and clothing; each brigade establishes a health station offering medical care at normal cost; children are indoctrinated and educated in commune schools and adolescents are completely disciplined and involved in social production. They travel to other parts of the country to lend a hand, whenever needed, on large projects, such as dams, canals and bridges. A propaganda team in each brigade is responsible for political education; brigade members discuss ways of improving farm production and their lives.[119]

Most of rural China now lives under the commune system. A single commune may consist of only a few villages or more than 200 organized in brigades, each brigade, a Revolutionary committee representing the army, the party, and the peasants. Thus the commune is the body in which the Communist Party has been organized in rural areas, served by subsidiary organizations, especially the youth and women's Leagues and also by the three organizational levels of commune, brigade and the team. These three levels serve as agricultural machinery repair and manufacturing network, and should repair and manufacture at county level, repair and assemble at commune level, and merely repair at brigade level, that is, minor repair work should be carried out within the brigade, medium work within the communes and major work at county level enterprises.[120] According to Chinese press reports in 1971, 90 per cent of the counties have set up fledgling three-level networks, but it seems to take some time before all the stations are fully equipped with machine tools and manned with skilled workers.[121]

In Kwong-li commune in Kao-yao district, Kwangtung province, water and fertilizer must be brought to the hills because the land in the mountain is not fertile enough for peasants' production teams to make a living. Men, women and children are Hakkas from the hills, who number one-sixth of the commune's total population of 42,000 souls. The vice-Chairman of the Revolutionary Committee said that 2,850 hectares of the commune produced 23 million kilos of rice in 1972 against an output of 20.5 million kilos in 1965. The commune kept 13 million kilos of grain for its own use in 1972. The rest had been sent to the state.[122] The state brings pressure to bear on the commune for better agricultural results. The target was raised from the national plan by the regional authority and then transmitted through the county government to the commune and its 28 production brigades and 221 production teams. The commune members are also encouraged to work private plots on a household basis. The average size of private plots was 0.3 hectares, but each household was allotted extra land to rear pigs and poultry and grow vegetables according to the number of mouths. Although the distribution of earnings from agriculture is regulated on a basis of large income inequalities within the commune, the official policy sees to it that every member is offered the necessities of life.

Mechanization is a more complex problem; it is the state that determines the annual volume of machinery and other industrial products for agriculture. Agricultural mechanization appears to be achieved where the greatest amount of labour is being used. Hence such operations as ploughing and hoeing should be mechanized only, but mechanization should conform, first, to the county's condition of intensive farming and be suited to the varied natural conditions; secondly, it should be produced in medium and small factories and the big ones alike. Given the present limited capacity for making farm machines, this manufacture should play an important role in agricultural production, save more manpower, use up less material, and require the shortest time to build.[123]

The Kwong-li commune produced educated young people capable of modernising its farming methods; it has 6,000 children in primary school and 1,350 in middle school, and 32 of its youngsters attend university. Unfortunately a proportion of children stops short in their education at the primary level because their families need more hands to accumulate the work points in the fields.[124]

There are problems about incentives because of this theory of the commonwealth.

(1) The work point system was adopted in the early 1960s and has not been discarded ever since; points record the tasks performed each day by the individual peasant. Work points are used in agriculture to goad the peasants into fighting tooth and nail in the fields. Until recently, the highest number of work points (wages that are converted into cash, food, etc . . .) a woman could receive was eight, whereas a man could earn up to ten. At Red Star Commune, about 80% as many women receive ten points as among the men; yet due to the housework that has left women little time to spend in the field they can scarcely compete equally with men.[125] As for cash distribution, the production team is unaware how much cash will be available for distribution among its members until the harvest and other products have been sold. After the production team has paid taxes on an annual basis and made contribution to various commune funds, it will distribute the remainder among the members according to the work points they accumulated.

Probably about 60 per cent of the output of Chinese agriculture is distributed every year on the basis of the work point accumulated by each member of production team and harvests. Part of the output is allocated to meet the costs of fertilizer or new machinery and also to keep up the village's welfare funds and reserves. Only 25 to 30 per cent of the crop is delivered to the central and provincial governments or authorities.

This quantity of produce which represents and meets the agricultural tax ranges between 5 per cent and 15 per cent of the harvest. Each province is encouraged to be self-sufficient and self-reliant. Supposing the annual crop yields 150 million tons of grain, these 80 million tons are dealt with at the local level, and 70 million tons is distributed within the province of its origin. It is estimated that only about four million tons of grain go across provincial boundaries. During the Cultural Revolution when the mayor of Shanghai appealed to the Communist Party Committee of Chekiang province for urgent supplies of foodstuffs, the First Secretary of that province retorted: 'Chekiang is not a colony of Shanghai'. [126] In fact, not all communes have the same fertile soil and the same irrigation and drainage system, so that a yield per acre cannot be the same. Hence the range of wage differs, though the peasants in poor communes work as well hard as those in rich communes. This shows that the principle 'to each according to his work' cannot fully be realized. In face of this problem Peking has to winkle out all the surplus gain from these opulent provinces, such as Szechuan, Kirin and Heilungkiang and to organize its transport to the areas needed. The government tries to hurdle this problem by a seven per cent tax levy on the produce of rich communes, whereas poor communes have paid only 2 per cent of produce in taxes.

Small collectives - teams - still remain the mainstay of agriculture. The levelling of land, made feasible through the introduction of machinery and large-scale irrigation and drainage systems has made modern large-scale agriculture possible; and responsibilities are thus transferred from teams to brigades and further to communes. Prerequisite now is the elimination of the considerable differences which still exist between teams even when they are geographically contiguous.

(2) Another problem the state has to solve with the communes is corruption and the communes' financial mismanagement, that is, from the account-keeping and maintenance of the work point system. Party workers had to be sent from cities to rural communes; for the cadres of production teams sometimes take advantage of their authority for personal gain. The government endeavours to brace and purify the commune system from the seeds of revisionism shown by tendencies to relaxation-the campaign of 'Si-ching' translated as the 'four clean-ups movement' in the communes. [127] The cleaning-ups aim at capital construction in the political, economic and organization fields according to the principle of thorough-going socialist revolution and a profound class education among the masses; as a result, proletarian ideology must be promoted and bourgeois ideology eradicated. A Chinese pamphlet asks: 'Is our society today thoroughly clean?' The answer is negative; classes and class struggle still remain, and we can still see speculative

activities by old and new bourgeois elements and desperate forays by embezzlers, grafters and scroungers. According to David Bonavia, in rural China officials have difficulty in finding signs of class struggle. At a commune in Kiangsi province a work brigade leader called attention to the existence of rich peasants in his brigade and to the struggle between them and the poor and the lower middle peasants. In reality, rich peasants were here no longer in existence. Some of them were indeed employed as labourers without rights of commune members until they endured the brain washing. So what class struggle seemed really to mean was that conflict between two types of attitude, the selfish and public spirited. Bonavia told us what the theatrical sketch 'Half Baked Peanut' purports to mean that a young girl and her mother endeavour to divert this small luxury from the commune's joint earnings to their own use.[128]

Another instance in point is: the Tachai people's commune can illustrate how capitalist elements still exist in many communes. The village of Tachai with hardly over 800 families is in Hsiyang county, Shensi province. A small number of Party bigwigs were allegedly still hankering for capitalism and deprecated the thought of Mao. In Tachai commune there was a struggle between the two classes, and two Party lines from two headquarters. In 1964 a group worked out a reactionary line 'left in form and right in essence'. Tachai was on the socialist road as a brigade, but it encountered thorny problems: there were staff grievances and Party members who lodged false accusations against the cadres at the basic level and then brought pressure on the poor and lower middle peasants in an effort to sow discord between the cadres and the masses; anyone opposed to their directives was branded as counter-revolutionaries or degenerate. The handful of Party bosses accused the Tachai people of concealing the acreage of their arable land and giving false figures of their total output.

(3) Here the problem is concerned with a rich peasant economy. After the Great Cultural Revolution there was in rural communes a vast individual peasant economy and a rich peasant capitalist economy; the latter insisted on taking the capitalist road and espoused revisionism.[129] In Hopei province a propensity towards egalitarianism was rife. A good many communes fell short of the principle of 'to each according to his work', and a secondary production of the family was crushed.[130] In Yunnan province an almost insurmountable obstacle contrary 'to each according to his work' was excessive egalitarianism.[131] In Ninhsia autonomous region, the principle 'to each according to his work' and an exchange of equal value could not be put in practice; many peasants of communes were prevented from such side-line economic activities as growing crops and raising domestic fowls from private allotments.[132]

Worse still, peasants were loath to increase the yield per mou (1/3 an acre); instead, they exaggerated their grain output year after year, so that the total volume had decreased. On the other hand, due to competition for more honorable records of grain output, peasants neglected their secondary production. The sequel was that the yield appeared higher, while the average income of brigade members declined considerably. So the central committee demanded a revision of the total production programme, that is, both the average productive quantity of each individual and the total volume of production.[133] These shortcomings threw light on the reason why Chou En-lai complained of the 4 per cent decline in total grain output during 1972.[134] In fact, neither in 1969 nor 1970 did the total output of grain increase. A question is: Has China ever reached egalitarianism? A foreign newsman wrote from Peking: 'In a society that professes to be the world's most egalitarian' there is a striking departure from it in China. There are eight monthly grades ranging from 14 dollars (people's currency) for apprentices to 285 dollars for the most senior officials'. Likewise an army unit in Szechuan province admitted at the end of February 1975 that bourgeois rights - the opportunities for individuals to enjoy different incomes levels - were retained under socialism. In fact, the People's Republic of China has never claimed egalitarianism, let alone having the most of it. The shocking inequality of centuries between a privileged few and poverty-trodden masses has been done away with.[135] However, great efforts are being made to restrict and whittle down the unequalness. Yao Wen-yuan has warned that should the 'bourgeois rights' be strengthened in any way, a small number of people will acquire increasing amounts of commodities and money through certain legal channels and numerous illegal ones. . . . Public property will be turned into private property, and speculation, graft and corruption, theft and bribery will rise'.[136]

The Agriculture Production and Commune

(1) Fertilizer. Fertilizer is one of important factors that increase the yield per acre. Although the yield per acre in any commune increases by means of irrigation canals and crop rotations, the Chinese have always relied on natural fertilizer, both animal and human manure, but the Chinese have a distrust of too regular a use of artificial fertilizer: for instance, in the Sino-Albania Friendship Commune outside Peking, the cadre director cast doubts on the overuse of fertilizer; such attitudes may well account for lagging fertilizer production. Despite her basic need for 40,000,000 tons of fertilizer a year according to European Nitrox, China produced in 1972 only between 10,000,000 and 12,000,000 tons.[137] Production in tons is as follows:

1949	27,000
1955	426,000
1960	2,500,000
1966	5,500,000
1968	4,800,000
1969	5,800,000
1970	7,400,000
1971	9,600,000
1974	30,000,000

Nowadays many Chinese are employed in the fertilizer plants. Perhaps with the help of East German model there is a new drying rotary kiln, made in China for the urea-making process; the area has a 40 per cent nitrogen content. At the industrial exhibition in Shanghai one can see developments in azotobacterial* fertilizer. Research is being carried on the problems of human waste disposal and recycling; an analysis of wastes is being made for toxic and nutrient composition, and is concerned about the effects of spreading slurry on the land.

China's peasants need to be trained for the application of chemical fertilizer as against manure-the supply of which is limited. Although the growth of large numbers of small fertilizer plants is remarkable, China still imports large quantities of chemical fertilizer and has scouted around for potash.

The land shortage in China raises interesting question: What impact does a cemetery exert on commune property? Where arable and fertile land has become commune property, 'burial' lots are not permitted and the peasants have been persuaded to remove the old graves of their family from fields needed for cultivation. Cemeteries which have encroached in course of time on the environs of the city have also been removed.

(2) The land shortage. The obstacle to cremation is the reluctance of the masses whose religious beliefs the Communist Party has stigmatized as the remnants of feudal thinking. In traditional China 65 thousands mou of land (13,000 acres of land) are occupied by graves. One mou yields 300 kg of grain. Under the given conditions 19.5 million kg of grain which is adequate to feed 110,000 people for a year could be grown upon the land taken by graves in China; and 3.25 million square meters of timber are used for coffins, a colossal quantity of timber that would suffice to build 325,000 rooms in homes;[138] 9.75 million kg of iron nails, 65

---

* Azotobacterial is a genus of large flagellated from negative rod-shaped bacteria occurring in soil and sewage that fix atmosphere nitrogen in the presence of carbohydrates and derive growth energy from oxidation of carbohydrates.

million man-days for labour and 6.5 million kg of varnish and paint are expended annually for making coffins;[139] so a considerable sum of money and material could be saved, if cremations were introduced. Considering the ritualistic extravagance of funerals, the government has taken strong measures against them and converted cemeteries into arable land in rural communes. A report says that cemeteries still remain in some communes, though the government has encouraged people to resort to cremation. There is no permission for burial mounds, and graves instead must be flattened so that vegetables can grow there.[140]

We may adduce that the present leaders have shown keen interest in commune system. Nevertheless on the basis of the foregoing analysis it may be assumed that in future the commune will tend to operate primarily as an administrative unit, engaging in industrial activities which are supported by the farm units' functioning.

The Social and Economic Function of Collectives

Millions of Chinese can benefit from the balance of industry and agriculture. The small-scale industry serves agriculture, and makes the machines the agriculture needs and supplies necessary fertilizer. All this can be done within the old administrative unit of the county (hsien-district) with a population ranging from 200,000 to 500,000 in the most populated areas.[141] Apart from the supply of fertilizer the most important task the small-scale industry has performed is the service station operated by the commune, where repair and maintenance are the main tasks. There can be no doubt that this economic pattern has shown considerable results. The arguments of self-help or self-reliance, the maturing experience of effective local industry since the great leap forward in 1958 together with the growth of local political initiative, the sequel of the Cultural Revolution, have all combined to afford China much stability.

Not every area is capable of establishing repair and maintenance networks without outside help; however, central subsidies in the form of finance and the transfer of skilled workers and used equipment are a matter of course.[142] In areas where the land is enormously fertile, agriculture has developed very rapidly. In Kiangsu and Chekiang provinces the countryside is emerald green with young wheat, fruit and vegetables in abundance. The surplus of farming produce and ample raw materials make more industry possible. On the other hand, some areas have a rather poor economic foundation, so that intermediate administrative units will build more factories there. Still other areas have industries run by the province or state. The agencies for internal distribution of produce are handled by the commercial departments of the provincial and municipal governments who act as the natural coordinating agencies between demand and supply. Given these circumstances regional authority can go too far. Time and again *Red Flag* protested against those who regard the area they administer as an independent realm.[143] Yet one should not mistake this independence for anything apolitical. Local loyalties have traditionally been encouraged with sound economic initiative and development; party administration at the local levels progresses with much more confidence than it yet does in the provincial capitals. Under such circumstances, the communes would gradually be superseded by the collectives. The indication that the government has revived the people's communes was revealed in an article published in both *Red Flag* and *People's Daily*. This official announcement should prove that China is still a great distance from the Communist ideal of a classless society.

From the preceding description and research we come to the following conclusion: first, the commune or its variant will not vanish in spite of its many deficiencies and continual modifications; second, there is no doubt that China has succeeded remarkably in removing the traditional family system to help industrialization and make women participate in production in rural and urban areas. Third, weakening a good deal the traditional family, the Chinese Communists have not destroyed the family as an economic unit as well as a social unit, but established nurseries and kindergartens where old women are called for taking care of babies while their mothers are free to work outside home. Fourth, as all Chinese families have joined communes in productive units, they have had a stable base of agriculture and small-scale industry that is self-reliant. The family continues to be an economic unit, though the state has brought home to people the greater importance of the state.

6. THE IMPACT OF POPULATION POLICY ON THE FAMILY

> *To protect women and children and bring up and educate our younger generation in a way conductive to the health and prosperity of the nation, we agree that a due measure of birth control is desirable.*
> CHOU EN-LAI

The Malthusian theory of population presents a melancholy picture; Malthus ascribed the suffering of the poor to the fact that food supplies could not keep pace with the increase of population. Marxists, on the other hand, maintained that what causes the suffering of the poor lies not with any deficiency of nature but with production, which fetters the development of productive forces; the true cause, in fact, is social, not natural. Population growth would not be a problem, if the Marxist hypothesis were true; and it was on such a basis the Chinese Commuinists believed population increase to be an asset in a country with vast new lands and unexplored natural resources.[144] Population growth, they feel, threatens resources only in countries under the capitalist system of production in which the masses are denied the benefits of technological development, while under socialism the benefits of technological development are equally distributed among the workers, who are the producers of all wealth. Yet the Communists seem to have shown great flexibility in modifying Marxist orthodox doctrine in the face of the rapidly rising population.[145]

(1) Birth Control. The birth control programme in China aroused great surprise in the Western world.[146] Many authors who adopted the Marxist theory that 'man is the nation's greatest wealth' attempted to clarify their position. In fact, the dissemination of knowledge about birth control had nothing in common with either Malthusian or neo-Malthusian theory;[147] but the knowledge of birth control was mainly intended to improve the health of mothers and infants, and to allow mothers more time for work and study. Throughout 1955, numerous articles on contraception were published in various magazines, with the object of encouraging the masses to practise contraception. In February 1958, one newspaper editorial admitted that the total provision of contraceptives available in China was enough for only 2.2 per cent of all those in reproductive age groups. Another report states that reliable contraceptives are recommended for general use. This apparently runs counter to Marxist theory.

The method of contraception used in China since the Cultural Revolution includes a wide range of oral contraceptives. In 1970 two birth control pills made from progesterone and oestrogen were on hand in some areas, and it is said that their effectiveness has approached 99.56 per cent. The pills were to be taken for 22 days beginning with the fifth day of the menstrual cycle; a few women reported side-effects from these pills, which were said to disappear in proportion as the body adjusted to the hormonal changes.[148] On his visit to China in the winter of 1970-1971, Edgar Snow was told by a Peking doctor that the 22-day pills were immune from side-effects and 100 per cent effective when taken in accordance with instructions, but that irregularity in pill-taking was far too frequent.[149]

The Shanghai Health Clinic reported that a contraceptive injection made also from progesterone and oestrogen came into use in 1970. Although it was 98.59 per cent effective, it produced side-effects in a few cases, such as irregular menstrual cycle. At the time of Snow's visit, the Japanese development of a vaginal pill using prostaglandin aroused keen interest in Chinese medical research personnel.[150] The evidence of serious research in this fertility control technology is incontestable.

Intra-uterine devices of metal and plastic are still available in China, though they are regarded as about 80 per cent effective. The metal devices can remain for 4 to 6 years, and the plastic ones for 2 years; nevertheless they are insuitable for women with ulcerated cervix, inflammation of the uterine cavity, or vaginitis. Conventional contraceptives such as condoms, diaphrams and spermicides are also available, but these devices are likely to be replaced gradually by newer ones that are more convenient.[151]

As for abortion, it should not be counted on in place of contraception. The official policy stipulates that it may be performed when contraceptive measures have failed, or when a woman is unfit to give birth. But the woman was cautioned about the hazard the operation may bring to health.[152] Actually a considerable effort has been made to increase the suction abortion-facient machines throughout the country. During his last visit to China, Snow bore witness to the fact that abortion has now been performed without charge on demand of the mother alone.[153]

Sterilization was available for both men and women. In the rural areas 'barefoot' doctors bring contraceptives and the operation to the peasants by means of mobile operation rooms where are prepared basic surgical equipment and instruments.[154] In 1973 abortion and operation for voluntary sterilization including hospitalization and gynaeocological X-Ray examinations were freely offered. Factory workers and staff members drew direct pay during the sick leave.[155] To banish disgust at sterilization, the Shanghai Health Clinic instructed applicants to have 'three straightening-out treatments,' that is, straighten out the thinking of the applicant, of his family and of the old folk so as to get rid of all apprehensions.[156] Literature about sex knowledge is widespread at present moment.

(2) Planned Parenthood. Feudal society granted women no say in their own fate. Their position could not be enhanced unless they give birth to a male child; failing this, they would be spurned by their husband as well as by their parents-in-law. Since China's liberation, the feudal oppression of women has met a bitter attack; innumerable women have been emancipated and gained economic independence. Nowadays planned parenthood is in vogue and universally supported. The present policy of the Communist government as to size of family has stipulated no more than two children as ideal. Family planning keeps the growth of population within the bounds of living standards; in China it is rather a new idea. Efforts to limit population growth where one out of every four people in the world is Chinese are not obstinately thwarted by some of the old ways between the sexes. Nevertheless we admit of some obstacles, such as the traditional Chinese large family and preference for male children that have to be hurdled in persuading people to have fewer children.

More medical and health workers are trained and more clinics set up to enlighten people about birth control and contraceptives. 38 per cent of all streets in Shanghai have set up co-operative health centers and have trained 30,000 health workers in the past few years. Lo-ting county of Hopei province in North China has equipped the county hospital and commune clinics with 435 gynaecologists and health workers for mother and child care. Likewise, in Kao-ping of Shansi province, the country and rural communes have all established 250 clinics to guide people in birth control.[157] Medical workers, scientific and technical personnel have succeeded in testing oral contraceptives which have proved reliable in clinical tests. The policy of family planning has brought good results; there has been some drop in the rate of population growth in densely populated areas: it is 4.8 per thousand for Shanghai and surrounding countryside; 9.7 per thousand for Peking and surrounding countryside; 12 per thousand for Kiangsu province. The government believes that family planning benefits many aspects of life: National construction, the emancipation of women, protection of mothers and children, and better health for the people. It is, in a word, in the interests of the people.[158]

(3) **Does Birth Control Break up Family Solidarity?** In traditional China, as a result of the veneration of ancestors and the need for increasing labour, there existed an overwhelming desire to beget sons. The Communists, however, have endeavoured to control the high birth rate, which is regarded as an obstacle to economic development. The following comments on the possible consequences suggest themselves.

A reduction in the number of people within a family would weaken its solidarity. Durkheim developed this principle in his analysis of group unity and group feeling. He held that the greater the diversity of relatives the closer the links attaching the individual to the group.[159] Our hypothesis is that the larger the number of persons living together in a family, the more family solidarity tends to develop and the stronger becomes the position of the father as the directive authority. By the same token, a family which has been limited by birth control will suffer from the point of view of solidarity. Again the larger the family group the more cohesive it is, and the more dominant are one or two members. A large group of persons of differing ages and sexes requires some degree of organization and authoritarian control. This may mean a dominant role for the father, the mother, or possibly an older brother. This would suggest that the authoritarian family, symbolic of Chinese society, was originally the product of the large family.

Another hypothesis is that the large family tends to perpetuate traditional family virtues and mores. What one can do depends upon what others do. Filial piety can be instituted more readily in a large family and reinforced by faimly codes. Strict restraint has decreased in Chinese society juvenile delinquency. Undoubtedly as the size of the family is compulsorily limited, the government birth control policy will no longer be necessary.

Birth control frees women from enslavement and introduces voluntary planned parenthood. This freedom has enabled women to enter factory work, and with their entry into outside production, the single family ceases to be the economic unit of society. As we have seen, the interruption of family functions weakens the interdependence of members and the solidarity of the family group, as may be well verified by the high rate of divorce in the beginning of the Communist Revolution. However, we cannot safely assume that the Chinese family is weaking and its ties are breaking. As in industrial societies the Chinese family at present has become a small residential group for which life has waned in many respects: the commune, the factory, the office, the school and the hospital have dissociated the family members for many hours a day and changed relationships and interests. In other words, modern China has reduced child care activities, amusement, recreation and emotional exchange within the family.

Smaller families do not imply the disappearance of filial piety and the loss of binding family virtues. There can be no denial that the Communist Revolution at first assailed the feudal nature of Chinese family structure; the divorce rate was also rampant owing to the practice of child marriage and enforced marital alliance. Worse than that were women oppressed by parents-in-law and the absolute authority of husbands. A few years after the Revolution the Communist government has evidently reversed its original policy on the family. For example, the government is loath to grant divorce without convincing grounds, so we now embark on examining to what extent the Communist authorities have altered its original policy in this matter.

The Marxist Doctrine of Population in China

Let us now analyze the effect of population growth in China alongside Marxist doctrine, which attributes the population problem entirely to the capitalist system. The central interest lies in exploring some political implications involved in industrial development. The vacillation of official policy on population, particularly on birth control, marks a fundamental divergence from Marxist dogma. The official position seems to have varied by stages from a faithful adherence to the Marxist doctrine, which led to the ignoring of population problems during the early years of revolution, to an admission of overpopulation, and the adoption of birth control from 1953 to 1958, and finally a renewed disregard of population problems after June 1958.

Our questions are: did the population policy actually change? What are the official statements intended to mean? Did the early position represent a desire for rapid population growth in accordance with the Marxian denial of population problems? Did the birth control programme indicate an effort to accelerate the inevitable economic development? A study of the abundant Communist written materials can be helpful in reaching some conclusions.

Orthodox Marxist Doctrine on Population

In 1955 and 1956 the Communist Party briefly deviated from Marxist doctrine and adopted the Malthusian theory; their experimental birth control programme was short-lived, and has been suggested that the policy was discarded because it hinted at official pessimism concerning the Communist future in China. Later the Peking government resumed a policy of family limitation, which sinologists considered a real challenge to the Communist regime, but there had apparently been no alternative to reducing the population pressure. Failure in farm production confirmed that the government could not afford any unchecked population increase. In fact, it was widely felt that Mao must decrease the Chinese birth rate or be confronted by severe food shortages.

On October 14, an article appeared attacking 'rightists' who advised curtailing population growth. There was an increasing tendency in 1959 to criticize those who, for economic reasons, had advocated birth control. Individual charges were levelled against Ma Yin-chu, the noted economist and President of Peking University, and Fei Hsiao-tung, President of the National Institute for Minorities, both ardent supporters of birth control. In November 1955 Ma published an article in which he contended that his population theory was not concerned with Malthus in terms of food production and population growth.[160] He maintained that the enormous population of China was an obstacle to progress and that population control would lead to improve 'human quality'; but Ma was charged with arrogance and ignorance of Marxism; in April 1960, Peking announced that Ma Yin-chu had been discharged from his post as president of Peking University.

In opposition to Ma and Fei's views the government abandoned birth control. They held that a large reserve of labour was essential if the millions of men needed for colossal construction projects, such as dams, irrigation canals, were to be recruited. Yet it has been reported in the *New York Time* that an open campaign for birth control is gaining momentum in China chiefly through magazine articles.[161] The reversal of Marxist doctrine on population will be presented in greater detail below.

Reversal of Marxist Theory on Population

Shifting policy on birth control in opposition to Marxist theory gave rise to speculation. The Communist government began the birth control policy in 1956, but abandoned it within two years. Whether this reflected popular resistance to it, or deference to the Marxist and other economists' doctrine which claims that human labour is a source of wealth, and that the population is therefore treasure is not known. Marx, Engels, Bebel, and Kautsky, the early prophets of Marxism all disapproved of the Malthusian theory. Yet Peking carried on a campaign against the teeming birth rate. L.A. Orleans suspects that the primary factor in the shift of policy is the difficulty of supplying and popularizing contraceptives, and of changing the attitudes of the peasants. Thus the birth control campaign was the direct reaction to the rapidly growing population which, according to a report given in 1962, was officially estimated at 700 millions.[162] It was also reliably reported that from March 8 to April 20, 1962, an exhibition of planned parenthood was held in the Canton Culture Park where over 10,000 visitors saw the display of charts, modes, and speciments during the first two weeks.[163] Peking was then attempting a carefully planned control programme aimed at reducing the birth rate by up to 50 per cent.

The measures were as follows:

(1) In order to facilitate the use and distribution of contraceptives a revised schedule of import duties on incoming travellers' baggage and personal effects and on articles sent by mail was approved by the State Council in January 1962. The new custom regulations provide, among other things, that contraceptive appliances and drugs may be imported into China duty-free.[164]

(2) A provision of the means of abortion and of contraceptives was designed to extend the spacing of births by six months to one year. This was intended to decrease the birth rate further by between 10 to 20 per cent.[165] New contraceptive measures were adopted, though some were of doubtful efficacy.

Victor Zorza, records one method, as published in the Chinese press, advising the swallowing of 24 live tadpoles, which could be readily found in fishponds and which were said to cause sterility for five years![166]

(3) A provision for sterilization. A large number of young parents in their middle and later twenties are required to resort to sterilization after they have had two or three children. By this means the birth rate should be further reduced by between 10 and 20 per cent.

(4) Other measures of birth control have been suggested. Yeh Kung-shao, Dean of the Department of Public Health at Peking Medical College recommended late marriage in an article 'What is the most suitable age for marriage'.[167] In commenting on Article 4 of the Marriage Law 'A marriage can be contracted only after the man has reached 20 years of age and the woman 18 years of age', Yeh said that this is simply a statement of minimum requirement; it does not encourage young people to be married at 20 and 18. 'The best age', he continued, 'for a woman to get married is between 23 and 27, and for a man between 25 and 29'.[168] The state suggests that women have their first child generally at the age of 26 or 27 and the second one after three to five years.[169] If this plan were successful, it could cut back the birth rate between 10 and 20 per cent. Meanwhile the Peking government not only discouraged early marriages but warned young people against falling in love. According to Yeh, love will affect the quality of a student's work. He said:

> I feel that in opposing early marriage we must oppose falling in love at too early an age. . . . A family should have only two children and certainly no more than three.[170]

Married couples are being urged most strongly to practise contraception. Sterilization of husband or wife is recommended, and abortion is tolerated. Clinics dispensing birth control information to the public have been expanded in every city. Shop windows displayed a complete range of contraceptive devices.[171]

One may readily question how the attempt to curb the population explosion in Communist China can be consistent with the Marxist doctrine preached during the 'great Leap forward' when a large population was considered an asset. The Peking government has camouflaged this dilemma by concentrating publicity for birth control on the health and welfare aspects without mentioning considerations of population.[172] This official position comes close to the Malthusian theory, which advocates the postponement of marriage as one of the checks to a high birth rate. We should keep in mind the specialists' forecast that Peking will encounter difficulties in encouraging later marriage or contraceptive practices. However, medical facilities in the countryside must be inadequate; so in order to meet this shortage Peking planned to train 150,000 doctors in 1962-72 and to assign most of them to rural areas.[173]

The classic Marxist doctrine attacks birth control as a 'reformist diversion' and argues that if production and distribution are stabilized on the basis of equality, there will be no poverty and misery, and thus no fear of over-population. Jean Freville contended that a classless society will provide work for everyone, and will adapt production to its needs. There will be neither 'relative' overpopulation, nor 'absolute' over-population.[174] Marx was particularly critical of Malthus and the concept of over-population as a bourgeois and capitalist dilemma. Nevertheless, the present policy of Communist China certainly is contrary to Marxist doctrine and embraces Malthusian or rather neo-Malthusian theory. Alfred Sauvy wrote:

> The Chinese conversion is gradually forcing Marxism to change its position, and to tone down judgments too visibly inspired by the desire to fight capitalist Malthusianism and also to insist on certain aspects which until then had only been evoked with the most extreme discretion.[175]

True, it may be inferred that whenever the Communist Party promotes a birth control programme, it acts against basic Marxist belief. As regards loyalty to Malthusian doctrine, the editor of *Cheng-chih Hsuëh-hsi* (Political Study) replied that Malthus was a reactionary, bourgeois economist whose position had nothing in common with the Communist Party policy. In short, in disguising their departure from Marxist doctrine, the Communists have tried to rationalize and interpret the Marxist stand in favour of planned limits on population.

(5) New developments in regard to the birth control and planned parenthood have been supported by various reports. By the beginning of 1968 it was reported that early marriages and lavish weddings attracted youths, and young people of 18 or 19 were prone to get married; the government opposed early marriages and curbed luxury wedding ceremonies.[176] On January 15, 1968, the Shanghai Municipal Revolutionary Committee issued a notice on strengthening planned birth and advocating late marriage deliberately to curb population increase.[177] In spite of Mao's exhorting people to delay marriage, they defied late marriage by indulging in love affairs, romances and siring natural offspring; this trend was conspicuous in factories, rural areas and schools. There can be no surprise that in April, 1968 the young people were reprimanded for their slander that the promotion of late marriage and birth control was part of the 'bourgeois reactionary line'.[178] Professor Sailer noted that planned parenthood is a great target in China now. Medical doctors instil planned parenthood into people's minds and discourage the pristine tradition of large families.[179]

The rationale for the late marriage and birth control campaign on the ebb of the Cultural Revolution was strengthened by a few new arguments. In July 1970 it was stipulated that in a socialist country where everything is planned population growth must equally be planned.[180] The phrase 'show concern for the growth of the younger generation' has reflected Mao's authorization for discouraging early marriage. However, the works of Mao, like these of Marx, Engels and Lenin, contain little that can be truly construed as an endorsement or support of family limitation. Maoist approval of birth control is a crystal-clear indication that the campaign has undoubtedly been supported at the highest level. Birth control and late marriage bring home to people the importance of changing habits, altered customs and transforming the world.[181]

Another rationale for the birth control campaign arises from population pressure on the food supply. In July 1970, it was reported that planned childbirth and late marriage would give rise to self-sufficiency in food and that the population of the production team was not increased in the previous three years.[182] A radio broadcast from Peking in November 1970 announced that grain production was linked to the solution of over-population problems with a brigade in Chekiang province.[183] In November 1971, Vice-Premier Li Hsien-nien in a discussion of China's economic development with a Cairo newsman said that 'We have been in great haste to cope with the enormous increase of population' and he added: 'what can be said in this matter is that, in spite of the enormous population, we have been able to find a basic solution to the problem of food. We have guaranteed that no citizen will die for want of food or clothing'.[184]

Semi-official estimates of the United Nations Statistical Office places the number of the population of mainland China at 800.72 millions in 1972.[185] It is believed that at present about 20 per cent of the inhabitants on earth live in China. The crude birth rate is about 32.3 per 1,000 between 1965-1970 and 30.6 between 1970-1975. The crude death rate of China is estimated at 19.0 per 1.000 between 1965-1970 and 17.5 between 1970-1975. The stupendous Chinese population and the differential of population among the most populated countries are tabulated as follows:

Estimates of Mid-year population (in millions)[185]						Latest official[186] estimate (in millions)
Countries	1970	1971	1972	1973	1974	1975	1976
China	773.66	787.18	800.72	814.29	. . .	838.80	. . .
India	539.86	551.83	563.49	574.21	586.05	598.08	. . .
The Soviet Union	242.76	245.09	247.46	249.74	252.06	254.38	256.70
The U.S.A.	204.88	207.05	208.84	210.39	. . .	213.61	215.00
Indonesia	121.20	124.89	128.67	124.60	127.58	136.04	. . .
Japan	103.39	104.66	105.99	108.34	109.91	110.95	. . .
W. Germany	59.43	59.18	59.60	61.97	62.04	61.83	61.53
The United Kingdom	55.75	55.57	55.79	55.93	. . .	55.96	. . .

In point of fact, a grand total of 800.72 millions may be safely assumed with the annual rate of increase approximately at 2 per cent. The goal today in China is to cut the rate of population down to 10 per 1,000 in cities and 15 per 1,000 in the countryside. The present policy of the government recommends that each family should be limited to two children. Sharp reduction in infant mortality and adult death rate, as a result of living conditions and medical care, have been the *raison d'être* of the need for family planning. Infant mortality has been once as high as 200 per 1,000 births in some areas: the average in Peking at present is less than 20; in other areas it is lower still.[187]

The government has introduced family planning to regulate the birth rate. Birth control, contraceptives and related medical services are free. With government and social organizations at all levels publicizing and explaining the advantages of family planning, an increasing number of people wish to practise it. This policy has entailed good results. There has been a decline in the rate of population growth in densely populated areas. It is 4.8 per 1,000 for Shanghai and surrounding countryside; 9.7 per 1,000 for Peking and surrounding countryside; 12 per 1,000 for Kiangsu province.[188] The decline in the birth rate is uneven in different areas, but continued effort is needed.

Granted that the estimate of population size in China is reliable, the Communist authorities feel that birth control is indispensable because they believe that an enormous population will consume all they have produced and thus China is in fear of its prolific, growing colossal population. It is also their belief that limiting population is an effective way of relieving the strain on national resources and so permitting an easier transition to the final stage of communism.

Another rationale for birth control is concerned with the health of mothers. Family planning and birth control is being carried throughout China to benefit the health of mothers. The word 'planned control' means not only birth control, but the adoption of different measures in accordance with different circumstances. Population control has much bearing on the development of medical health work both in cities and rural areas, maternity and child care and raising people's living standards. Various kinds of contraceptive methods are available and couples resort to them according to their age, health and number of children. In cities the health department provides contraceptives to hospitals or clinics in factories, schools, government offices and neighbourhoods, and the local medical workers then distribute them to individuals. In rural areas the "bare foot doctors" supply the peasants with contraceptives. Health workers enlighten people on birth control and various methods of contraception. How do people react to contraceptives? A British doctor reported that two groups reacted differently. The older peasants regarded a number of children as honour and prosperity, while the youngsters felt enthusiasm for a planned family.[189]

What about postponement of marriage? Late marriage has helped to slow down population growth. Whereas the Marriage Law in 1951 enacts the age of 18 for women and 20 for men, at present the government's stipulation is for women to marry at around 25 and men at about 28.[190] Here two communes can serve to illustrate the postponement of marriage. The Tung Chin rural commune in Kiang-su province is composed of 6,300 families with a population of 30,000. In 1971 two hundred couples contracted marriage; their marriage age averages at 27 for males and at 24 or 25 for female.[191] In Ch'a Pei commune of Ju Tong district in Kiang su province Miss Ts'ing Mei-chen is a member of a productive brigade and married Wu Yung-shien when she was 24. Their postponement of marriage was influenced by the Communist policy. They felt that an earlier marriage would hinder learning and concentrating on revolution and social production.[192]

One may ask whether the commune affects the birth rate. It seems too early to predict the effects; but were the husband and wife not living together in the commune, the birth rate would be affected.

To sum up, in support of the Marxist doctrine of population, Malthusian theory—food supply will be outstripped by population increase—was dealt a heavy blow during the early years of the Chinese Communist Revolution. But in recent years all the population policy is reminiscent of the Malthusianism that marked official attitudes towards birth control and planned parenthood and Mao's own position during the 'hundred flowers' period (1958–1962). In 1977 men and woman were permitted to marry only at 28 and 25 respectively, and the family must be limited to two children.

7. MARXIST DOCTRINE ON THE FAMILY IN CHINA

Investigating the modification of Marxist theory on the family in China seems necessary to discover the validity of prediction in shaping the modern social system. It is the Communist principle that a revolution always begins with a destructive phase and moves, at an appropriate time, to the constructive stage. The Chinese Communists are striving to reverse some of their original policies and to consolidate and re-establish the family. On the strength of Communist documents we are confronted with no difficulty in seeing that the Chinese family has not faded away. Marriage may be somewhat frail, but marriage does exist, and it aims to rear staunch and useful citizens. Under this policy the Marxist tenet that the family eventually withers away in a socialist state has been challenged.

The Marxist dialectic process—the thesis, antithesis and synthesis—[193] may be of use in an attempt to study various phases of the Communist policy on the family. By this means the modification in the Marxist doctrine will soon become apparent.

The Restoration of Human Relations in the Family

(a) *Filial piety.* Tradition requires that children and young people should show filial piety to their parents. Failure to discharge this duty would incur ostracism. With the establishment of the Communist government came the antithesis—negating the value of the old family system. The Communist Party argues that filial piety, the first of all virtues has elevated the male to the headship within the family and lent support to his absolute authority.[194] Similarly, in discussing the patriarchal family system Engels declared:

[The Patriarch] had under him wife and children and a number of slaves . . . The wife became the first domestic servant . . . He (the man) is the bourgeois; the wife represents the proletariat.[195]

From 1956 to 1957 the Communist authorities began to revise somewhat their earlier policy in relation to family relationships. They contended that despite the exploitation of filial piety on the part of the feudal ruling class, it was not desirable actually to eliminate this virtue which is in human nature. The magazine *Chinese Youth* criticized young people for their lack of respect for their parents and their failure to support them.[196] Young people were encouraged to love and support their parents, so long as this did not lead to feudal attitudes or preoccupation with family interests at the expense of the state. They greeted the new policy with some scepticism, however, as they had previously been emboldened actively to oppose the outmoded feudal authority of their parents.[197]

The Communist effort to accelerate industrial development accounts for the re-emphasis of support for parents. The Communists conceded that the socialist programme was still in its initial stage and not all old parents could work for a living. The state would be compelled therefore to assume the obligation which had been in the past the responsibility of children towards parents.[198] In fact, the Marriage Law insists that children shall support their parents in the interest of society as a whole.[199] According to the census of 1953, there were 64,000,000 old folk: women over fifty and men over sixty years of age. To support this group, the total cost of the government, at the rate of about £17 per year per person, would amount to £1,000,000,000.[200]

In enforcing the support of parents according the degree of the Marriage Law, the courts took a firm line with defaulters. In Harbin City, Kao Yi-sheng and his wife faced public trial in the Harbin Municipal People's Court on January 17, 1957 on a charge of mistreating their mother.[201] The court sentenced the man to six months and his wife to two years, but a suspension was granted because both of them rectified the wrongdoing.[202] The Communist Party held that a daughter-in-law's obligation to respect and support her father and mother-in-law is as great as a son's or daughter's duty to his or her own parents.[203] It was claimed that in a socialist society people should abide by filial piety more scrupulously than in the past. Those who neglected their parents were remiss in their filial duties which are opposed to socialist morality. Sons and daughters-in-law should care for their parents, and society is responsible for supporting those old people who have none.[204]

Furthermore, the Communists emphasize the responsibility of parents towards their children; the parents must teach their children to fulfil the requirements of the new society. The family is not only the place where children's health and physical development are property looked after, but also where they receive their initial education. It is the responsibility of the family to mould the new generation physically, mentally and morally, whereas the children should emerge as working people with socialist consciousness. The education of children is the duty of both the state and the family, and parents must play their role.[205] Since children spend most of their time at home, parents' words, deeds and attitudes have a far-reaching influence.[206] Children usually regard their parents' behavior as a model and endeavour to imitate it; they also adopt their standards for distinguishing between right and wrong. In the face of growing juvenile delinquency in China, parents are often criticized for their negligence towards their children; hence the necessity occurs for re-affirming parental authority.

Professor Chen Hsing-shen, a distinguished mathematician paid a visit to China. Asked whether the family structure has undergone any change, he said that there is no considerable change; his relatives have loving care for their children and are very anxious about their whereabouts. The young people are dutiful towards their parents. Although the social system has changed, it has not had much repercussion throughout the family. Many people are under the impression that the family institution must act counter to Communist doctrine, but in truth, the family institution has not drastically changed.[207]

(b) *The Family Relationship.* In the beginning of the Communist Revolution family life was patterned in accordance with Marxist doctrine. Engels pointed out that individual family life must not remain the basic unit of society; private household affairs were to be transformed into social industry, and the upbringing of children would become a public undertaking.[208] Similarly, Lenin condemned the aspect of 'household slavery', emphasizing that no real emancipation of women was possible, while they were oppressed by the 'pettiest, dirtiest, heaviest and dullest toil, that of the kitchen and of the individual family household in general'.[209] The earliest Communist policy was devised to disrupt close, affectionate family life. Communists denied that conventional family life is immutable; they reasoned that family life is a product of social development, which is subject to alteration and change just like any other social institution.

The following excerpt illustrates an attempt of the Chinese Communists to separate husband and wife:

A young accountant in Szechuan province turned to the editor of *Chinese Youth* for satisfaction. Comparing himself to the herd-boy in the legend of the Magpie bridge,[210] he revealed that he worked in one city, while his wife was a nurse in another distant city. The couple had brief unions three times a year: on the May Day, National Day and a New Year's holiday. The wife, disgruntled at this way of life wanted to divorce. Both had applied time and again for the transfer but their superiors only chided them for putting-petty personal concerns before their work and the national interest![211]

Today a reversal of the earlier policy was evidently been made. The Communists insisted that the enforcement of a collectivized life would not aim at the segregation of husband and wife. For there is an ethical relationship between husband and wife and their children, and their feelings can be even more genuinely expressed in a socialist society.[212] In fact, despite the Communist campaign against the inequality of the sexes, and the Marriage Law enforcing the equality and emancipation of women, it cannot be denied that the inequality of the sexes still persists.[213]

In the political sphere Chinese women still suffer inequality. The Ninth Congress of the Chinese Communist Party elected 170 persons as full members of the Central Committee in 1969 of whom only 13 were women. A political bureau which was elected by the Central Committee in 1969 is composed of 21 full members and four alternate members of whom only two were women, Chiang Ching, the wife of Mao Tze-tung and Yeh Chun, the wife of Lin Piao.[214] Notwithstanding the disparity in their official position, there can be no doubt that men and women are approaching equality. Toward the end of 1974, 230 women had been promoted to cadres at the higher level in the production brigades or the commune itself. Of the 1,200 cadres in the category, one-third now are women.[215] In the Fourth National People's Congress, the country's highest organ of power, 22 per cent of the deputies were women; three vice-chairmen and 39 members of its standing Committee were women. In Linhsi county, Hopei province, 1,926 women have taken over leading posts since the beginning of the Cultural Revolution.[216] There are women machine-tool operators, pilots, navigators, spray-painters, engineers and scientific researchers.

In the economic field equal pay is given for equal work, and special protection is provided for women workers. They receive pre- and postnatal care free, and a 36 days' maternity leave with full pay. When women industrial workers retire at age 50, they will draw from 50 to 70 per cent of their wages as pensions. An increasing number of women participate in farm work, and in some places half of the women join in collective labour. This has raised their social status considerably.[217] But in a recent past, women have not yet received equal pay for equal work in the rural areas. Men had a prejudice against paying women equally on the grounds that women are, on the average, physically weaker.[218] The Chinese peasant worker is paid according to a system of work points, which are allocated on the basis of physical strength and productivity.[219] At present with an increasing adoption of automatic tractors and ploughs the thorny problems of equal pay for equal work on the farm are being tackled. Some women at Red Star Commune are now getting maximum work points and 89 per cent receive the same pay as men. In March 1975 over half of the 13,000 commune members called out for a rush river-dredging work were women.[220] Article 27 of China's Constitution says: 'Women enjoy equal rights with men in all respects'. The status of women is in conformity with what was taught by Lenin: 'Let women participate in social production by throwing off the domestic yoke. Women should not be confined to cooking and caring for children'.

In theory, the old family system has to be departed from in order to conform to Marxist doctrine. There were many cases in which wives complained against their husbands and petitioned for divorce. In practice, however, family relations have not been disrupted as one of the more extreme statements might suggest. It would be interesting to learn the extent to which human relations in the family are gradually being subordinated to political considerations. Is love in the marital relationship valued because it is conducive to the stability of the state and thus to greater output by both as workers? Is it valued because each personality is thereby enriched? We are aware that the Chinese Communists made a considerable effort to destroy the patriarchal family system; family relations undoubtedly have been altered, but it would be an exaggeration to say that family life, particularly as regards husband and wife, has been completely discarded. In his visit to China, a *Times* correspondent commented that in China, the separation between husband and wife, because of work, is nothing to be surprised at. Yet the government tries to assign husband and wife to work in the same place, so that they spend their week-end together!

The title 'collective living'[221] might gradually foment resentment if it means the breakdown of marital private life. Mere communal eating and communal workshops do not, in fact, constitute collective living and thus they disrupt by no means family relations. While priority in new building is given to factories, no new design for communal living seems immediately likely.[222] As an evidence, Construction Department built, experimentally, houses which correspond to the present living standards and habits of peasants. In Miyun and in the suburbs of Peking, the old rural houses built in wood have been replaced by small-sized prefabricated steel and concrete structure. In Miyun itself some 2,170 concrete houses were built.[223] Ming Hong, a new town 20 miles from Shanghai has new blocks of flats among its shambling slums. Here the unit of living space is the 'set' with three rooms, kitchen and bathroom. This is allotted to one large family or two ordinary families. At another housing estate, there was a family of four living in a room 12 feet square, and sharing the kitchen with three other families.[224] Again according to Wickbom's report, most of the workers in the new industries are housed in the blocks of flats built of the simplest possible kind. There has been more building of family flats which consist of one room or perhaps two with a kitchen often shared between two or three families.[225]

Before the liberation one-fifth of the population of Shanghai, China's largest industrial city with a population of more than 3,000,000 lived in squalid rude huts of wood or mud or in sheds made of mats in over 300 slum areas. Quite a few people had to sleep or huddle under the eaves for shelter the year around. These slums have now disappeared and been replaced by new workers' villages or flats. Within twenty-four years' time, the government built almost 10,000,000 square meters of new housing in Shanghai and renovated an additional 14,000,000 square meters, ending the housing problem for more than 2,000,000 people.[226] In Kwangchow, 11,000 families of Pearl River fisherfolk, who had lived on their small boats, have moved into new four to six story flat buildings. At Peking in 1949, there were only 13,000,000 square meters of housing, built within the previous 500 years. Within twenty-four years' time almost 20,000,000 square meters of new housing were constructed, 1.5 times the original floorspace.[227] In Paotow in the Inner Mongolia Autonomous Region, the new floorspace is 3.4 times that at the time of liberation; in Loyang, Honan province it is well over four times and in Hofei, Anhwei province eight times the old. The new residential district is accommodated with clinics, restaurants, club, post office, kindergartens, tailor shop and schools.[228] In Harbin City, Manchuria, many new apartment houses of three to five stories have been put up. The new buildings have a total floor space of 3,110,000 square meters. At Szuerkou now stand some 80 multi-story apartment buildings with gas, running water, electricity and steam heat. The average rent amounts to between three to five per cent of a working family income.[229] State-built housing is run by the housing administration of the local people's governments, and the state or factory is in charge of all maintenance.

In view of the preceding survey, there are no grounds for the suggestion that there will be no parental and marital love in the socialist society. Not only will there be such love, but the relations between family members will become still stronger and more genuine. Moreover, the Communist government has made every effort to renovate housing and provide people with more spacious shelter which indicates to all intents and purposes the important role of the family, not its 'withering away'.

(c) *Free Love*. Through the *Origin of the Family, Private Property and the State* Engels used first the institution of private property and then capitalistic production as the framework of his analysis of the remaining social institutions. In this context he laid an emphasis on the institution of marriage. His basic thesis was that love was proclaimed as a human right, and indeed not only as a *droit de l'homme,* but also as a *droit de la femme.*[230] As the leading adherents of Marxian thought showed, in their private lives and conduct, no inclination to what is called 'free love', this same subject exerted a profound influence upon the attitude of youth.[231] It was, in fact, the chief contributory cause of formulation of the Marriage Law in Communist China.[232]

> We have often seen some young comrades who deal with problems of love and marriage with extreme levity. Some of our comrades are poisoned by this kind of freedom of love. They believe that love should be absolutely 'free' and should not be restricted in any way.[233]

Hasty marriages and the fashion for marriage among very young people were fully attacked in the mainland press. To counteract such attitudes, the government resorted to all possible means of enlightenment. The campaign was undertaken in schools, work teams, and youth league. It was stated that high school students were not mature enough to make the important choice of a marriage partner. The abuse of freedom of marriage, and especially freedom of divorce, became so serious that the stability of family relationships was adversely affected.

To counter this abuse, the government first attempted to clarify the concept of 'freedom of love'; freedom of love was not to be interpreted as meaning 'sexual' freedom. Liberation from the past sex tradition and inhibition should by no means result in a leap into libertinism and promiscuity. It is interesting to note that in the traditional China most women did not particularly emphasize pure physical love; they felt that their duty was to give birth to children. Until a woman is entirely freed from past inhibitions she will not be able to adopt a more receptive attitude.[234] Next, the government endeavours to enforce the Marriage Law as a method of preventing reckless marriage, a new approach to the family on the basis of mutual love, respect, and trust. All members of the family, it was hoped, would then live happily and contribute more to the socialist cause.[235] *China Youth* reported that there are still women who retain bourgeois ideas in the selection of a marriage partner and are tempted by material benefits, and they aim in marrying at simply being supported by their husbands. This is undoubtedly repugnant to the socialist principle that love is one side of life and happiness must be based on mutual companionship and common interests. Instead, it is the belief of youth today that love is founded on money, material comfort and indulgence.[236] There is the story of a woman worker who was seduced by a well-dressed man in a wool worsted sweater and shiny shoes and was engaged secretly. A co-worker recognized the man and exposed him as having a wife and five children.[237] Naturally, this case does not represent the behaviour of all young people, but it reflects the trend among youth in China. Yang Liu wrote:

> The traditional ideas and customs left behind by the system of private ownership and of class exploitation do not vanish overnight with the disappearance of this system. In our socialist society Communist elements are growing up steadily, and at the same time there are still vestiges, though constantly diminishing ones of the old society.[238]

In July 1968, it was reported that to fall in love has become a 'fad' among young workers. They had lost their revolutionary spirit and were interested in romance. These tendencies were branded as the anarchist trend. In an article entitled 'stem the evil wind of early marriage' the Chinese frown on free love and sex; even the word 'free sex' can hardly exist. [239]

The government declares that inordinate passions must be controlled by male and female until marriage.[240] 'Puritanism' in China is frequently looked upon in bewilderment, if not outright dismay, by new visitors. Strangers in China often regard the absence of pre-marital sex as the result of harsh official measures against transgressors. Some suspect that the women in China have been de-sexed as recently one United States medical writer reported that 'girls and young men are dressed alike, usually in loose trousers and jackets'.

That people frown upon public display of affection between the sexes is as old as China itself: couples holding hands have seldom been seen. Newcomers might come across a young couple holding hands; but as far as can be ascertained, such visitors have yet to stumble upon a man and woman kissing in public.

Some observers have thought that the lack of pre-marital relationships in China results from the stark absence of sexy advertising, nudity and pornography as well as rigid social and moral values. Although tradition plays its part in inhibiting the affectionate display between the sexes, the government has imposed the restraints on sex mores. City teenagers walk, boys with boys, girls with girls in groups of twos, threes, fours or more on the way home from schools, and there is little mingling between the two sexes in school. We have seldom, if ever, found a young man in his mid-twenties photographed with his girl friend, unless they are very serious about getting married.[241]

What has become of divorce nowadays? The government defines the grounds for divorce. They rule that the bond of affection between the partners must be proved to be irreparably damaged. One party's determination to divorce the other party must be absolute. Also, a special procedure requires that this party must publish the facts and the reasons for divorce in the newspapers and in the notices issued by the courts. As a further discouragement, it is prescribed that the courts should collect more fees in divorce cases. In a divorce suit reported by the *Sunday Times*, the judge heard plaintiff husband and defensive wife; complaint was that his wife beat his daughter by previous wife; but her defence was: 'I confess I beat the daughter, but I beat my own daughter as well'. The verdict was 'divorce refused'.[242]

Divorce is only permissible on the condition that mutual consent must be given and a convincing reason is required; the divorced woman will not bring disgrace on herself. On the strength of the Marriage Law promulgated in 1950, a good many women made a petition for divorce ever since the liberation. What underlay this petition most was the 'forced' and child marriage. This anomalous marital alliance is in conflict with the rights and freedom of a woman. In her visit to China, Dr. Han Sui-ying recollected a divorce suit. The judge is female and the two assessors are male. Both the plaintiff and the defendant are young workers of a poor peasant family, and are married out of their freedom of choice and love. They live with their mother; on account of her disatisfaction at her daughter-in-law, the mother forced her son to beat his wife. As a result, the wife sued for divorce, but the judge refused to grant divorce. Nevertheless the man and his mother were severely reprimanded, while the wife was told to bear her mother-in-law until she reformed her conservative and uncouth attitude.[243]

The Tung Ching commune has attested the fact that if a marriage is on the brink of breaking up, the productive brigade committee makes every possible effort to make the couple be on good terms. If they insist on divorce, they have the permission to resort to it. As regards the children, the parents may, by mutual consent, raise them separately. The local government issues them a divorce certificate which legalizes their remarriage if they want to. As a result, among 6,000 families in Tung Ching commune in South Kiang-su province there were not more than two couples ending their marriage in divorce in 1971.[244]

The Emancipation of Women

Engels anticipated the emancipation of woman from household chores and her participation in public production. His thesis was that in order to establish actual equality between the sexes, the family would have to cease being an economic unit of society, i.e., the wife should be relieved of household duties so that she would be free to engage in productive labour.[245]

There are two ways in which the Communists have modified Marxist doctrine with reference to women's status.

While before 1952 women were encouraged to participate in productive labour, in 1955 women were told to wait to be called whenever their work was needed. At the same time, they were indoctrinated with the belief that to be a 'family woman' was socially valuable. According to *New Chinese Women:*

> If women who stay at home can encourage their husbands and children to take part in socialist reconstruction, and educate their children to become members for the next shift in the work of socialist reconstruction, then their domestic service already has revolutionary and social value, and the salaries and income of their husbands and other family members already are the result of their own labour.[246]

Moreover, as unemployment spread in cities it was proposed, in the spring of 1957, that employed women should be sent back to the family so that the number of unemployed men would be reduced. *The New York Times* has reported that it is now the government's policy to force people to return from cities to the countryside.[247] There is no denying that married women workers have to undertake a great deal of work in looking after children and running a house, and the handling of such problems has a direct bearing on production. In the First Maintenance Center of Peking Municipal Omnibus Corporation[248] there were 347 married women workers. Most of them had children, and families were large, but the nurseries and nursery homes sponsored by the Center would accommodate only 80 children.

(a) The arrangement of marriage. A report in Shensi province revealed that most marriages were arranged by the parents. Is this situation representative of other parts of China? The answer is that the situation in Shensi could somehow represent the general social pattern. Before the liberation the marriage was arranged and decided by the mother of the prospect fiancée; the fiancée must have 600 yuan (Chinese dollars) as dowry. The fiancée ought to send 'betrothal' money; this seems to be business-like transaction. A government official, Chen Hung-ting fell in love with a school girl named Liu Mu-hsuh, and they wished to marry; yet Liu's mother strongly opposed this saying that Chen's income was too meagre. Although Liu knew her mother was unfairly prejudiced, she was indebted to her for having brought her up, and was very distressed by her attitude. At present, parental arrangement of marriages has not been entirely ruled out. In discussion with college students on love and marriage Chung Kian reported that the students do not wish to marry young, but because of family pressure, they are forced to do so.[249] Parental authority over children on the subject of marriage arrangement can be illustrated by this story. One girl angered her mother and was therefore refused the financial help in her education because she was reluctant to comply with the marriage arranged by her mother.[250]

In 1965 a press and radio compaign against feudal custom brought down its fire on the traditional Chinese wedding ceremony which clearly showed that even after fifteen years of the Communist government vestiges of so-called bourgeois custom can still be observed among the peasants; they maintain extravagant wedding feasts. The repast offers two pigs, thirty or more ducks and chickens, several hundred pounds of rice, plenty of rice wine and half a dozen hired cooks. Such a lucullan rite would sink the peasant financially for two years. There was also the bride price, since in China the sons are expected to pay the wife's family more often than a dowry is undertaken by the girl. Apart from the aforementioned expenses, the astrologer's fee to forecast an auspicious wedding day, the mirrors with congratulatory messages in gilt and the red matching scrolls with propitiously written inscribed couplets were exorbitant.

The delay in launching a mass campaign against family arranged marriages seems to re-assert the traditional system of marriage. If this situation is in fact widespread in many parts of China, one would suspect that the Communist government which has uncritically adopted Marxist doctrine has modified equality of women whenever it fails to meet the social needs of their society.[251] This leads us to believe that although the views of parents are not always acceptable, they are not yet to be discarded altogether. Today free love and marriage without the consent of parents have been encouraged on the stipulation that the photos of the prospective couple should be attached to the petition form and sent to the Revolutionary committee; and the marriage licence will be issued. After the marriage the wife continues to keep her maiden name and children can take the name either of their father or mother.[252] The Marriage Law decrees that husband and wife have the right to use his or her own family name. (Art. 11). Again traditionally, a new bride would be uprooted from her own family to join the household of her husband and his kin. Nowadays events have taken another course. Socialist newlyweds can now move in with wife's parents.[253]

(b) The emancipation of women from household chores. The heritage of male supremacy in China dates back to some 2,000 years. Nonetheless the husband holding sway over the household has recently come under fire. One production brigade made a scene; both Jan and his wife engaged in farm work. Yet it was she who fetched the water, cooked and attended the chickens after work. One day back from work earlier than his wife, Jan found no water in the house; on his way to the well he saw his wife approaching to throw the water there. He feared that if he had to fetch water he would have to do the rest of household chores.

Bai Shiu-min estimates approximately 120 families in The Red Star Commune struggle to get rid of old ways. As a result of anti-Confucius campaign against male chauvinism more men are doing some of the domestic chores. Bai Shiu-min, a vigorous proponent of equality, succumbs to no new or old suffragette. Her ideas may differ from those of the feminists visiting from abroad who fume over Chinese women's opinions that the female sex in general is better suited to cooking, sewing and looking after small children.[254]

Are there equal job opportunities and equal pay for men and women? After liberation when the Communist Party exhorted housewives to come out of their homes and participate in the building of socialism, there was a sharp rise in employment of women. In the West City district of Peking alone 30,000 women took up jobs in industrial and service trades. In Peking more than 40 per cent of scientific and technical personnel were women; in the hospitals 35 per cent of the senior doctors were women. As for pay, in the old society women workers' pay was only a half that of men. After the establishment of the Communist Party, chairman Mao pointed out that men and women should receive equal pay for equal work in factories, government offices, stores, educational and cultural units.[255]

8. MARX'S THEORY OF COMMUNISM IN PERSPECTIVE

As the second Five-Year Plan (1958-1962) introduced the 'Great Leap Forward' and the creation of the communes, Chinese Communists were more and more convinced that Mao had discovered a new organization leading to full communism; in fact, they conceded that it was Marx, Engels, Lenin and Stalin who had developed almost all of the general principles that foreshadow the Communist society of the future. Undoubtedly, Stalin had instituted the commune but it was Mao who has elaborated and implanted the idea embodying the Chinese commune system; and his great contribution, it is claimed, lies in his fashioning of the people's communes out of the Chinese masses.

One may ask what is the validity of the Communist claim in regard to the communes. Is Mao to be credited with having developed and expanded the Marxist theory? Whereas it is admitted that Mao has introduced some innovations since he gained political power, these have been primarily applications of Marxist revolutionary theory coloured by practical considerations, at least until his death in September 1976.

One Chinese Communist slogan is 'politics takes command'[256] and indeed if the words 'over theory' are added, it fits perfectly into Mao's philosophy. The way Mao understands Marxism is that though he may distort it, theory is primarily an implement to be manipulated for the purpose of rationalizing a policy which is based on pragmatic considerations. The same principle is clearly enunciated by Lenin when he said: 'Marxism is not a dogma, but a guide to action'. This signifies that Marxism must not be taken literally, but must be adapted to changing social conditions. Similarly at the 18th Russian Party Congress in 1939, Stalin told the Party members that they must not expect to find the answer to all their problems in Marx, Engels, or even Lenin himself, and that it was their duty to work them out for themselves in accordance with general Communist principles.[257]

The Political Struggle and the Cultural Revolution

It appears that the great proletarian Cultural Revolution which was launched in August, 1966 and which gradually receded from 1969 aimed at liquidating anti-Maoist revisionists. Nonetheless in its further development the Cultural Revolution betrayed a considerable split in Party ranks. Mao directed urban young people to settle in the country.[258] As the struggle intensified in exasperation there are no secrets that its roots lay in repercussion against Maoist policies which failed to reach the goal in the Great Leap Forward and communes; this also entailed Maoist loss of authority. By means of the Cultural Revolution, Mao and certain loyal elements sought to overthrow Liu Shao-ch'i and the entire power structure in opposition to Maoism. The Cultural Revolution was thought to represent radicalism and caused a striking decentralization of economic and political decision-making.

Faced with losing control of the Party and government apparatus Mao called upon youth staunch to him throughout the country. The shock troops of the Cultural Revolution were the Red Guards, young people and students whose mandate was to weed out all traces of creeping revisionism in Chinese society. Included are bureaucracy, prerogatives, and political cliques, excessive reliance on material incentives, failure to use local resources to tackle local problems and many other abuses that tend to creep into socialist systems. The Red Guards were instructed to destroy the vestiges of traditional and foreign culture and crush Mao's contemporary rivals. However, the lack of employment in urban areas diverted large numbers of the urban workers to agricultural employment.

Some of the transferred workers were purged of bourgeois attitudes, and returned to their urban work in the end; others were permanently consigned to rural life. Although the majority of the students had volunteered to undertake rural tasks, many of them grumbled at their assignment that tilling the land was out of tune with their education and was of no avail to their future. The young people were told that the rural areas offered a world of promise and prospects, and that they should not go into tantrums but accept their rural assignment with a good grace in the spirit of patriotism.

Many students found rural life arduous and distressing and they cast doubt on what Mao and the party told them they would discover an endless bright and promising future in the countryside. The 'transfer' policy was fully in conformity with Liu Shao-ch'i's instructions on 'How to be a good Communist'; and it was also congruent with Mao's ideas about the opportunities for youths to bring revolution into the vast countryside and reach the goal of eliminating the differences between educated people and peasants. Mao commanded youths to march from city to city and exchange experiences with other revolutionary groups and to attack local Party officials not in line with Mao. Late in the Cultural Revolution Liu Shao-ch'i was charged that his agents sent young people to rural areas to the detriment of their health and prevented them from leaving for urban life. The youths felt justified in rebelling against this policy.[259] When the youths became so recalcitrant in the winter of 1966-1967, the Maoist leaders issued an order to those still on the farms to stay where they were.[260] In April of 1967 it was intimated that those intractable youths were branded as 'capitalist roaders'.[261] In December of 1967 the Party brought accusations against Liu that he provoked young people to leave rural areas.[262] At any rate, Liu was a scapegoat.

Regardless of how true were Maoist charges, they would serve to rally first the young people round Mao and later push them off to rural areas when their violence was beyond control. The Cultural Revolution leaves us short of statistical data, so the balance of the Cultural Revolution in Chinese economic or industrial production is hard to assess; but there can be no doubt that the Cultural Revolution delayed the absorption of imported technology and entailed the decrease of industrial production and reduced export capacity.

The Chinese leaders would argue that political unity has benefited from the Cultural Revolution. Socialism assumes that men will work hard in the interests of society, and not only for their own benefit. The doctrine 'to each according to his work' still holds since it is closely linked with workers' political attitudes; for all policy aims at raising production towards economic self-sufficiency.

The economic decentralization which resulted in the Cultural Revolution was also associated with the political situation and a new outlook of economic system. Preoccupied with politics, such as factional fightings or mass travel from city to city by Red Guards, the leadership encouraged more regional incentives in the economic planning; it also encouraged the ideas of self-reliance and regional self-sufficiency within certain limits.[263]

Education has certainly been adversely affected by the Cultural Revolution: the universities were closed for almost four years, and even at present they seem not have reached the normal academic standards of most universities.

Efforts are being made to redress the disruption of higher education which has been spread more evenly around the spheres of production. Workers are offered short technical courses at universities, and, as graduates they use their skill to help peasants and workers. Thus the educational hiatus caused by the Cultural Revolution can be closed through a great effort in a few years. Today there are two types of education at universities: one for regular students in the three year courses, most of whom are aged about 20; the other is for students enrolled in the short training courses run for factories, communes, and other units. They must study to meet the requirements of their jobs and meanwhile receive regular pay. The Chemistry Department of Futan University in Shanghai offered a short course in analyzing three quantities of mercury with a new instrument used in monitoring industrial waste. It has now been necessary for students of any subject, if they are to contribute to social construction, not only to have a university training but also to have carried out intensive field experiments. In 1974, Futan University held 31 short-run training courses and trained a nucleus of 2,600 worker and peasant theorists.[264] Chiao Tung University in Shanghai, for instance, ran 15 courses on cold extrusion, training about 2,000 technicians for some 200 factories.[265] By December 1974 there were 130 'July 21' Workers' Universities in Shanghai with an enrollment of 10,000 students. At present 3.6% have graduated and become the technical core of their plants.[266] A mother works in the People's Radio Plant; lacking enough schooling and taking care of her children she must grind at learning, but in the end she learns the technique of production and alignment of TV channels.

The special feature for factory-run universities was that the three-year course was divided into four stages dovetailed with the design and manufacture in the plant: a brief study of basic principles which are put to the test by practice, that is, students are helped to understand theory on the basis of practice. On July 21, 1968 Mao said that students should be selected from among workers and peasants with practical experience, and they should return to production after a few years' study.

A bitter wrangle about Liaoning University standards took place in

1974. A poster written by seven automation students at Shenyang College of Mechanical and Electrical Engineering was read: 'we will never just be ordinary workers. . . . We should not equate the two—students and workers. Otherwise we should fail to make the best of our training.' This poster was counterattacked by a group of 12 students from the foundry class, which stated: 'we think we should be nothing but ordinary workers, the more ordinary the better'. The Communist Party dismissed the argument that graduates could not be average workers since they had been trained to operate at a higher level of skill as a version of the outlawed mandarin tradition. The Party also feared that this poster would encourage intellectual snobbery.[267]

The conflict appears to lie in the struggle over status. The 9,000 full-time students at the Liaoning province's 29 institutes of higher learning do three-year courses; but persons classified as graduates are turned out also by small factory and commune-run universities. In 1973, Shenyang, the capital of Liaoning province had 24 such institutions with 1,200 students, and its factory universities had graduated 480 students.[268]

The Communist government has made practice weigh down theory in education. I feel that knowledge in one or other way influences conduct, but whether social or natural sciences have, or will have, any immediate practical use, seems to be a matter of secondary importance. One of Oxford's greatest men has well said that knowledge is not merely a means to something beyond it,. . . . but an end sufficient to rest in and to pursue for its own sake.

Agriculture was more favourably affected by the Cultural Revolution: the sending of young zealots and technicians to rural areas may have improved electrification and mechanization; the peasants were driven to construct more irrigation work, use more fertilizers, and weed out pests. Notwithstanding this, side production suffered through the denunciation of production on private lots. This defect has now been retrenched, leading to more productive and diversified agriculture.

On the political plane, officials (who denounced the Cultural Revolution as bureaucratic) in search of material benefits for themselves are likely to avoid arousing such resentment and indignation in the future; this is conducive to efficiency and loyalty towards the Party.

Whether there will be other cultural revolutions in the future remains to be seen. In the context of international relationships China has established, probably she will not be prepared to sever her diplomacy and foreign trade again. On the other hand, in face of a developing country's problems, the Chinese would consider that the cultural revolutions, for all their excessives, are the only effective way to make a socialist economy a going concern.

Mao's Thought and the Marxist Principles of Class Struggle

It is Mao's tenet that the application of Marxist principles of class struggle varies with different cultures in society. In his conversation with E. Snow, Mao has challenged Marxist principles considerably. He said that 'the youth of today and future generations would assess the work of revolution according to the values of their own: man's condition on this earth was changing with ever-increasing rapidity. A thousand years from now, all of them, even Marx, Engels, and Lenin would possibly appear preposterous'.[269] If one accepts this it is understandable that Mao, in manipulating theory to achieve political objectives, would have to deviate from the Marxist principle.

Marx held that social needs in contrast to the survival needs, such as food, drink, sex and shelter arise when an individual attempts to adapt himself to his particular society. For example, money develops among members of bourgeois societies. The notion of changeability in human nature is that human beings undergo constant evolutionary change. Productive labour in pursuit of survival establishes man's form of interaction with nature through which the organization is changed. The idea of changeability of man derived from classical Marxism exerts paramount influence in China.

Maoism links man's social nature and his economic base. In government policy certain thought is related to social relationship. For instance, a bourgeois intellectual can gain a proletarian nature by working with peasants. Maoism makes an effort to bring factories to farms, thereby giving peasants industrial experience; again through education an individual peasant may be changed into a collective peasant and thereby a communist; soldiers born into peasant and petty bourgeois families can also change into a proletarian soldiers.[270] Here lies the concept of 'self-reform' referring to the changing of the individual's thought. It is man's social being that determines his thinking.[271] Social being changes from place to place, and specifically, from city to countryside. A university professor or a scientist, when engaging in farming work, will remould his thoughts and accomplish thereby a change in his personality. There is no doubt that Marx and Engels believed in the class struggle and social change, though what direction it leads to depends on different cultural settings. But Marx, Engels and Lenin have been dead for a good many years: Marx has been dead for ninety years, Engels for about eighty and Lenin for half a century (1924). Had they have been alive today, they would have formulated different ideas from those which face China at present; many of their prophecies have proved terribly mistaken. For example, the *Communist Manifesto* of 1848 forsaw that in capitalist societies the poor would get poorer and the rich richer until the middle classes would be out of existence altogether. Actually, in this century the middle class has increased more rapidly than either end of the social scale.[272] Likewise Marx and Engels predicted that family would wither away in a socialist society when the state encroaches upon the functions of the family. As for Lenin's prophecy that in consequence of the proletarian revolution, the state would wither away in the end, it has proved hitherto fallacious and disillusioning.

It is true that like many religions, Chinese communism has its orthodox books; its bibles are the works of Marx, Engels, Lenin and, of course, Mao. It requires every citizen to pore over these texts. But in harnessing modern technology to a reasonable standard of living the Chinese are confronted with colossal problems to solve, for which the Marxist classics will be of no avail. If the Chinese continue to be assiduous in the study of Marxist bibles, their effort will end in disillusion. We are thus not surprised to see that Mao has not applied Marxist ideas which can industrialize China and serve the public weal. On the other hand, we should bear in mind that the rise in the standard of living carries out a threat to the egalitarian objectives of Chinese communism. When people have easy access to material goods, their inclination to personal acquisitiveness may well increase, and revive social class divisions.

9. WORKING WOMEN AND FAMILY BUDGET

> *Unite and take part in production and political activity to improve the economic and political status of women.*
> MAO TZE-TUNG

If Communist official sources are credible, Chinese women have fought long and hard to break the shackles of oppression so that they can play an important role in economic progress; experience has taught them that they can win genuine liberation only when they succeed in reaching equality and economic independence. The Communist Party emphasizes the training and promotion of women workers, many of whom are entering productive careers. In Changchow, Kiangsu province, of the nearly 270,000 residents 160,000 wage-earners are housewives.[273] The people's government found jobs for unemployed women and also placed the indigent relatives of dead revolutionary heroes. In Peking, for instance, about 100,000 housewives either have organized their own production or engaged in service occupations: today the overwhelming number of women have jobs.

Now we ask: are women paid the same as men? Are women's wages enough to live on? How much money can women save? In sum, what is the cost of living for an average family in China? Let us look at an average family by way of illustration.

A textile worker named Tan Ken-ti and her husband Yang Yu-chuan live in Shanghai's Puto district. Tan Ken-ti works in the Shanghai No. 2 State Cotton Mill, and she rents a second floor flat in a workers' building; the rooms are not spacious, but they are simply and neatly arranged. Both Tan Ken-ti and her husband Yang Yu-chuan are war veterans; Tan's base pay is 70 yuan—dollars (the people's currency) a month, and Yang is paid 76 yuan a month; the total monthly income is 146 yuan. The family spends about 18 yuan a month on rice, the best quality of which stands at 0.328 yuan a kilogram for years. As for clothing, they bought 31.7 meters of cotton cloth a year before. They pay between 70 and 80 yuan for the cloth and tailoring, and they have also spent between 30 and 40 yuan a year for some clothing of wool and of a cotton-dacron fabric. For rent of two rooms which have a floor space of 25 square meters they have paid 5.68 yuan a month. Water, gas and electricity cost their family 6.30 yuan a month.

The couple has three children. The tuition for the Yen-jung, the oldest girl 13 years of age and 11 year old sister Yen-ping is 3 yuan a term, with an average of 1 yuan a month for two of them. I-wen, the youngest girl is still in a day-care center which costs 1 yuan a month, so the education total is 2 yuan a month for three children; the family also spends about 2 yuan a month for newspapers and stationery. Other miscellaneous items come to about 5 yuan a month; about 25 yuan go for extras. After these outlays, the family put 20 yuan a month in the saving bank.

The couple has made the following list of monthly expenses:[274]

Item	Amount Reminbi (RMB)	Income%
Food	60.00 yuan	41.09
Clothing	10.00	6.85
Rent, water, gas, electricity	11.98	8.20
Tuition, day care, newspapers, stationery	4.00	2.74
Miscellaneous	5.00	3.45
Money sent to Yang Yu-chuan's mother	10.00	6.85
Extras	25.02	17.12
Savings	20.00	13.70
Total	146.00	100.00

As for medical insurance, if people work in a state-owned factory, half their medical expenses are paid for the whole family; and the cost of medical care has dropped sharply since liberation: the cost of medicines has come down 80% since 1950. What is more, labour insurance has been well provided for when working people retire; they receive 70% of their salary as a pension. If they are taken ill, the state pays the medical expenses and hospitalization.

A question may be raised: what has become of people's living conditions in case of inflation? There has been no problem of inflation in China. The value and purchasing power of the people's currency—reminbi (RMB)—has not declined for the past 25 years. Prices of necessities such as food, cotton cloth and fuel have remained suprisingly stable; indeed medicines have gone down and cost only one-fifth as much as in 1950. Rents, water, electricity, postal and public transport rates have remained unchanged.

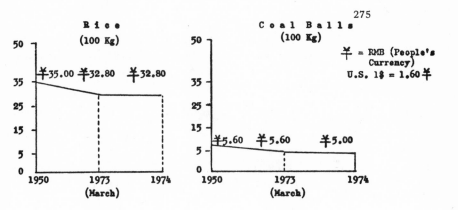

Independence and a firm determination for self-sufficiency are the backbone of the Chinese people's currency. The RMB has no fixed relations with any foreign currency nor has it belonged to any monetary bloc for many years. Thus price fluctuations in New York, London or Paris exert no influence on the RMB. In March 1950 China kept a firm hand on the national revenue and expenditure, banking and distribution of materials. This enabled the government to balance budgetary revenue, expenditure, and holdings and outpayments by the banks, and to improve the supply of commodities.

In 1953 the purchase and supply of principal farm products by the state broke the links between the capitalist forces in the cities and countryside and brought about the socialist economy. Once the means of production have been owned by the socialist state, industrial and agricultural production and commerce came under unified state planning; and the production is aimed no longer at private profit, but at the public weal. Here again, prices of industrial and farm products in China are planned and regulated by the state, ignoring any 'supply and demand' principle. This has prevented, despite wage increase, price fluctuations, i.e., falling prices due to a surplus and rising prices due to a shortage of commodities. And products of state enterprise are reserved by the state, while farm and side-line products of communes, other than those put aside for their own use, are purchased by the state at reasonable prices and sold again on the market at stable and fixed prices.

China has her foreign trade under strict control. Imports and exports are under the unified management of foreign trade departments. A commodity's home price and export price are fixed differently: exports are sold at fluctuating prices on the international market, while imports for domestic consumption are dealt in at domestic prices and are immune from price fluctuations on the international market. This aims to procure a stability and security for the people's livelihood and gives impetus to the expansion of production and economic development.

Chinese women have contributed much to the national economy. At the No. 2 Motor Vehicle Reconstruction Plant in Peking 14 women workers have been recruited.[276] Freeing themselves from such ideas as 'women are backward' and 'women should devoted themselves to their husbands' they have improved the designs of dies for casting heavy steel parts and raised work efficiency 400%. Since liberation, there has been a great influx of women into workers' ranks; many have been trained to be skilled technicians. They design new engineering projects, drive locomotives and pilot planes. For instance, twenty per cent of the staff workers of the Taching oil field are women. In the people's communes women work shoulder to shoulder with men to transform mountains, harness rivers and mechanize farm implements so as to raise agricultural yields. The people of Hsiyan county in Shansi province have achieved 620 water control projects and improved 30,000 hectares of land and thirty per cent of the work has been done by women. Mao pointed out in 1934 that 'our fundamental task is to adjust the use of labour power in an organized way and to encourage women to do farm work'.[277]

It would seem that at long last China may be free-very largely- from want; the economic situation has no doubt been improving from 1973 to 1975, and the Chinese may have abolished unemployment as they claim, but her citizens are by no means free from fear, and the price they have paid for doing away with unemployment is thought control.

NOTES

1 The joint family consists of parents, their unmarried children, their married sons and sons' wives and children. O. Lang, *Chinese Family and Society*. New Haven: Yale University Press, 1950, p. 14.

2 Fei Hsiao-tung, 'Peasantry and Gentry in China', *Am. Journal of Sociology*, 52 (1946-47), p. 5.

3 Arthur H. Smith, *Proverbs and Common Sayings from the Chinese*. New York, 1965, p. 302.

4 D.H. Kulp, *Country Life in South China*. New York, 1925, pp. 135-37.

5 Han Yu-shan, 'Moulding Forces', in H.F. MacNair, ed., *China*, University of California Press 1946, p. 7.

6 Lee Shu-ching, 'China's Traditional Family: Its Characteristics and Disintegration', *American Sociological Review*, 18 (June 1953), p. 278.

7 Lin Yu-tang, *The Gay Genius*, New York: John Day Co., 1947, pp. 40-43.

8 *Ibid.*, p. 255.

9 There is a common saying: 'A wife is married for her virtue; a concubine is for her beauty and fecundity'.

10 Florence W. Ayscough, *Chinese Women, Yesterday and Today*, Chicago: University of Chicago Press, 1934, pp. 104-05.

11 Chou Chia-ch'ing, *Hun-yin Fa Chiang-hua* - Talks about the Marriage Law, Peking, 1964, pp. 76-82.

12 H. Maspero, *La Chine antique*, Paris, 1927, pp. 117f.

13 M. Granet, *Fêtes et Chansons anciennes de la Chine*, Paris, 1915, p. 126.

14 P'ang Yu-mei, 'Village Women', *The Sociological World*, VI (Peking, 1933), p. 172; Li Ch'ing-han, *Ting Hsien, A Sociological Survey*, Peking, 1933, p. 397; Fei Hsiao-tung, *Peasant Life in China*, London, 1939, p. 40.

15 F. Engels, *The Origin of the Family, Private Property and the State*, New York: International Publishers, 1942, pp. 49-50.

16 *Ibid.*, p. 56.

17 *Ibid.*, p. 63.

18 *Ibid.*, p. 65.

19 *Ibid.*, p. 51.

20 Schlesinger, *Op. cit.*, p. 44: 'Decree on the Legalization of Abortions'.

21 *Ch'en Ch'eng's Papers*, Reel No. 14 Document No. 0086, 1029, 0246, pp. 96-97.

22 *Marriage Regulations of the Chinese Soviet Republic of 1st December 1931*, from Ch'en Ch'eng, *Ch'ih-fei fan-tung wen-chien hui-pien*, Vol. I. Ch. 8, p. 1595.

23 'On Coalition Governments', April 24, 1945, *Selected Works*, Vol. III, p. 288. Cited in *Quotations from Chairman Mao Tse-tung*, Peking: Foreign Languages Press, 1966. p. 296.

24 'On Widening the Scope of Women's Work in the Agricultural Co-operative Movement' (1955), *The Socialist Upsurge in China's Countryside*, Chinese edition, Vol. I

25 *The Marriage Law of the People's Republic of China*, adopted by the Central People's Government Council at Its 7th Meeting on April 13, 1950. Peking: Foreign Languages Press, first edition 1950.

26 Teng Ying-ch'ao, 'On the Marriage Law of the People's Republic of China', *The Marriage Law of the People's Republic of China* (Peking: Foreign Languages Press, 1950), pp. 25-26.

27 Despite the age limit provided by the law there arises the difficulty of enforcing the age requirement. The most desirable age for childbirth for a woman was around 25. *Chung-kuo fu-nü*, No. 4, April 1, 1957

28 M.J. Meijer, *Marriage Law and Policy* (Hong Kong University Press, 1971), p. 78.

29 Lu Chien-hsiang, 'Marriage in the Village-Yesterday and Today', *China Reconstructs*, July 1962, p. 10.

30 Engels, *Op. cit.*, pp. 66-67.

31 'Do not be greedy for small benefits and favours', *Union Research Service*, Vol. 28, No. 5, July 17, 1962.

32 This recalls the Communist ideology in Soviet Russia which requires the leaders to regulate their behavior in order to serve the interests of the revolutionary struggle.

[33] *China Youth,* No. 6, March 6, 1962.
[34] Lucy Jen Huang, 'Some Changing Patterns in the Communist Chinese Family'. *Marriage and Family Living,* 23 May 1961, p. 137.
[35] How China's Marriage Law Works', *China Reconstructs,* Vol. XI, July 1962.
[36] *China Youth,* No. 6, 1962.
[37] How China's Marriage Law Works', *Loc. cit.,* p. 12.
[38] *Women of China,* August 1958, pp. 18-19.
[39] With the patriarchal family the household became a private service; the wife became the head servant. Engles, *Op. cit.,* p. 65.
[40] Engels, *Op. cit.,* pp. 58, 60.
[41] Ibid., p. 65. The Chinese Communist Party stresses that since woman is acquired as a commodity in capitalist societies, her unequal status is determined from the beginning. *People's Daily,* April 23, 1963, Tao Yen, "Brief Discussion of Matrimonial Case."
[42] *The Marriage Law,* Art. 2.
[43] Lao Chen, "The Most Praiseworthy Thing", *Women of China,* No. 2, 1960, p. 12.
[44] Lu Chen-hsiang, "Marriage in the Village—Yesterday and Today", *Op. cit.,* p. 11.
[45] *The Marriage Law,* Art. 2.
[46] Engels, *Op. cit.,* p. 59.
[47] Viscount Montgomery, "My Talks with Mao," *The Sunday Times,* June 19, 1960.
[48] Sripati, Chandraseckhar, *Red China,* New York: Praeger, 1961, p. 83f.
[49] All prostitutes in China were re-educated into other professions. A distressed Frenchman Werther, reported that once-bawdy Shanghai was 'almost pasteurized', its palatial 'Grand Monde' brothel remoulded into an all-purpose amusement centre in which ten operas were performed simultaneously in ten separate theatres. 'Red China,' *Time Magazine* (Weekly), July 31, 1964, p. 34.
[50] Dr. Ronald Ma, M.D. delivered a speech on 'How did the Communist Party eliminate prostitution' on May 6, 1975 at William Paterson College, Wayne, New Jersey. He was personally engaged in the rehabilitation of prostitutes in China in 1950. He left China in February 1975.
[51] Lesley Oelsner, 'World of the City Prostitute is a tough and lonely Place', *The New York Times,* August 9, 1971.
[52] Chen Fei, 'A Report on Prostitutes in Hong Kong', *Ming Pao* (Weekly), February 21, 1971.
[53] *The Marriage Law,* Art. 13.
[54] *The Marriage Law,* Art. 17.
[55] Engels, *Op. cit.,* p. 55.
[56] *Ta Kung-pao* (Daily), Shanghai, March 4, 1950.
[57] Wu Chih-p'u, 'From Agricultural producers' Co-operatives to People's Communes', *Red Flag,* Peking No. 9, 1958.
[58] Peking, *People's Daily,* June 16, 1962.
[59] K. Marx, *Selected Works.* Moscow, 1935, II, p. 474. In an address to the General Council of the International Workingmen's Association, published as the 'Civil War in France', Marx said that communism would be a system under which united co-operative societies are to regulate the national production under a common plan.
[60] 'The people's commune Advances Women's Complete Emancipation', *Red Flag,* No. 5, 1960. Cited in *Peking Review,* March 8, 1960, No. 10. Liu Shao-ch'i, *The Victory of Marxism and Leninism* in China, Peking: Foreign Languages Press, 1959, pp. 32-36.
[61] Liu Chao-ch'i, *Op. cit.,* p. 32.
[62] Since the establishment of the Communist government, there have been three good harvests in China: in 1952, 1955, and 1958. Each marked the inauguration of some major new policy; the first Five-Year Plan, collectivization of agriculture and nationalization of industry, and the introduction of the communes respectively. A. Eckstein, 'A Study in Economic Strategy', *Survey.* Hong Kong, October 1961, pp. 154-55.
[63] Rebecca S. Kwan, 'The Commune, the Family, and the Emancipation of Women', *Contemporary China,* ed. by Stuart Kirby, Hong Kong University Press, 1960, p. 146. Engels, *Op. cit.,* p. 159.
[64] The people's commune has represented a direct institutional response to the serious

economic problems which have always afflicted the Chinese Communists and which became acute by the summer of 1957. Donald S. Zagoria, 'Russian and China', *Survey*, No. 38, October 1961, p. 141.

[65] *Rural Work Bulletin*, Semi-Monthly, No. 10, 1958.

[66] *Red Flag*, No. 9, 1958, p. 22.

[67] *Communique by the State Department of Statistics*, April 14, 1959.

[68] Chu Li and Tien Chieh-yun, *Inside A People's Commune*, Peking, Foreign Languages Press, 1974, pp. 12-15. The Chilying People's Commune is located in Hsinhsiang County, Honan Province.

[69] China Revises Plan for Communes,' *The Manchester Guardian*, April 23, 1959, p. 5.

[70] An urban commune is not an economic and social unit in the same sense as a rural commune. Its aim is employment in small-scale factories. In a suburb of Peking with a population of 75,000 there were only 4,000 women organized in the 19 factories set up and only about another 1,000 remained to be 'volunteer'. The rest of people worked outside the area in offices or factories where they were already 'communized'.'Industry and the Urban Communes', *The Times*, July 13, 1960.

[71] D.E.T., Luard, 'The Urban Communes', *The China Quarterly*, July-September, 1960.

[72] By November 1959, 200,000 Peking housewives were working in 590 neighbourhood work shops, with 1,750 productive teams, which were managed on a co-operative basis under the guidance of the Communist Party in the districts. *New China News Agency*, November 19, 1959 and April 8, 1960.

[73] Yang Liu stated in the *Amoy Daily:* 'Municipal and ch'ü (ward) government should be asked to transfer the control of some of their factories and shops to the communes so as to expand the basis of production within the commune and increased its sources of revenue', *Amoy Daily*, China, October 9, 1958.

[74] Engels, *Op. cit.*, p. 70. He said: 'That the mutual affection of the people concerned should be the one paramount reason for marriage. . . . was and always had been absolutely unheard of in the practice of the ruling classes.

[75] According to *New China News Agency*, December 30, 1958, about three million nurseries in the countryside looking after 24 million children, and kindergartens were taking charge of 25 million children in 1958. About 58 per cent of the pre-school children in countryside were in nurseries and kindergartens. This reflects Engels' proposition that through the introduction of large-scale production, the care and education of children become increasingly a social responsibility.

[76] 'What to do when the mother is at work', *People's Pictorial*, No. 6, 1972.

[77] *Ibid.*; Itti Chan, 'Head Start in the Socialist Way', *New China*, January 1976, p. 16.

[78] Tsui Hsiu-mei, 'Home Life', *China Reconstructs*, January 1973, p. 33.

[79] David Bonavia, 'The Sunny Face of Flower Mountain Commune', *The Times*, March 21, 1973, pp. XIV-XV.

[80] Engels, *Op. cit.*, p. 148. Lenin, 'Tasks of the Working Women's Movement in the Soviet Republic', *Selected Works* (New York: International Publishers, 1943), Vol. IX, p. 496; Lenin, 'A Great Beginning', *Selected Works*, Vol. II, Part 2, pp. 233-234.

[81] If women want to take part in public production and earn independently, they cannot carry out family duties. Engels, *Op. cit.*, p. 65.

[82] Susan K. Kinoy, 'Growing Old in New China', *New China Quarterly*, Spring 1975, pp. 18-19.

[83] The commune seeks to replace the constant anarchy of capitalist production by a form of production that would regulate material production upon a common plan, and this would be communism. 'The Civil War in France', *Selected Works of Marx*, I, p. 474.

[84] Marx, *The Communist Manifesto*. Chicago: Charles Kerr and Company, 1947, p. 44.

[85] *Selected Works*, I, pp. 50-51.

[86] Marx, *Anti-Dühring*, p. 171.

[87] 'The Civil War in France', *Selected Works*, I, p. 51.

[88] What a prolitarian society should be is fully stated in Lenin's *The State and Revolution* where the commune must be formed.

[89] *The People's Daily* issued throughout October and November 1958 espouses the ideas of the Marxists.

[90] The theory of uninterrupted revolution is adopted in the Soviet Union, but is now greatly emphasized in Mao's declaration in the post-revolutionary period.

[91] *Associated Press Dispatch*, Tokyo, December 29, 1960.

[92] Victor Zorza, 'Better times ahead for the Chinese', *Manchester Guardian Weekly*, October 11, 1962.

[93] According to the projected targets, the annual output of grain within three years north of Yellow River and in the Northeast was expected to reach 400 catties to the'mou' (Chinese acre), and South of the Yangtze, 800 catties to the 'mou'. 'Large-scale readjustment of communes', *The Peking Informers*, Vol. II, No. 1, January 1, 1961, p. 4.

[94] *The New York Times*, April 18, 1962.

[95] Marx, *Selected Works*, II, p. 20.

[96] Wang Hao, *'Some Points of Impression Reported in His Visit to China'*, Hong Kong: Pan Ku Publisher, February 1973, p. 15.

[97] David Bonavia, 'Cultural Revolution: Effects Linger On', *The Times*, March 21, 1973, p. VIII.

[98] Wang Hao, *Loc. cit.*, p. 16.

[99] *People's Daily*, Peking, August 27, 1959.

[100] Cheng Chu-yuan, *The People's Communes*, Hong Kong: The Union Press, 1959, p. 136.

[101] The production teams were in essence the same as the small co-operatives created back in 1956, and their formation constituted a clear ideological revisionism for the communism.

[102] André Piettre, 'The People's Republic of China', *World Justice*, Vol. III, Peking, 1961-1962, 4 June 1962, p. 459.

[103] 'Red China Gives Farms Priority'. *The New York Times*, April 17, 1962.

[104] Dick Wilson, 'Delicate Balance of Food Group Shareout', *The Times*, march 21, 1973, p. XV.

[105] *The Constitution of the People's Republic of China* adopted on January 1975 by the Fourth National People's Congress of the People's Republic of China at its First Session. Foreign Languages Press, Peking 1975.

[106] *People's Daily*, June 28, 1962.

[107] *Nan Fan Jih Pao*, China June 14, 1962.

[108] *The Liberation Magazine*, Shanghai, No. 22, 1960.

[109] Hedley Rhodes, 'Chinese Hopeful on food supply', *The Observer*, October 4, 1962.

[110] Canton, *Nan fan Jih pao*, June 14, 1962.

[111] 'Communist China's Economy Falters On', *Current Scene* - Development in Mainland China (Hong Kong), April 1963, p. 5.

[112] 'Peking to Tighten Political, Economic Hold on People', *New York Herald Tribune* (International Edition), March 26, 1964.

[113] Marx, *Selected Works*, I, pp.50-51.

[114] N. Jones, 'China Now', *The Observer*, May 19, 1963.

[115] 'Frisian Bull in a Chinese Commune', *The Times*, May 12, 1964.

[116] *Ibid.*

[117] Robert Guillain, 'Les communes populaires continuent', *Le Monde*, 23, Septembre 1964.

[118] 'Life Inside a Showpiece Commune in China', *The Times*, May 10, 1965, p. 12.

[119] A. Topping, 'Returning to Changing China', *National Geographical Magazine*, December 1971, p. 830.

[120] 'Agricultural Mechanization in Hopei', *Hopei Radio*, 30 September 1971.

[121] 'Follow Chairman Mao's Directives for the Road Forward of Agricultural Mechanization', *People's Daily*, 17 September 1971.

[122] Leo Goodstadt, 'Poverty: Frequent Theme', *Far Eastern Economic Review*, May 21, 1973, p. 49.

[123] John Sigurdson, 'Long-term Changes Stem from Impact of Technology on Country-Side'. *The Times*, March 21, 1973, p.XV.

[124] Leo Goodstadt, *Loc. cit.*, p.49.

[125] Joan Hinton, 'Women gain equal pay and men share household at Red Star Commune', *New China*, June 1976, p.32.

[126] Dick Wilson, 'Delicate Balance of Food Crop Share-out', *The Times*, March 21, 1973, p. XV.

[127] 'Flattening China's Social Pyramid', *The Times*, April 27, 1965.

[128] David Bonavia, 'Rural China Learns to Look for Political Implications even in a Handful of Peanuts', *Loc. cit.*

[129] This report was broadcast in Kwangchow, February 1972.

[130] A report was broadcast in Shihkiachung, March 31, 1972.

[131] The Editorial in *Yunnan Daily*, March 11, 1972.

[132] A report was broadcast in *Yin Chuan*, March 10, 1972.

[133] Chao Fung-nien, 'The Summary of Total Practical Realization', *People's Daily*, October 18, 1972.

[134] *People's Daily*, September 23, 1972.

[135] Julian Schuman, 'Dateline Peking', *Ta Kung pao*, July 10, 1975, p. 13.

[136] Leo Goodstadt, 'Guideline from the Top', *Far Eastern Economic Review*, March 14, 1975, p. 27.

[137] T. Dalyell, 'Learning Lessons from Donkeys and Petrol', *The Times*, March 21, 1973, p. XVI. *China Quarterly*, Vol. 64, December 1975, p. 713.

[138] 'The Cost of Dying: Ancestors Are Out', *Atlas*, the Magazine of the World Press, Vol. 12:39-40, 1966.

[139] *Ibid.*

[140] 'The Bas-relief of Modern China', *Ming pao Monthly*, Vol. 8, No. 2, February 1973, p. 90.

[141] R. Harris, 'Looking at China from the Bottom Upwards', *The Times*, April 21, 1973, p. 14.

[142] Jon Sigurdson, 'Long Term Changes Stem from Impact of Technology on Countryside', *The Times*, March 21, 1973, p. XV.

[143] R. Harris, 'Looking at China from the Bottom Upwards', *Loc. cit.*, p. 14.

[144] This is in conformity with Ricardo's doctrine of wealth distribution. D. Ricardo thought that Malthus was substantially right in his day, but that a rising tide of the wealth has submerged his principle. Ezra Bowen, *An Hypothesis of Population Growth*, New York: Columbia University Press, 1931, p. 49.

[145] John Aird, 'The Present and Prospective Population of Mainland China', *Milband Memorial Fund, Population Trends in Eastern Europe, the USSR and Mainland China* (1960), p. 93.

[146] W.P. Mauldin, 'Fertility Control in Communist Countries Policy and Practice', *Milband Memorial Fund* (1960), p. 179.

[147] Thomas R. Malthus, *An Essay on Population*, (1798) Vol. I, London: J.M. Dent and Sons, Ltd., 1914, pp. 18-19.

[148] Shanghai Municipal No. 1 Health Clinic for women and infants, 'Planned Birth', in 'Planned Childbirth and Promoting Later Marriage', in *I-liao wei-sheng tzu-liao* - Medical and Health Data, Shanghai, No. 5, July 1970.

[149] Edgar Snow, 'Population Care and Control', *The New Republic*, May 1, 1971, pp. 21-22.

[150] *Ibid.*

[151] Shanghai Municipal No. 1 Health Clinic for women and infants, *Loc. cit.*

[152] *Ibid.*

[153] Edgar Snow, 'Population Care and Control', p. 21. In both operations acupuncture was substituted for anaesthesia.

[154] 'Struggle to raise the health level of women', *People's Daily*, March 3, 1971.

[155] 'The promotion of family planning results in decreasing birth rate in China', *Ta Kung pao*, March 8, 1973.

[156] 'Shanghai Municipal No. 1 Health for women and Infants', *Loc. cit.*,

[157] *Ta Kung-pao*, March 9, 1973, p. 3.

[158] 'China on the Population Question', *China Reconstructs*, November 1974, p. 13.

[159] George Simpson, *Emile Durkheim on the Division of Labour in Society*. New York: The Macmillan Company, 1933, Book II, p. 109.

[160] For a detailed discussion of Professor Ma's dismissal see Schattman, 'The Case of Mr. Ma Yin-chu', 63 *Listener*, 8, 1960.

[161] *The New York Times.* August 16, 1962.

[162] Richard Hughes, 'China's 700 million people', *The Sunday Times,* August 26, 1962.

[163] Canton, *Yang-cheng Wan-pao,* March 25, 1962.

[164] Hong Kong, *Ta Kung-pao,* January 16, 1962.

[165] Robert Brunn, 'Peking Veers to Malthus', *The Christian Science Monitor,* December 15, 1962.

[166] Victor Zorza, 'Birth Control Again Respectable in China', *Manchester Guardian Weekly,* August 30, 1962.

[167] *China Youth Daily,* April 2, 1962.

[168] *Ibid.*

[169] Robert R. Brunn, 'Peking Veers to Malthus', *Loc. cit.*

[170] 'Peking Reviving Birth Control Bid', *The New York Times,* August 16, 1962.

[171] Robert Trumbull, 'China's Birth Control', *The New York Times* (International Edition), June 20, 1963.

[172] 'Various Methods of Birth Control', *Women of China,* No. 2, 1963, p. 29, and No. 3, 1963, p. 30. Maryan Jones, 'China Now', *The Observer,* May 19, 1963, p. 21.

[173] Robert R. Brunn, 'Peking Veers to Malthus', *Loc. cit.*

[174] Jean Freville, *L'épouvantail malthusien,* Paris, May 1956.

[175] Alfred Sauvy, *Fertility and Survival,* New York: Criterion Books, Inc., 1961, p. 210.

[176] *Shanghai Radio,* January 13, 1968.

[177] 'Go quickly into action to carry out the Patriotic public health movement with elimination of the four pests as key', *Wen-hui pao,* Shanghai, April 22, 1968.

[178] 'Paper boats and bright candles light the way to the skies' *Wen Hui-pao,* Shanghai, April 22, 1968; Chu Yin-hsing, 'Revolutionary Youths should take the lead in changing prevailing bad practices and customs', *Wen Hui-pao,* April 23, 1968.

[179] 'American Professor's Home-coming After 23 Years', *Ta Kung-pao,* May 17, 1973.

[180] 'Under the guidance of Mao Tze-tung's thought, do a good job to promote late marriage of young people, in planning childbirth and promoting later marriage', *I Liao Wei-sheng Tzu-liao* (Medical and Health Data), Shanghai, No. 5, July 1970.

[181] 'Practice of planned births and later marriage is formed at state cotton mill', *Kung-jen tsao fen pao* (Worker Rebel Paper), Shanghai, February 1, 1970.

[182] *I Liao Wei-sheng Tzu-liao* (Medical and Health Data), July, 1970, p. 311.

[183] Peking Radio, *New China News Agency Dispatch,* November 29, 1970.

[184] Manduh Rida, 'Days in China-an interview with No.3 man in China', *Al Jumhurian Cairo,* November 18, 1971, p.9.

[185] *United Nations Monthly Bulletin of Statistics.* New York: United Nations, May 1973, Vol. 27, No.5, pp.1-5.

[186] *Population and Vital Statistics Report,* U.N., 1975 and 1976.

[187] Julian Schuman, 'China's Policy on Population growth', *Ta Kung pao,* June 14, 1973.

[188] 'China on the Population Question', *China Reconstructs,* Vol.22, No.11, November 1974 p.13.

[189] Han Sui-ying, *Woman, Family and a New Life.* Hong Kong, 1971, pp.45-46.

[190] *Ta Kung pao,* July 14, 1973, p.14.

[191] 'The Bas-relief of Modern China', based on the report by Chin Ten Jen Chih, *Ming pao,* No.86, February 1973, p.88.

[192] 'Why We postpone Marriage?' *Ta Kung pao,* March 9, 1973, p.3.

[193] The term 'dialectic' is defined as the theory of the union of opposites. The dialectical process thus involves three laws: the thesis-the first law-affirms a proposition: A is A; the antitheisis-the second law of contradiction-denies, or in Engelian terminology, negates; the synthesis-the third law-is the reconciliation of the contradiction or the negation of the negation, and brings us one step nearer to reality. R. Ozborn, *Freud and Marx* (London: Victor Gollancz, Ltd., 1937), pp.238-39.

[194] Feng Ting, 'Love and support of Parents is also necessary virtue in the Socialist society', *Chinese Youth,* No. 24, December, 1956.

[195] Engels, *Op. cit.,* pp.51, 65-66.

[196] 'Care for parents should not conflict with the interests of the state', *Chinese Youth*, 1957, February 16, 1957; Feng Ting. 'Love and support of parents is also necessary virtue in the Socialist society', *Op. cit.*

[197] *People's Daily*, December 24, 1956.

[198] In criticizing the disrespect for the old on the part of youth, the Communist Party has emphasized the important role of the old in terms of socialist construction. *Workers' Daily*, April 20, 1963.

[199] *The Marriage Law*, Art. 13.

[200] Chi Ya, 'A few arguments and answers concerning the support of parents', *Chinese Youth*, January 16, 1957, p.26.

[201] The word 'their' means the mother of the husband and the mother-in-law of his wife.

[202] *Heilungkiang Jih-pao*, January 21, 1957

[203] Peking, *Chinese Youth*, May 12, 1962, p.15.

[204] *Ibid.* On the Chinese New Year's Day, 1964, a dinner party was arranged by the government to entertain and pay respect to all officers and their wives aged over 70 years. Those present numbered 248 compared with 218 in 1963, Chou En-lai greeted them and toasted their health. *People's Daily*, January 2, 1964.

[205] Peking, *People's Daily*, June 1, 1962, p. 6.

[206] Canton, *Nan-fan Jih-pao*, July 3, 1962.

[207] 'The Report of Professor Chen Hsing-shen on his visit to China', *The Seventies Montly*, Hong Kong, No. 4, June 1973, p. 11.

[208] Engels, *Op. cit.*, p. 148.

[209] Lenin, 'Programme and Statute of the Communist International', *Works*, IV p. 3.

[210] 'The Bank of the Celestial Stream', *Folktales of China* ed. by W. Eberhard. The University of Chicago Press, 1968, p.43.

[211] Morton F. Fried, 'The Family in China: the People's Republic', in the *Family*, ed. by Ruth N. Anshen. N.Y. Harper and Brothers, 1959, p. 162.

[212] Engels, *Op. cit.*, p.72. An official in a certain factory was promoted to a higher position, and thus he felt that his wife could not match his new social status, and he divorced her. 'Some young people in Tientsin involved in hasty marriages, divorces. Peking, *People's Daily*, March 9, 1957.

[213] The Communist doctrine and the Western democratic idea of 'equality of the sexes' exhibit a rapprochement. A man and a woman may be equal as persons in society, but as husband and wife, playing their masculine and feminine roles in marriage, they are different. David and Vera Mace, *Marriage East and West*. New York: Doubleday and Company, Inc., 1960, p.328.

[214] Ian Stewart, 'China's Woman still faces inequality', *The New York Times*, March 14, 1972, p.16.

[215] Julian Schuman, 'Women in Red Star Commune', *Ta Kung pao*, April 17, 1975, p.13.

[216] 'Questions People Ask About Chinese Women', *China Reconstructs*, June 19, 1975, p.10.

[217] *New Women in New China*, Peking: Foreign Languages Press, 1972, pp. 1-3; *Ta Kung-pao*, Hong Kong, March 8, 1973.

[218] Carma Hinton, 'Women: The Long March Towards Equality', *New China Quarterly*, Spring, 1975, p. 32.

[219] Shirley MacLaine, *You Can Get There from Here*, New York: W.W. Norton and Company, Inc., 1975, pp. 159-60.

[220] JulianSchuman, 'Women in Red Star Commune', *Loc. cit.*, p. 13.

[221] 'Industry and the Urban Communes', *The Times*, July 11, 1960. The title 'collective living' means that, on the basis of division of labour, men and women work under the same roof of factories.

[223] Peking, *People's Daily*, July 29, 1962.

[224] M. Jones, 'China Now', *The Observer*, May 19, 1963.

[225] *The Times*, January 13, 1964

[226] Chung Chen, 'New Housing for the Working People', *China Reconstructs*, January 1973, p.38.

[227] *Ibid.*

[228] *Ibid.*

[229] Miao Chuang, 'The Port of Luta-from Colony to Socialist Society', *China Reconstructs,* No.4, April, 1975, p.31.

[230] Engels, *Op. cit.,* p. 72.

[231] Lenin condemned 'free love' as a reflection of the decay of bourgeois society, of 'lower-middle class radicalism'. Lenin, *Documents,* 1 and 5. Lenin's disapproval of 'free love' serves the interest of revolutionary movements by eschewing the reproaches of his opponents and gaining supporters. R. Schlesinger, *Op. cit.,* pp. 14-15.

[232] Divorce shall be granted when husband and wife both desire it. *The Marriage Law,* Art. 17.

[233] Shu P'ing, 'A talk to young Comrades on love and marriage', *Taiyuang Jih-pao,* March 8, 1958.

[234] Simone de Beauvoir, *The Long March,* New York: The World Publishing Co., 1958, pp. 153-54.

[235] Ma Y nu-erh, 'Implement the Marriage Law', Urumchi: *Sinkiang Jih-pao,* January 31, 1959.

[236] *China Youth,* No.6, March 1962; Wang Kung and Wang Chih, 'Breaking up with Romantic love', *Women of China,* No. 1, 1965, p. 23.

[237] Canton: *Yang-ch'eng Wang-pao,* No. 1, 1963.

[238] Yang Liu, 'Reform of Marriage and Family Systems in China', *Peking Review,* March 13, 1964, p. 19.

[239] 'Stem the evil wind of falling in love and getting married early among literary and art circles', Shanghai: *Wen-hui pao,* July 28, 1968.

[240] Han Sui-ying, *Woman, Family and a New Life,* Hong Kong: Nan Yueh Publisher, 1971, pp. 15-16.

[241] Julian Schuman, 'China's policy on population growth', *Ta Kung pao,* June 14, 1973, p. 13.

[242] *The Sunday Times Magazine,* October 10, 1965.

[243] Han Sui-ying, *Loc. cit.,* p. 12.

[244] Ch'ing Kuei, 'The Bas-relief of Modern China', Hong Kong: *Ming pao monthly,* Vol. 8, No. 2, February 1973, p. 89.

[245] V.I. Lenin, 'The Task of the working women's movement in the Soviet Republic', *Selected Works,* New York: International Publishers, 1943, Vol.IX, p. 496.

[246] 'How should family women better serve socialist reconstruction?' *New Chinese Women,* Peking No. 10, October 1955, pp. 18-19.

[247] Tad Szule, 'Peking's Economic Woes said to democratize people', *The New York Times,* August 8, 1962.

[248] *Women of China,* No. 12, December 1, 1962.

[249] Chung Kiang, 'Love and Marriage', *Women of China,* No. 3, Peking 1963, p. 17.

[250] *Women of China,* No. 5, 1963, p. 29.

[251] That the modification of the Marxist doctrine in relation to the woman's status in China is expected. Mao asserts that Communist theory should be welded to the particular national background; it means the sort of blending of Communist ideas with national culture in China. Mao Tze-tung, *China is New Democracy,* Bombay: People's Publishing House, 1950, pp. 40-41.

[252] 'The Report of Professor Chen Hsing-shen on his visit to China', *The Seventies Monthly,* No. 4, June 1973, pp. 11-12. See also Julian Schuman, 'Women in Red Star Commune', *Ta Kung pao,* April 17, 1975, p.13.

[253] Philip C. Huang, 'Women', *New China,* New York Summer 1975, p. 18.

[254] Julian Schuman, 'Women in Red Star Commune', *Loc. cit.,* p. 13. 'Between Husband and Wife', *China Reconstructs,* Peking June 1975, pp. 17-18.

[255] 'Questions People Ask About Chinese Women', *China Reconstructs,* June 1975, pp. 10-11.

[256] Dr. A. Klochko gave a first-hand account of the waste and misdirection of a 'politics taking command'—one of the Great Leap Forward slogans, forcing scientists to spend three full days a week in meetings and discussion and to waste their time in manual labour on dams. 'Shield among the Chinese', *The Times,* February 11, 1965. For a detailed account see M.A. Klochko, *Soviet Scientist in China.* London: Hollis and Carter, 1965.

257 Joseph Stalin, *Leninism.* Moscow, 1940, p.659.
258 'Educated Young People Settle in Chinese Countryside', *New China News Agency*, September 27, 1966.
259 *Ko Ming ch'ing-nien* (Revolutionary Youth), Canton, November 10, 1973; 'Three years of Blood and Tears', *Chih-nung hung-ch'i* (Aid-Agriculture Red Flag), Canton, No. 7, January 1968.
260 'Central Committee Issues Emergency Directive', (Peking Dispatch), *Mainichi*, Tokyo, January 17, 1967.
261 'Wen-hui pao tells students not to leave units', *Shanghai Radio*, April 22, 1967.
262 'The Correct Orientation of Making Educated Youth Go to Mountain and Villages Must be Firmly Followed', *Hung-se Ch'ing-nien* (Red Youth), Canton, No. 72, December 21, 1967.
263 David Bonavia, 'Cultural Revolution: Effects Linger On', *The Times*, March 21, 1973, p. VIII.
264 'Taking Society as a Factory—Educational Revolution in Futan Univertsity', *China Pictorial*, No. 6, 1975.
265 'Higher Education in Shanghai Walks on Two Legs', *China Reconstructs*, April 1975, p.43.
266 'July 21 Workers' University', *China Reconstructs*, July 1975., '135 July 21 Workers' Colleges in Peking', *Ta Kung pao*, July 31, 1975, p.6.
267 Leo Goodstadt, 'Defining the Work of a Worker', *Far Eastern Economic Review*, June 20, 1975, p. 22.
268 *Ibid.*
269 'No War with the United States over Vietnam', *The Sunday Times*, February 14, 1965.
270 *A Company's Managing Educational Work*, Shanghai: People's Publisher, 1965, p.4.
271 Mao Tze tung, 'Where Do Correct Ideas Come From', in *Four Essays on Philosophy*, Peking: Foreign Languages Press, 1963, p.134.
272 Barbara Wooton, 'Journal to China', *Encounter*, June 1973, p.22.
273 'No More Unemployment', *China Reconstructs*, August 1975, p.12.
274 'Two Family Accounts', *China Reconstructs*, April 1975, p. 34.
275 'Two Family Accounts', *Loc. cit.*, p. 35.
276 Hsu Kuang, 'Women's Liberation—Part of the Revolutionary Movement', *China Reconstructs*, June 1975, p. 6.
277 Mao Tze-tung, 'Our Economic Policy', January 23, 1934, *Selected Works*, Vol. I, p.142.

SUMMARY AND CONCLUSION

This study focuses on the sociology of the family and women's status, investigating a variety of evolutionary theories bearing on these subjects. This concluding section serves to recapitulate the general proposition which made up our understanding of the Marxist doctrine on the family institution in socialist societies.

In his *Mutterrecht* Bachofen threw into relief and postulated the existence of the matrilineal family, and sexual promiscuity. Taking a leaf out of Herodotus' account of the Lysians as matrilineal, Bachofen established a kinship system which is antithetical to the patriarchal principle. Kinship through females presumably preceded kinship through males, with the result that women ruled the family as well as the state, and accordingly children adopted their mother's name. After reading Bachofen's *Das Mutterrecht* and Darwin's *the Descent of Man,* Morgan postulated that any matrilineal organization preceded a patrilineal one and that the family emerged from the primitive horde – a period of sexual promiscuity, which was followed by four stages of evolution to the modern monogamous family. Maine contended in his *Ancient Law* that the patriarch, with his absolute power over the life and death of the members of the family, was dominant in early societies. McLennan, Tylor, and Frazer, on the other hand, supported the theory of the matriarchate. McLennan held that polyandry was a general social phenomenon and the first modification of promiscuity. Briffault regarded institutions such as sororate, levirate, sex hospitality, and the exchange of wives as representing early stages of group marriage.

These evolutionary ideas, with some variations, are undoubtedly implicit in Marxist writings. Bachofen's postulation of matrilineal descent led Marxists to reject the concept of the supremacy of males. Maine's theory of absolute patriarchal power underlay Marxist belief in the patriachal system, and McLennan's theory of marriage by capture lent further support to the idea of male supremacy. Lubbock's and Briffault's theory of communal marriage buttressed the Marxist attack on the 'concealed prostitution' of capitalist societies. Finally, it was in the light of Morgan's *Ancient Society* that Engels wrote the *Origin of the Family, Private Property and the State* which discussed the matriarchate, the emergence of private property, and the inferior status of woman.

It is often supposed that the disintegration of the family institution began with the decadence of the bourgeoisie. Marx contended that in the eighteenth century the family had already showed signs of dissolution. The inner ties of the family, the individual concepts of family life such as

196

obedience, affection and conjugal fidelity, had vanished. But the real life of the family, property relations and enforced communal living, the conditions that were determined by children and by the development of capital, persisted despite considerable modifications.

Marxists proclaimed the equality of women and argued that the bourgeois monopoly of the means of production tore the family from its sentimental bonds and reduced it simply to an economic unit. Transferring the means of production to public or communal ownership would deprive the family of its functions as an economic unit, and extirpate both public and private prostitution. House-keeping would be transformed into a social or communal task, and the care of children, whether legitimate or illegitimate, would become a social responsibility, freeing the wife from oppressive drudgery in the home and facilitating the development of real, true affectionate relations. Thus the only remaining motive for marriage would be mutual attraction based on individual love. The public ownership of the means of production, Engels predicted, would make freedom of selecting marriage partners a reality, reducing to a minimum anxiety about bequeathing and inheriting, and would make love, rather than money, the basis of marital choice!

The emancipation of women was used by Marxists as an index by which the general freedom of mankind might be measured. It was their belief that the solution of the problem of making women simultaneously housewives and social workers was feasible only under socialism but they seriously weakened their own case by ignoring the measures taken in the capitalist societies where women have been offered, though to a different extent, opportunities of working outside home.

The situation with regard to the family and women's status in Soviet Russia not only challenges the Marxist presumption that the family would disappear as an institution in a socialist society but also suggests that this presumption will not be tested given the actual state of present family policy. There are, on the contrary, ample indications of state attempts to strengthen the family by rendering divorce more difficult and abhorring frivolous love. The Marxist may argue that the 'withering away of the family' refers in effect to the 'bourgeois' family. Yet a careful inquiry into the functions of the Soviet family shows that, although the family institution theoretically follows the Marxist blueprint, it is distinctly akin, all ideologies apart, to the capitalist model. If the Marxist prediction on the point at issue cannot be borne out by supporting evidence, it has a limited degree of validity. Nevertheless, Marxist doctrine exerted a strong influence on the family institution and women's status in socialist societies. In Soviet Russia and the People's Republic of China, Communist leaders have endeavoured to mould the family institution in accordance with it.

On December 18th and 19th, 1917, the Russian government issued two decrees which brought about drastic changes in marriage and family. These included the secularization of marriage, the recognition of monogamy as the basic form of marriage, the granting of divorce without a hearing to petitions by the Civil Registry's Bureau, the acknowledgement of the equality of spouses, and the protection of mothers whether married or unmarried as well as their children. On May 31, 1918 coeducation was regarded as a prerequisite for equality of access to the professions without which equality of rights between the sexes was bound to be fictitious. Since 1936 equality of rights for both sexes and the free access of women to all professions was strictly enforced and women were encouraged to be engaged in any occupation for which they were physically fit. Nonetheless the Soviets abandoned in 1936 the idea that women's primary duty was a social function and undermined the basis for the socialist feminist claim to equality of the sexes.

The 1944 legislation enacted again a new foundation for material equality: it provided for the mother who devoted her life solely to motherhood, and women won medals for bearing a large number of children. In short, there were no important changes in Soviet policy concerning women during 1926 and 1936. In 1926, for instance, most people, particularly in rural areas, opposed *de facto* marriage and permitted divorce only if it were demanded by two parties. This petition was akin to the legislation of 1918 and 1936, though the 1944 divorce law went further still. Article 26 of the law of 1944 rendered divorce difficult and empowered the courts to refuse divorce even when reconciliation failed.

China's the new Marriage Law of 1950 was laid down in the light of Marxist doctrine. Back in 1931 the National government promulgated the family law which honoured the principle of equality of the sexes in all respects, the right of the parties to marry at their own free will, the right to divorce by mutual consent, the right of inheritance and maintenance and guardianship of the children. Thus the essential principles contained both in the Family Law of the National government and the Marriage Law are not significantly poles apart. Although the New Marriage Law is not a reproduction of the Family Law of the National government, it stands to reason that the latter exerted an influence on the former. However, to the extent that the People's Republic of China relies on means of control other than laws, its system and goals differ basically from those of the National government in the past. The pressure that is brought to bear upon people in this regard is strong and admits of no alternative but compliance.

The New Marriage Law in China is no doubt a potent force for changing family relationships and serves to emancipate women by granting freedom in the selection of marriage partners and enabling them to participate in outside social production. The socialist system has enabled women to approach equal status with men in political, economic, cultural and family life. The revised Constitution adopted on January 17, 1975 by the Fourth National People's Congress provides that 'women enjoy equal rights with men in all respects'. In the Soochow No. 1 Silk Mill, for instance, women make up over 80% of the 1,563 workers. At the Muchiayu Commune outside Peking work attendance among women rose from 70% to over 90%. At home now husbands and wives share the housework: whether this lasts remains to be seen.

Although the commune system is viewed as a method of breaking family ties leading to ultimate communism, it seems to have little purpose. As for the population problem, instead of abiding by Marxist doctrine that population is not a problem in socialist societies, the Chinese government has encouraged birth control.

This book has investigated the Marxist doctrine of the family and women's status as applied in the Soviet Union and the People's Republic of China. Our central inquiry has been the extent to which Marxist theory has markedly changed the family institution in the two socialist societies and the extent to which the theory itself has obviously modified in response to the needs and interests of the given societies. We have expounded in detail the Marxist doctrine of the family as contained in Marx's own writings and the works of Engels, Bebel, Lenin, Stalin and Mao Tze-tung. Further, we have investigated and evaluated what influence evolutionary theories have exerted on Marxist doctrine to show that deficiencies in the former invalidate the latter. Moreover, in terms of a comparative evaluation we have described the social structure of the pre-revolutionary family in both Russia and China. This serves to trace the changes which have occurred in the transition to the post-revolutionary period. In support of this research I have studied most available documents, records, reports and legal proclamations in English, French, German, & Chinese. I have aimed to state in this book what has occurred to the family in Soviet Russia as well as in the People's Republic of China. It goes without saying that I am eager to see that further research along these lines will be carried on in the years to come. Both Russian and Chinese governments have found it indispensable to modify official policy and deviate from orthodox Marxism though in every case they have supplied rationalizations for doing so. Doubtless Marxist predictions have not be borne out by evidence in these two socialist societies, as they have been belied elsewhere.

Difficulties, taken singly or together in this book, explain convincingly how it is that so little of what is aimed at has been reached. It is for this reason that the author in no way claims that this study has been exhaustive. Here we deal with values, sentiments, purposes and political ideas as well as with historical circumstances in the socialist societies. Everyone is aware that in political affairs it is impossible to predict with exactitude what will happen. Tomorrow's decisions which are made to play their part in shaping future development, whether economic or political, are unknown today and at best can only be vaguely foreseen. In the Great Leap Forward in 1958, the Communist authorities set a goal of 750,000,000 catties of grain, but in fact less than 500,000,000 catties were yielded. What has appeared in the Russian and Chinese Communist press, whether on income or social welfare ought to be discounted.

Undoubtedly Communist authorities have continuous choice in the direction of their affairs, and, if a decision is found at fault, it is not beyond their wits to make a second to rectify the first. The fact emerges that neither the Soviet Union nor China has ever maintained a consistent position as regards the Marxist doctrine of the family and the women's status. Economic and political exigencies have taken priority over doctrinaire adherence to the Marxist fanaticism. Montesquieu in *the Spirit of Laws* wrote this celebrated passage: 'Man, as a physical being, like other bodies, is governed by invariable laws. As an intelligent being, he incessantly transgresses the laws established by God, and changes those which he himself has established'.*

---

*Baron de Montesquien, *The Spirit of Laws*, Paris, 1950, p.4.

BIBLIOGRAPHY

1. Books

Alison, A., *The Principles of Population.* London: T. Cadell, 1940, 2 vols.

Alt, H., and Edith, *Russia's Children.* New York: Bookman Associates, 1959.

Aristotle, *Politics, Book II.*

Ayscough, F.W., *Chinese Women, Yesterday and Today.* Boston: Houghton Mifflin Compamy, 1937.

Bachofen, J.J., *Das Mutterrecht.* Basel: B. Schwabe, 1897.

———, 'Myth, Religion and Mother-right', *Selected Writings of Bachofen,* trns. from the German by Ralph Manheim. Princeton U. Press, 1967.

Bebel, August, *Women in the past, Present and Future.* London, trans. by H.B.A. Walther, 1902, 4th edition.

———, *Women and Socialism.* New York: Socialist Literature Co., 1910.

Bergson, A., *Economic Trends in the Soviet Union.* Harvard University Press, 1963.

Bottomore, T.S. and Rubel, M., *Karl Marx—Selected Writings in Sociology and Social Philosophy.* London: Watts and Co., 1956.

Bowen, E., *An Hypothesis of Population Growth.* New York: Columbia University Press, 1931.

Burns, Emile, *Handbook of Marxism.* London: Victor Gollancz, 1935.

Carr, E.H., *Karl Marx—A Study of Fanaticism.* London: J.M. Dent and Sons, 1934.

Chu Li and Tien Chieh-yun, *Inside a People's Commune.* Peking: Foreign Languages Press, 1974.

Cournot, A., *Considérations sur la marche des idées.* Paris, 1872.

Darwin, Charles, *The Descent of Man.* New York: D. Appleton and Co., 1872.

Eastman, *Marx, Marxism, Is It Science?* New York: W.E. Norton and Co., 1940.

Engels, F., *The Condition of the Working-Class in England in 1844.* trans. and ed. by W.O. Henderson and W.H. Chaloner. Oxford: Basil Blackwell, 1958.

———, *The Origin of the Family, Private Property, and the State.* New York: International Publishers, 1942.

———, *Anti-Dühring.* trans. by Emile Burns. New York: International Publishers, 1966.

Fahmy, M., *La condition de la femme dans la tradition et l'évolution de l'Islamisme.* Paris, 1913.

Fairchild, M., *Factory, Family and Women in the Soviet Union.* New York, 1935.

Fei Hsiao-tung, *Peasant Life in China.* New York: Dutton, 1939.

Feuerbach, L., *Selected Works.* II.

Fischer, M., *My Lives in Russia.* New York, 1937.

Fortune, R., *Sorcerers of Dobu.* London: George Routledge and Sons, 1932.

Freville, J., *L'Épouvantail malthusien.* Paris, 1956.

Gaskell, P., *The Manufacturing Population of England.* London, 1833.

Glasson, E., *Le mariage civil et le divorce.* Paris, 1880.

Goldenweisser, A., *Anthropology*—An Introduction to Primitive Culture. New York: F.S. Crofts and Co., 1946.

Gray, A., *The Socialist Tradition.* New York: Longmans, Green and Co., 1946.

Gregoire, F., *Aux Sources de la Pensée de Marx, Hegel, Feuerbach.* Louvain: L'Institut Supérieur de Philosophie, 1947.

Handy, E.S., *The Native Culture of the Marquesas.* Bernice: P. Bishop Museum Bulletin 9, Honolulu, Hawaii, 1932.

Hu Shih, *The Chinese Renaissance.* The University of Chicago Press, 1934.

Hunt, R.H., Carew, *The Theory and Practice of Communism.* New York: The Macmillan Company, 1954.

Kollontai, A., *The Family and the Communist State.* London: Workers' Socialist Federation, 19—?

Kovalevsky, M., *Tableau des origines et de l'évolution de la famille et de la propriété.* Stockholm: Samson and Wallin, 1890.

Kroeber, A.L., *Zuni Kin and Clan.* Anthropological Papers of the American Museum of National History, Vol. 18, Part II, 1917.

Kulp, D.H., *Country Life in South China.* New York: Teacher's College, Columbia University, 1925.

Lenin, V.I., *International Woman's Day.* 1918.

————, 'The Woman Question', *Selections from the Writings of Marx, E. Engels, V.I. Lenin and J. Stalin.* New York: International Publishers, 1951.

————, *Women and Society.* New York: International Publishers, 1958.

Lichtheim, G., *Marxism: An Historical and Critical Study.* London, 1961.

Liu Shao-ch'i, *The Victory of Marxism and Leninism in China.* Vol. III. Peking.

Lowie, R.H., *The History of Ethnological Theory.* New York: Rinehart and Company, 1957.

————, *Social Organization.* New York: Rinehart and Company, 1949.

Lubbock, John, *Prehistorical Times.* London, 1869.

McLennan, J.F., *Primitive Marriage.* London, 1865.

————, *Studies in Ancient History.* London and New York, 1896.

Malthus, T.R., *An Essay on Population.* Vol.1, London: J.M. Dent and Sons, Ltd., 1914.

Mandel, William M., *Soviet Women* (New York: Garden City-Anchor Books, 1975).

Mao Tze-tung, *China is New Democracy.* Bombay: People's Publishing House, 1950.

Marx, K., *Correspondence to P.V. Annenkov.* December 28, 1846.

————, 'Wage, Labour and Capital,' *Selected Works,* I. Moscow, Progress, 1968.

————, 'The Civil War in France,' *Selected Works,* I. Moscow, Progress, 1968.

————, *Capital.* Vol. I.

Marx-Engels Gesamtausgabe. abt. I, Band 5. Moscow, Bego, 1968.

Marx, K. and Engels, F., *The Communist Manifesto.* Chicago: Charles H. Kerr and Co., 1947.

Marx, K. and Engels, F., *The German Ideology.* New York: International Publishers Co., 1939.

Maspero, H., *La Chine Antique.* Paris, 1927.

Meek, R.L., (ed.) *Marx and Engels on Malthus.* trans. by Dorothea L. Meek and R.L. Meek. New York: International Publishers Co., 1954.

Mejer, M.J., *Marriage Law and Policy.* Hong Kong: Hong Kong University Press, 1971.

Morgan, Lewis H., *Ancient Society.* New York: Holt, New Edition 1907.

————, *System of Consanguinity and Affinity.* Washington, 1871.

Müller-Lyer, *The Family.* London, 1931.

Osborn, T., *Freud and Marx.* London: Victor Gollancz, Ltd., 1937.

Plato, *The Republic,* Book V.

Poincare, H., *La science et l'hypothèse.* Paris, 1908.

Proudhon, P.J., *Qu'est-ce que la propriété?* Paris, 1840.

River, W.H.R., *Social Organization.* New York, 1924.

Schlesinger, R., *Marx, His Time and Ours.* London: Routledge and Kegan Paul, 1950.

Serebrennikov, T., *Women in the Soviet Union.* Moscow: Foreign Languages Publishing House, 1943.

Shershenevich, G.F., 2 Text Books of Russian Civil Law. 11th ed., 1915.

Smith, W., and Robertson *Kinship and Marriage in Early Arabia.* London, 1903.

Stalin, J., *Problems of Leninism.* Moscow.

————, *Selected Writings.*

Stern, B.J., *The Family, Past and Present.* New York: D. Appleton and Co., 1938.

Starke, S.N., *The Primitive Family in its Origin and Development.* New York: D. Appleton and Co., 1889.

Symons, J.C., *Arts and Artisans at Home and Abroad.* Edinburgh and London, 1839.

Teuton, A.G., *Les origines du mariage et de la famille.* Paris, 1884.

Winter, Ella, *Red Virtue, Human Relationships in the New Russia.* New York: Harcourt, Brace and Co., 1933.

Zetkin, K., *Lenin on the Woman Question.* New York: International Publishers, 1934.

2. Periodicals and Newspapers

Aird, John S., 'The Present and Prospective Population of Mainland China', *Milbank Memorial Fund, Population Trend in Eastern Europe, the USSR and Mainland China* (1960).

Aid-Agriculture Red Flag, 'Three Years of Blood and Tears', January 1968, China.

Atlas, 'The Cost of Dying: Ancestors are Out', New York, July 1966.

Banavia, D., 'Cultural Revolution: Effects linger on', *The Times,* London, March 21, 1973.

————, 'The Sunny Face of Flower Mountain Commune', *The Times,* London, March 21, 1973.

————, 'Rural China Learns to Look for Political Implications even in a handful Peanut', *The Times,* London, March 29, 1973.

Belova, V.A., 'Family Size and Public Opinion', *The Soviet Review,* 1972–1973, No.4.

Berman, H.R., 'Soviet Family Law in the Light of Russian History and Marxist Theory', *The Yale Law Journal,* 56, November 1964.

Boldyrev, Y., 'The Study and Prevention of Juvenile Delinquency', *The Soviet Review,* May 1961.

Bolotin, Y., 'Profit in the USSR', *Soviet Life,* Moscow, March 1972.

Chao Fung-nien, 'The Summary of Total Practical Realization', *People's Daily,* Peking, October 18, 1972.

China Pictorial, 'In agriculture learn from Tachai', Peking, 1968.

————, 'Shaping up in Struggle—Women Cadres of Linhsi', Peking, No. 6, 1975.

China Reconstructs, 'How China's Marriage Law Works', Peking, July 1962.

————, 'China on the Population Question', Peking, November 1974.

————, 'July 21 Workers' University in Shanghai', Peking, July 1973.
————, 'Higher Education in Shanghai: Walks on two Legs', Peking, April 1975.
————, 'Two Family Accounts', Peking, April 1975.
————, 'Between Husbands and Wives', June 1975.
————, 'Questions People ask About Chinese Women', June 1975.
China Youth, 'Care for Parents Should not Conflict with the Interests of the State', Peking, February 16, 1957.
Ch'ing Kuei, 'The Bas-Relief of Modern China', *Ming pao,* Hong Kong, No. 86, February 1973.
Chung Chen, 'New Housing for the Working People', *China Reconstructs,* Peking, January 1975.
Chung Kiang, 'Love and Marriage', *Women of China,* Peking, No. 3, 1963.
Davis, K., 'The Sociology of Prostitution', *American Sociological Review,* 10 (October 1937).
Demographic Yearbook, United Nations Publications, 1959.
Dunham, Vera S., 'Sex in the Soviet Union', *The Russian Review,* Moscow, 10, 1951.
Eason, W.E., 'The Soviet Population Today', *Foreign Affairs,* 37, 1959.
Economist, 'Changing Russia', London, June 1, 1963.
Fan Jo-yu, 'Why We Have Abolished the Feudal Patriarchal Family System?' *Peking Review,* III, Peking, March 8, 1960.
Frankland's Report on Siberia 'The Land of the Long Rouble', *The Observer,* April 14, 1963.
Georgiyev, Y., 'The Census Findings', *Soviet Life,* Moscow, September 1972, No. 9.
Golod, S.I., 'Sociological Problems of Sexual Morality', *Soviet Review,* Moscow, Summer 1970.
Goodstadt, L., 'Poverty: Frequent Theme', *Far Eastern Economic Review,* Hong Kong, May 21, 1973.
————, 'Guideline from the Top', *Far Eastern Economic Review,* Hong Kong, March 14, 1975.
Gsovski, V., 'Family and Inheritance in Soviet Law', *The Russian Review,* Moscow, Autumn 1974.
Harrison, J.F.C., 'Social Reform in Victorian Leeds, the Work of James Holl, 1820', *Thoresby Society Monograph,* No. 3, London, 1954.
Harris, R., 'Looking at China from the Bottom Upwards', *The Times,* London, April 21, 1973.
Hazard, J.N., 'Soviet Property Law: A Case Study Approach', *British Journal of Sociology,* 4, 1953.
Hinton, Carma, 'Women, the Long March towards Equality', *New China,* New York, Spring 1975.
Huang, Lucy Jen, 'Some Changing Patterns in the Communist Chinese Family', *Marriage and Family Living,* 23 (May 1961).
Huang, Philip C., 'Women', *New China* New York, Summer 1975.
Kharchev, A.G., 'The Soviet Family', *The Soviet Review,* Moscow, May 1961.
Kinoy, Susan K., 'Growing Old in New China', *New China,* New York, Spring 1975.
Kleek, van M., 'Women in Industry', *The Encyclopedia of the Social Sciences,* Vol. XV. 1931.
Kuznetsova, L., 'Choosing a Partner in Marriage', *Soviet Life,* March 1974.

Layard, J., 'The Family and Kinship', *The Institutions of Primitive Society.* Glencoe, Illinois: The Free Press, 1954.

Liu Tung-kao, 'Treat Marriage Seriously', *People's Daily,* Peking, May 29, 1959.

Lu Chien-hsiang, 'Marriage in the Village—Yesterday and Today', *China Reconstructs,* Peking, July 1962.

Luard, D.E.T., 'The Urban Commune', *The China Quarterly,* New York, July-September 1960.

Manchester Guardian Weekly, May 1, 1944; April 23, 1959; June 16, August 30, September 27, October 11, 1962.

Marus, A., 'National Attitudes on Abortions', *The Observer,* London, August 26, 1962.

Maulin, V. Parker, 'Population Policies in the Sino-Soviet Bloc', *Law and Contemporary Problems,* XXV, Summer 1960.

Ma Y nu-erh, 'Implement the Marriage Law', *Sinkiang Jih-Pao,* China, January 31, 1959.

Le Monde, 'Les communes populaires continuent', Paris, 23 September, 1964.

Moscow News, 'Women in Soviet Society', Moscow, March 8-25, 1975.

Motzenck, M., 'Youth Has Its Say on Love and Marriage', *The Soviet Review,* Moscow, August 1962.

Munthe-Kaas, H., 'China's Four Clean-ups', *Far Eastern Economic Review,* June 9, 1966.

New China, Spring 1975; January 1976, June 1976, New York.

New China News Agency, 'Educated Young People Settle in Chinese Countryside', September 27, 1962. Peking.

The New York Times, 'Soviet Programs Compared—Lenin in 1919 and Khrushchev Today' August 6, 1961.

————, 'Soviet Surgery Advances Found by Visiting American Scientists' by W. Sullivan, July 1, 1959.

————, 'Peking's Economic Woes Said to Democratize People' by Tad Szulc, August 8, 1962.

Novikova, Y., 'An Equal Member of Society', Moscow, *Moscow News,* No. 9, March 8-15, 1975.

The Observer, 'Russia! A Home of One's Own?' London, August 12, 1962.

————, 'Cruel Pressure upon Wives', April 7, 1963.

Oelsner, L., 'World of the City Prostitute is a Tough and Lonely Place', *The New York Times,* August 9, 1971.

Orleans, L.A., 'Birth Control: Reversal or Postponement', *The China Quarterly,* No. 3, July-September, 1960.

Orlova, N., 'Women in Soviet Society' Moscow, *Soviet Life,* March 1973.

Peking Review, 'Reform of Marriage and Family Systems in China', Peking, March 13, 1964.

People's Daily, Peking, November 15, 24 and 27, 1956; March 9, 1957; July 22, November 1958; May 1, August 27, 1959; June 1, 16 and 28, July 29, Nov. 15, 27, 1962; January 2, 1964; September 23, 1972.

————, 'Struggle to Raise the Health Level of Women', March 3, 1971.

People's Pictorial, 'What to do When the Mother Is at Work', No. 6, 1972. Peking.

Petersen, W.N., 'Marx versus Malthus: The Man and the Symbols', *Population Review,* July 1957.

Piettre, A., 'The People's Republic of China', *World Justice,* Vol. III, July 1962.

Prudkova, N., 'Marriage and the Family', *Soviet Weekly,* Moscow, May 16, 1963.

Rhodes, H., 'Chinese Hopeful on Food Supply', *The Observer,* London, October 4, 1962.

Shalayev, S., 'Housing, Health and Pension in the USSR', *Moscow News,* June 17, 1973.

Shatman, 'The Case of Mr. Ma Yin-chu', *Listener* 8, 1960, London.

Sigurdson, J., 'Long Term Changes stem from Impact of Technology on Countryside', *The Times,* London, March 21, 1973.

Smith Robertson Hedrick, 'Soviet Feminists are beginning to speak out against Sexual Inequality', *The New York Times,* November 1, 1971.

Snow, E., 'Population Care and Control?' *The New Republic,* May 1, 1971.

Steward, I., 'China's Women still Faces Inequality', *The New York Times,* March 14, 1972.

Steward, Julian H., 'The Economic and Social Basis of Primitive Bands', in *Essays in Anthropology Presented to A.L. Kroeber.* Berkeley, California, 1936.

Su chung, 'Facts about China's Population', *Peking Review,* Peking, July 1, 1959.

The Sunday Times, 'Moscow Is now Building Plastic Flats', March 24, 1963.

————, 'No War with United States Over Vietnam', February 14, 1965.

Sverdlov, G.M., 'Milestones in the Development of Soviet Family Law', *American Review on the Soviet Union,* 9 August 1948.

————,

Svetlicnyj, B., 'Some Problems of the Long-Range Development of Cities', *Soviet Sociology,* Summer 1962.

Swanton, J.R., 'The Social Organization of American Tribes', *American Anthropology,* VII, 1905.

Ta Kung Pao (Hong Kong), 'Promotion of Family Planning Results in Decreasing Birth Rate', March 7 and 8, 1973.

————, 'Why We Postpone Marriage?' March 9, 1973.

————, 'American Professor's Home Coming After 23 Years', May 17, 1973.

————, '135 July 21 Workers' Colleges in Peking', July 31, 1975.

Teng Ying-chao, 'On the Marriage Law of the People's Republic of China' *The Marriage Law of the People's Republic of China.* Peking: Foreign Language Press, 1950.

The Times, London, 'China Indicts Russians as Bourgeois', July 31, 1963. March 21, 1964.

————, 'Farm Incentives Urged in Russia', February 29, 1964.

————, 'Material Incentives for Russians', March 1965.

————, 'Flattening China's Social Pyramid', April 27, 1965.

Tolstoy, P., 'Morgan and Soviet Anthropological Thought', *American Anthropologist,* 54 (1954).

Tomasic, K., 'Interrelations between Bolshevik Ideology and the Structure of Soviet Society', *American Sociological Review,* 16 (April 1951).

Tsui Hsiu-mei, 'Home Life', *China Reconstructs,* January, 1973. Peking.

Wei Chih-p'u, 'From Agricultural Producers' Co-operatives to People's Communes', *Red Flag,* Peking, No. 9, 1958.

Wen-hui Jih-pao (Hong Kong), 'Go Quickly Into Action to Carry out the Patriotic Public Health Movement with Elimination of the Four Pests as Key', April 22, 1968.

Werth, A., 'Love among the Russians', *New Statesman* 61, London, January 1961.

Wilson, D., 'Delicate Balance of Food Crop Share-out', *The Times,* London, March 21, 1973.

Women of China, 'Various Methods of Birth Control', Peking, No. 2 and 3, 1963.

————, 'Love and Marriage' No. 3, 1963.

————, 'A Few Views of Managing Marriage', No. 2, 1963 and No. 5, 1964.

Wooton, B., 'Journal to China', *Encounter,* London, June 1973.

Zorza, V., 'Better Times Ahead for the Chinese', *Manchester Guardian Weekly,* England, October 11, 1962.

Zvyazda, Moscow, September 13, 1970.

APPENDIX I

THE MARRIAGE LAW OF U.S.S.R.

DECREE ON DIVORCE OF DECEMBER 19, 1917* in USSR.

1. A marriage is to be annulled when either both parties or one at least appeal for its annulment.

2. Such appeal is to be made to the local court, in accordance with the regulation of local administration.

3. On the day fixed for the hearing of the appeal the local judge will summon both parties or their representatives.

4. If the whereabouts of one of the parties liable to summons be unknown, the appeal for annulment of marriage is allowed, provided the applicant states the last known address of the absent party.

5. If the whereabouts of one of the parties liable to summons be unknown, the date for the hearing of the case is to be fixed not less than two months after the day on which the court-summons has been published in the Gazette of the local administration.

6. When the judge has convinced himself that the appeal for annulment of marriage has been made by both parties or by one of them, he shall of his own authority declare the marriage void and issue a certificate to that effect.

7. Where a marriage is annulled by mutual consent both parties must include in the declaration which they submit a statement of the surnames they and their children propose to use.

8. In cases of divorce by mutual consent the judge . . . shall declare which of the parents is to keep the children born during the marriage and which of the two parties shall provide for the maintenance and education of the children.

9. If consent is lacking, the husband's share in providing for the maintenance and upkeep of his divorced wife in the event of her being destitute or without private means and unable to work, as well as the

* *Collection of Laws and Decrees of the Workers' and Peasants' government,* 1917, No. 152 *The Marriage Laws of Soviet Russia* (Complete text of first Code of Laws of the Russian Socialist Soviet Republic dealing with Civil Status and Domestic Relations, Marriage, the Family and Guardianship), New York: The Russian Soviet Government Bureau, 1921.

allocation of the children, shall be decided upon in the general order of suits by the local court independent of the amount of the suit.

10. Suits relating to the annulment and invalidation of marriages shall henceforth be heard in the local court.

11. This law shall bind all citizens of the Russian Republic irrespective of their religious denomination.

12. All suits relating to the annulment of marriage now under consideration by the religious consistories of the Orthodox Church and other faiths, by the Governing Synod and by any departments of other Christian and non-Christian denominations and by responsible persons in the administration of the affairs of the various denominations, are by virtue of this law declared invalid and are to be transferred to the local district courts.

THE ORIGINAL FAMILY LAW OF THE RUSSIAN SOVIET REPUBLIC
The Code of Laws concerning the Civil Registration of Deaths, Births and Marriages, of Oct. 17, 1918*

Necessary Conditions for the Conclusion of Marriages

66. Persons intending to enter into marriage must have attained marital age. The marital age is fixed for females at 16 years and for males at 18 years.

67. Marriage cannot be entered into by any persons who are already in a state of marriage, whether registered or non-registered, where the latter has the validity of a registered marriage.

69. Marriage cannot be entered into by relatives in the ascending or descending lines, or by consanguineous or half-consanguineous brothers and sisters.

70. Marriage shall not be contracted unless the mutual consent of the parties to be married is obtained.

71. Difference of religion between persons intending to enter into marriage does not constitute an impediment.

72. The monastic state, priesthood or the diaconate are not impediments to marriage.

73. Marriage is not prohibited to persons who have taken a vow of

---

* *Collection of Laws and Decrees of the Workers' and Peasants' Government,* 1918, Nos. 76–7, art. 818.
The Marriage Laws of Soviet Russia

celibacy even if such persons are members of the white (Catholic) or black regular clergy.

Invalidity of Marriage

74. Marriage can be considered void only in those cases foreseen by the law.

75. Legal proceedings to have a marriage declared void may be commenced by the husband or the wife, by persons whose interests are affected by the marriage, or by the representatives of the public authorities.

76. Suits relating to the annulment of marriage are decided by local courts pursuant to the regulations of the local jurisdiction.

77. A marriage is considered void if contracted by the parties, or by one of them, before the attainment of marital age.

78. Marriages are void if contracted by insane persons, or by persons in such a state as not to be able to act with discernment and to appreciate the significance of their acts.

79. Marriage is void if contracted at a time when one of the parties was already in the married state.

Divorce

86. Marriage may be dissolved by divorce so long as both parties are living.

87. The mutual consent of husband and wife, as well as the desire of one of them to obtain a divorce, may be considered as a ground for divorce.

88. The petition for the dissolution of marriage may be submitted either verbally or in writing, with the official report drawn up thereon.

89. The petition for dissolution of marriage must be accompanied by the marriage certificate, or, if that be lacking, by the signature of the declarant to the effect that the parties are married, with a statement where the marriage took place; the party who gives such information is responsible for its accuracy.

90. The petition for dissolution of the marriage is presented to the competent local court according to the place of residence of both the married parties; or to any local court chosen by both the parties to be divorced.

91. Subject to the mutual consent of the married parties, petitions for divorce may be presented to the local court as well as to the Registrar's Office at which the marriage was registered.

92. Upon verification that the petition for divorce actually issues from both parties, the Registrar must make an entry of the divorce and at the request of the former married parties deliver to them a certificate of divorce.

93. Divorce suits are heard by the local judge sitting in public and at his own discretion.

98. The decision of the local court on the dissolution of marriage is subject to appeal in the ordinary course to the Court of Appeal, and is not considered to have legal effect until the expiration of the time during which recourse may be had to the Court of Appeal, unless the parties shall have declared that they have no intention of having recourse to the Court of Appeal.

Rights and Duties of Husband and Wife

100. Married persons use a common surname (the matrimonial surname). On the registration of marriage they may choose whether they will adopt the husband's (bridegroom's) or wife's (bride's) surname or their joint surnames.

101. Married persons retain their matrimonial surname during marriage and also after the dissolution of the marriage by death.

102. When a marriage is dissolved by divorce, the petition for divorce must state by what surname the married parties wish to be known thenceforth.

104. Change of residence on the part of one of the married parties does not oblige the other to follow.

105. Marriage does not establish community of property.

106. Married parties may enter into any property relation permitted by law. Agreements by husband or wife intended to restrict the property rights of either party are invalid.

107. A party in need and unable to work is entitled to support from other party, provided that the latter is able to afford such support.

108. Should either of the married parties refuse to support the other if in need and unable to work, he or she is entitled to apply to the Department of Social Security of the local Soviet, according to the defendant's place of residence.

129. If the property of the deceased does not exceed 10,000 rubles in value and consists of house, furniture or working tools, it it left to the disposal of the surviving party, who has equal rights with other relatives entitled to inherit.

130. The right of a spouse in need and unable to work to be maintained by the other spouse is preserved even in the case of divorce.

131. If full accord upon the question of maintenance is secured between the parties to be divorced, the judge establishes the amount and form of maintenance to be paid by one spouse to the other at the time of the dissolution of the marriage.

Rights of Property and Obligations of Children and Parents

160. Children have no rights to the property of their parents, or parents to that of their children.

161. Parents are obliged to provide board and maintenance for their minor children, if these are in need and unable to work.

162. The duty of maintaining the children devolves equally upon both parents, while the amount of maintenance paid by them is defined in accordance with their means.

163. Children are obliged to provide maintenance for their parents who are in a needy condition and unable to work, unless the latter receive maintenance from the government in accordance with the law of insurance against illness and old age, or from measures of social security.

164. Should the parents refuse to provide maintenance for their children, or should the children be unwilling to maintain their parents in the cases mentioned in articles 161-3, the persons entitled to maintenance reserve the right to claim same in accordance with the rules prescribed in articles 108-18.

THE CODE OF LAWS ON MARRIAGE AND DIVORCE, THE FAMILY AND GUARDIANSHIP* NOVEMBER 19, 1926

Marriage and Divorce

General Principles

1. The registration of marriages is introduced in the interests of the State and society as well as for the purpose of facilitating the protection of the personal and property rights and the interests of husband and wife and of children. A marriage is contracted by registration at a Civil Registrar's Office.

Collected Laws and Decrees of the R.S.F.S.R., 1930.

2. The registration of marriage at a Civil Registrar's Office is conclusive evidence of the existence of the state of matrimony.

3. Where *de facto* conjugal relations exist between persons, such persons are entitled at any time to regularize their relations by registration, stating when so doing the period of their actual cohabitation.

Conditions Governing the Registration of Marriages

4. The following conditions are required for the registration of a marriage:

(a) there must be mutual consent to register the marriage; (b) both parties must be of marriageable age; and (c) the documents set forth in Section 132 of the present code must be produced.

5. The marriageable age is fixed at eighteen years.

6. It is unlawful to register the following marriages: (a) between persons one or both of whom is or are already married either with or without registration; (b) between persons one or both of whom has or have been adjudged weak-minded or insane, in the manner prescribed by law; (c) between relatives in the direct line of descent; also between brothers and sisters, whether of the full blood or the half blood.

Rights and Duties of Husband and Wife

7. On registering a marriage the contracting parties may declare it to be their wish to have a common surname, either that of the husband or of the wife, or to retain their antenuptial surnames.

8. On the registration of a marriage between a person who is a citizen of the R.S.F.S.R. and a person who is a foreign citizen, each party retains his or her respective citizenship.

9. Both husband and wife enjoy full liberty in the choice of their respective trades and occupations. A change of residence by either husband or wife does not oblige the other marriage partner to follow the former.

10. Property which belonged to either husband or wife prior to their marriage remains the separate property of each of them. Property acquired by husband and wife during continuance of their marriage is regarded as their joint property.

11. Section 10 of the present code extends also the property of persons married *de facto* though not registered, provided such persons recognize their mutual status of husband and wife, or their marital relationship is established as a fact by a court on the basis of the actual conditions under which they live.

12. Proof of joint cohabitation is sufficient for the court to establish marital cohabitation in cases where the marriage has not been registered, provided that in addition to proof of joint cohabitation proof of a common household be adduced and that statements have been made to third persons either in personal correspondence or in other documents tending to prove the existence of marital relations.

13. The husband and wife may enter into any contractual relations with each other regarding property provided they are lawful. Agreements between husband and wife intended to restrict the property rights of the wife or of the husband are invalid.

14. When either husband or wife is in need and unable to work he or she is entitled to receive alimony from the other conjugal partner, if the court finds that the latter is able to support the former.

16. The right to receive alimony both during marriage and after its dissolution extends also to persons who are married *de facto,* provided they fall within the purview of Sections 11 and 12 of the present code.

Dissolution of Marriage

17. A marriage is dissolved by the death of one of the parties to it or by a declaration of the presumptive death of either the husband or the wife through a notary public or court (May 27, 1929, *Collected Laws and Decrees of the R.S.F.S.R.,* 1929, No. 40, Sec. 422)

18. During the lifetime of both parties to a marriage the marriage may be dissolved either by the mutual consent of both parties to it or upon the *ex parte* application of either of them.

19. During the lifetime of both parties, the dissolution of a marriage (divorce) may be registered at the Civil Registrar's Office.

20. The fact that a marriage has been dissolved may also be established by a court, if the divorce was not registered.

21. When registering the dissolution of their marriage the husband and wife indicate what surname each of them wishes to use. In the absence of an agreement between the parties on this point, each resumes his or her antenuptial surname.

22. When registering the dissolution of a marriage it is the duty of the Registrar to consider the question of which child or children, if any, shall be entrusted to the custody of each parent, to what extent each parent is to bear the expense of raising the children, and the amount of alimony to be paid to a husband or wife unable to work.

24. In the absence of an agreement the question of the amount of alimony to be awarded to children is settled by an ordinary lawsuit.

The amount of alimony awarded to a husband or wife in need and unable to work must in the absence of an agreement likewise be decided by the court upon the institution of an ordinary lawsuit. (Decree of the Soviet of People's Commissars, May 21, 1930, *Collected Laws and Decrees of the R.S.F.S.R,* 1930, No. 38, Sec. 477).

DOCUMENT NO. 17

THE FAMILY LAW OF JULY 8, 1944

SECTION I

ON THE INCREASE OF STATE AID TO MOTHERS WITH MANY CHILDREN AND UNMARRIED MOTHERS

It is decreed:

Article 1

That in place of the existing regulation which gives State aid to mothers with six children at the birth of the seventh and of each subsequent child, State assistance shall be given to mothers (either with husbands or widowed) who have two children, on the birth of the third and of each subsequent child.

Article 3

To establish State assistance to single (unmarried) mothers for support and upbringing of children born after the publication of the present Decree, in the following amounts:

100 roubles monthly for 1 child
150   ″   ″   for 2 children
200   ″   ″   for 3 or more children

State assistance to unmarried mothers is paid until the children reach 12 years of age.

Unmarried mothers with 3 or more children receive the State assistance laid down in the present article, in addition to the regular assistance to mothers with many children which is received in accordance with article 2 of the present Decree.

Mothers of children born in 1944, before the publication of the present Decree, and not receiving alimony for them, have the right to receive the assistance provided by the present article.

Article 4

If an unmarried mother wishes to place a child to which she has given birth in a children's institution for its upbringing, the children's institution is obliged to accept the child, to support and bring it up entirely at the expense of the State.

Article 5

To increase the size of the lump sum assistance paid out for each new-born child from the Social Insurance Fund and Mutual Assistance Funds of the co-operative artels from 45 to 120 rubles.

SECTION II
ON THE INCREASE OF PRIVILEGES FOR PREGNANT WOMEN AND MOTHERS AND ON MEASURES TO EXTEND THE NETWORK OF INSTITUTIONS FOR THE PROTECTION OF MOTHERHOOD AND CHILDHOOD

Article 6

To increase the leave of absence for pregnancy and childbirth for women workers and women office employees from 63 calendar days to 77 calendar days, establishing the length of the leave of absence at 35 calendar days before the birth and 42 calendar days after the birth, assistance to be given during this period at the expense of the State to the amount previously laid down. In cases of difficult births or the birth of twins, leave of absence after birth is increased to 56 calendar days.

Article 7

Pregnant women from the 4th month of pregnancy not to be put on overtime work in factories and offices, and women with children at the breast not to be put on nightwork during the period the child is breast-fed

Article 8

To double the normal ratio of supplementary food for pregnant women, beginning with the 6th month of pregnancy, and for nursing mothers for four months of the nursing period.

Article 9

To instruct the directors of factories and offices to give aid to pregnant women and nursing mothers in the form of supplementary foodstuffs from their auxiliary farms.

Article 10

To reduce by 50 percent the fees for places in crèches and kindergartens for:

Parents with 3 children and earning up to 400 roubles a month.
Parents with 4 children and earning up to 600 roubles a month.
Parents with 5 or more children irrespective of earnings.

SECTION III
ON THE INSTITUTION OF THE "MOTHERHOOD MEDAL" AND THE ORDER "MOTHERHOOD GLORY", AND ESTABLISHMENT OF THE TITLE OF HONOUR "HEROINE MOTHER"

Article 12

To institute a "Motherhood Medal"—1st and 2nd class—for award to mothers who have given birth to and brought up:

5 children . . . . . 2nd class medal
6 children . . . . . 1st class medal

Article 13

To establish the Order "Motherhood Glory"—1st, 2nd and 3rd class —for award to mothers who have given birth to and brought up:

7 children . . . . . 3rd class
8 children . . . . . 2nd class
9 children . . . . . 1st class

Article 14

To establish that mothers who have given birth to and brought up 10 children shall receive the title of honour "Heroine Mother" with award of the Order Heroine Mother and certificate of the Presidium of the Supreme Soviet of the U.S.S.R.

Article 15

The award of the "Motherhood Glory" Order and the "Motherhood Medal" and award of the title of honour "Heroine Mother" are presented when the latest child is one year old and provided the other children of this mother are living.

SECTION IV
ON TAXES ON BACHELORS, SINGLE CITIZENS AND CITIZENS OF THE U.S.S.R. WITH SMALL FAMILIES

Article 16

As a modification of the Decree of the Presidium of the Supreme Soviet of the U.S.S.R. dated November 21, 1941, "On taxes on bachelors, single and childless citizens of the U.S.S.R.", to establish that a tax is paid by citizens—men between the ages of 20 and 50 years, and women between the ages of 20 and 45 years—having no children and citizens having 1 or 2 children.

Article 17

The tax to be paid in the following amounts:

(a) Citizens subject to income tax, where there are no children: 6 percent of income: where there is one child, 1 percent of income; where there are 2 children, ½ percent of income.

(b) Collective farmers, individual farmers and other citizens included in the farm personnel who pay agricultural taxes, where there are no children—150 rubles annually; where there is one child—50 rubles annually; where there are 2 children—25 rubles annually.

(c) From other citizens, where there are no children—90 rubles annually; where there is one child—30 rubles; where there are 2 children—15 rubles annually.

SECTION V
ON MODIFICATIONS IN THE MARRIAGE, FAMILY AND GUARDIANSHIP LAWS

Article 19

To establish that only registered marriage produces the rights and obligations of husband and wife laid down in the Code of Laws on Marriage, Family and Guardianship of the Union Republics. Persons having *de facto* matrimonial relations before the publication of the present Decree may formally establish their relationship by registering their marriage.

Article 20

To abolish the existing right of a mother to appeal to the court with a demand for the establishment of paternity and obtaining alimony for the support of a child, born of a person with whom she is not living in registered marriage.

Article 21

To establish that, when registering with the offices which register births, deaths and marriages the birth of a child by a mother whose marriage is not registered, the child is registered in the mother's surname, the patronymic to be given according to the wishes of the mother.

Article 22

A compulsory entry to be made in passports of the registered marriage, the surname, name and patronymic and date of birth of husband or wife, and the place and date of the registration of the marriage.

Article 23

To establish that divorce takes place in the public courts. On the request of the husband and wife, the divorce case may, in essential cases only, and by decision of the court, be heard in closed court sessions.

Article 24

In bringing a court action for dissolution of a marriage, the following conditions to be compulsorily observed:

(a) Presentation to the People's Court of a notice of the desire to dissolve the marriage, indicating the motives for the dissolution, and also the surname, name partronymic, year of birth, and place of residence of the husband or wife. Upon presentation of the notice for the dissolution of the marriage, 100 rubles is payable.

(b) The husband or wife to be summoned into court to become acquainted with the divorce statement of the wife or husband, and for the preliminary establishment of the motives of the divorce, and also for the establishment of witnesses to be summoned to court for examination.

(c) Publication in the local newspaper of the notice on the bringing of a court action for dissolution of marriage, the cost of publishing the notice to be borne by the husband or wife who gives notice of dissolution of marriage.

Article 25

The People's Court is obliged to establish the motives for notice of dissolution of marriage and take measures to reconcile the husband and wife, to which end both the divorcing parties must absolutely be summoned, and, where necessary, witnesses.

Article 26

The Regional, Territorial, District or Town Court or Supreme Court of a Union or Autonomous Republic, in the event of recognizing the necessity for dissolving a marriage, must:

(a) Determine with which of the divorced parties and which of the children will remain, and also which of the parents will bear the expense of the maintenance of the children, and to that amount.

(b) Establish the manner in which property shall be divided between parties seeking divorce, either in kind or on a business basis.

Article 27

On the basis of the decision of the Court, the office for registering births, deaths and marriages writes out a certificate of dissolution of marriage, on the basis of which an entry concerning the divorce is made in the passport of husband and wife and, by decision of the Court, from 500 to 2,000 rubles is charged to one or each party.

Article 28

To instruct the Supreme Soviets of the Union Republics, in accordance with this present Decree, to introduce the necessary modifications in the legislation of the Union Republics.

Article 29

To instruct the Council of People's Commissars of the U.S.S.R. to confirm the rules governing the procedure of allocation and payment of allowances to pregnant women, to mothers of large families and unmarried mothers, in accordance with the present Decree.

Article 30

To instruct the Council of People's Commissars of the U.S.S.R. to confirm the measures for regulating the registration of births, marriages and deaths, making provision for the introduction of a ceremonial procedure at the registration, the allocation for this purpose of suitable premises and equipment for them, and the presentation in the proper manner to the citizens concerned of a document fittingly designed.

THE MARRIAGE LAW OF THE PEOPLE'S REPUBLIC OF CHINA*

Chapter I
General Principles

Article 1

The feudal marriage system based on arbitrary and compulsory arrangements and the supremacy of man over woman, and in disregard of the interests of the children, is abolished.

The New-Democratic marriage system, which is based on the free choice of partners, on monogamy, on equal rights for both sexes, and on the protection of the lawful interests of women and children, is put into effect.

Article 2

Bigamy, concubinage, child betrothal, interference in the re-marriage of widows, and the exaction of money or gifts in connection with marriage, are prohibited.

Chapter II
The Marriage Contract

Article 3

Marriage is based upon the complete willingness of the two parties. Neither party shall use compulsion and no third party is allowed to interfere.

Article 4

A marriage can be contracted only after the man has reached 20 years of age and the woman 18 years of age.

Article 5

No man or woman is allowed to marry in any of the following instances:

---

*Adopted by the Central People's Government Council at Its 7th Meeting on April 13, 1950. Promulgated on May 1, 1950 by order of the Chairman of the Central People's Government on April 30, 1950.

a) Where the man and woman are lineal relatives by blood or where the man and woman are brother and sister born of the same parents or where the man and woman are half-brother and half-sister.

b) Where one party, because of certain physical defects, is sexually impotent.

c) Where one party is suffering from venereal disease, mental disorder, leprosy or any other disease which is regarded by medical science as rendering a person unfit for marriage.

Article 6

In order to contract a marriage, both the man and the woman should register in person with the people's government of the district or township in which they reside. If the proposed marriage is found to be in conformity with the provisions of this Law, the local people's government should, without delay, issue marriage certificates.

If the proposed marriage is not found to be in conformity with the provisions of this Law, registration should not be granted.

Chapter III
Rights and Duties of Husband and Wife

Article 7

Husband and wife are companions living together and enjoy equal status in the home.

Article 8

Husband and wife are in duty bound to love, respect, assist and look after each other to live in harmony, to engage in productive work, to care for their children and to strive jointly for the welfare of the family and for the building up of the new society.

Article 9

Both husband and wife have the right to free choice of occupation and free participation in work or in social activities.

Article 10

Husband and wife have equal rights in the possession and management of family property.

Article 11

Husband and wife have the right to use his or her own family name.

Article 12

Husband and wife have the right to inherit each other's property.

Chapter IV
Relations Between Parents and Children

Article 13

Parents have the duty to rear and to educate their children; the children have the duty to support and to assist their parents. Neither the parents nor the children shall maltreat or desert one another.

The foregoing provision also applies to foster-parents and foster-children.

Infanticide by drowning or similar criminal acts are strictly prohibited.

Article 14

Parents and children have the right to inherit one another's property.

Article 15

Children born out of wedlock enjoy the same rights as children born in lawful wedlock. No person is allowed to harm them or discriminate against them.

Where the paternity of a child born out of wedlock is legally established by the mother of the child or by other witnesses or material evidence, the identified father must bear the whole or part of the cost of maintenance and education of the child until the age of 18.

With the consent of the mother, the natural father may have custody of the child.

With regard to the maintenance of a child born out of wedlock, if its mother marries, the provisions of Article 22 apply.

Article 18

Neither husband nor wife may maltreat or discriminate against children born of a previous marriage by either party and in that party's custody.

Chapter V
Divorce

Article 17

Divorce is granted when husband and wife both desire it. In the event of either the husband or wife alone insisting upon divorce, it may be granted only when mediation by the district people's government and the judicial organ has failed to bring about a reconciliation.

In cases where divorce is desired by both husband and wife, both parties should register with the district people's government in order to obtain divorce certificates. The district people's government, after establishing that divorce is desired by both parties and that appropriate measures have been taken for the care of children and property, should issue the divorce certificates without delay.

When one party insists on divorce, the district people's government may try to effect a reconciliation. If such mediation fails, it should, without delay, refer the case to the county or municipal people's court for decision. The district people's government should not attempt to prevent or to obstruct either party from appealing to the county or municipal people's court.

After divorce, if both husband and wife desire the resumption of marriage relations, they should apply to the district people's government for a registration of re-marriage. The district people's government should accept such a registration and issue certificates of re-marriage.

Article 18

The husband is not allowed to apply for a divorce when his wife is pregnant, and may apply for divorce only one year after the birth of the child.

Article

In the case of a member of the revolutionary army on active service who maintains correspondence with his or her family, that army member's consent must be obtained before his or her spouse can apply for divorce.

Divorce may be granted to the spouse of a member of the revolutionary army who does not correspond with his or her family for a period of two years subsequent to the date of the promulgation of this law.

Chapter VI
Maintenance and Education of Children After Divorce

Article 20

The blood ties between parents and children are not ended by the divorce of the parents. No matter whether the father or the mother has the custody of the children, they remain the children of both parties.

After divorce, both parents continue to have the duty to support and educate their children.

After divorce, the guiding principle is to allow the mother to have the custody of a breast-fed infant. After the weaning of the child, if a dispute arises between the two parties over the guardianship and an agreement cannot be reached, the people's court should render a decision in accordance with the interests of the child.

Article 21

If, after divorce, the mother is given custody of a child, the father is responsible for the whole or part of the necessary cost of the maintenance and education of the child. Both parties should reach an agreement regarding the amount and the duration of such maintenance and education. Lacking such an agreement, the people's court should render a decision.

Payment may be made in cash, in kind or by tilling land allocated to the child.

An agreement reached between parents or a decision rendered by the people's court in connection with the maintenance and education of a child does not obstruct the child from requesting either parent to increase the amount decided upon by agreement or by judicial decision.

Article 22

In the case where a divorced woman re-marries and her husband is willing to pay the whole or part of the cost of maintaining and educating the child or children by her former husband, the father of the child or children is entitled to have such cost of maintenance and education reduced or to be exempted from bearing such cost in accordance with the circumstances.

Chapter VII
Property and Maintenance After Divorce

Article 23

In case of divorce, the wife retains such property as belonging to her prior to her marriage. The disposal of other family property is subject to agreement between the two parties. In cases where agreement cannot be reached, the people's court should render a decision.

In cases where the property allocated to the wife and her child or children is sufficient for the maintenance and education of the child or children, the husband may be exempted from bearing further maintenance and education costs.

Article 24

In case of divorce, debts incurred jointly by husband and wife during the period of their married life should be paid out of the property jointly acquired by them during this period. In cases where no such property has been acquired or in cases where such property is insufficient to pay off such debts, the husband is held responsible for paying them. Debts incurred separately by the husband or wife should be paid off by the party responsible.

Article 25

After divorce, if one party has not re-married and has maintenance difficulties, the other party should render assistance. Both parties should work out an agreement with regard to the method and duration of such assistance.

Chapter VIII
By-Laws

Article 26

Persons violating this Law will be punished in accordance with law. In cases where interference with the freedom of marriage has caused death or injury to one or both parties, persons guilty of such interference will bear responsibility for the crime before the law.

Article 27

This Law comes into force from the date of its promulgation.

In regions inhabited by minority nationalities in compact communities, the people's government (or the Military and Administrative Committee) of the Greater Administrative Area or the provincial people's government may enact certain modifications or supplementary articles in conformity with the actual conditions prevailing among minority nationalities in regard to marriage.

INDEX

abortion, 78–115, 121:178n, 157
adoption, 71, 128
adultery, 21
agricultural co-operatives, 135
alimony, 70, 71, 73–76, 78, 90, 93
All-Union Central Council of Trade
  Union, 96
All-Russian Central Executive Committee, 69, 76
All-Union Communist, 68
All-Union Congress of Shock Workers,
  37
American Federation of Labor, 54
ancestor worship, 128
ancestral graves, 142
Ancient Society, 2
Andaman Islanders, 46, 48
Anti-Dühring, 53, 142
Auls, 71
Azotobacterial, 153
Bachofen, J.J., 2, 3, 16, 32
barbaric stage, 17
barbarism, 21
barefoot doctors, 157, 166
Bebel, A., 4, 6, 17–18
Belgium, 85
bigamy, 67, 90, 131
birth certificate, 87
birth control, 156–161
  clinics, 158
  decline, 165
  pills, 156–158
birth rate, 108, 110
blood revenge, 63
Bolshevik, 68
Bolshevist, 25
bourgeois, 17, 67
  morality, 35
Briffault, R, 3, 5–6, 46
Briton, 13
capital, 24, 142
capitalism, 31, 47, 55, 57
  state, 49
Central Statistical Bureau, 93
Chiang ching, 169

Chiao Tung University, 181
child, 22–24
  betrothal, 130
  exploitation, 54
  illegitimate, 91, 130
  labour, 54
  marriage, 132
Chou En-lai, 143, 145, 152, 193:204n
church marriage, 26, 67
Civil Registry Authorities, 7, 90
clan, 123
class struggle, 49, 58, 151
Code of Laws, 75
collective farm, 28, 37, 99, 100, 134
collective living, 171, 193:221n
Communism, 188, 59n
Communist Manifesto, 19, 31, 82, 94,
  142, 183
communal mass hall, 28
communal property, 10
commune, 135–156, 186, 188; 64n,
  70n, 191:93n
  amendment of, 143–148
  Ch'a Pei, 166
  corruption of, 150
  definition of, 148
  Flower Mountain, 141
  Kwong Li, 148
  Lu Ku Chiao (Marco Polo Bridge),
  147
  Mar Chiao, 147
  and mechanization, 149
  mess hall in, 136
  Muchiayum, 198
  Red Star, 150
  residential district in, 171–173
  rural, 134–140
  Tachai, 145
  three levels of, 137
  three types of, 139
  Tung Chin, 175
  village, 64
  work team in, 138
co-operative house, 85
concubinage, 45, 132

227